Will You Happen, Past the Silence, Through the Dark?

Remembering Leonard Ralph Casper

Will You Happen, Past the Silence, Through the Dark?

Remembering Leonard Ralph Casper

by

Linda Ty-Casper

PALH

2022

Copyright © 2022 Linda Ty-Casper

All rights reserved. No part of this book may be reproduced or distributed in any form or by any means, or stored in a database or retrieval system, without prior written permission.

PALH
(Philippine American Literary House)
PO Box 5099
Santa Monica, CA 90409, USA
Palhbooks.com; palh@aol.com

FIRST EDITION

Library of Congress Control Number: 2022911961
ISBN: 978-1-953716-20-0 (Paperback edition)
ISBN: 978-1-953716-23-1 (Hardcover edition)
ISBN: 978-1-953716-22-4 (Ebook edition)

Cover by Ian Rosales Casocot

TO LEONARD CASPER'S PARENTS

LOUIS CASPER & CAROLINE EDER

CONTENTS

1	Will You Happen, Past the Silence, Through the Dark	1
2	In the Beginning	8
3	Fond Du Lac	10
4	World War II: Military Service	14
5	Short Stories: Southwest Review	20
6	University of Wisconsin	25
7	Len's Books	44
8	Letters: Universities of Wisconsin, Rhode Island, South Carolina	84
9	Len in Academe	97
10	Letters: Len to Linda	174
11	1961: Breadloaf: Middlebury College/Vermont	211
12	1980	218
13	1982	228
14	1983	242
15	1984	252
16	1985	268
17	1986	270
18	1987	275
19	1989	281
20	1990	286
21	1992	293
22	1998	297
23	2002	315
24	Leonard Casper Passes Away	318

PREFACE

This book is the Memoir that Len did not get to write. But the letters he wrote actually are his Memoir, evoking a life, the work that nurtured that life, the yearning for meaning that led to the creation of that essential self through his writings--plays, poems short stories, critical essays; through his planting trees and shrubs along the Sudbury River where we lived for over 60 years; through the carefully chosen trips to reconnect with memory and realize dreams. Len chose a life and a world in which to live it; became who he wanted to be.

The letters to Len reflect who he was to many friends, high school classmates, teachers and professors, colleagues in the Universities of Rhode Island, Ateneo de Manila University, University of the Philippines and Wisconsin, from editors of *Southwest Review* who encouraged Len to send stories from the European front during World War II; from Robert Penn Warren starting with his first letter of inquiry (two pages) when he began on his dissertation at the University of Wisconsin, the dissertation becoming the first book on Warren, which critics said showed the way for later books on the Southern writer. There are letters from Filipino writers Len grew to know as friends from years of teaching in the Philippines.

Besides academe, Len was part of the Filipino community of Greater Boston, including Friends of the Filipino People during the Marcos years; part of the Iskwelahang Pilipino where he took part in caroling (he sang bass) and festivals; part of Framingham where we lived for some 60 years, of the family of neighbors on Simpson Drive; part of the St. Jeremiah parish, of Boston College and its community until he retired after some 40 years.

This Memoir of letters shows a life lived with hopes, friendships, and abiding yearning for meaning which leads to that life without end.

Linda Ty-Casper

LEONARD RALPH CASPER
July 6, 1923-July 6, 2018

Leonard Ralph Casper wrote award-winning plays during high school. On the invitation of the editors of Southwest Review, he submitted stories from the European front during World War II. The *Review* published the stories, *A Lion Unannounced*, under a grant from the National Council on Arts. Len's dissertation at the University of Wisconsin became the first book on Robert Penn Warren with whom he corresponded for over ten years. After his Ph.D. he taught at Cornell University, the University of the Philippines, Ateneo de Manila University and Boston College, wrote articles, poems and pioneering books in American and Philippine Literature.

He has contributed over 100 articles to the *Americana Encyclopedia, Encyclopedia of Post-colonial Literatures in English, Encyclopedia of World Literature in the 20th Century, Philippine Studies, College English, Antigonish Review, Amerasia Journal, South Carolina Review, Pacific Affairs,*

Columbia Journal of American Studies, *Southwest Review*, *Popular World Fiction*, guest editor for *Literary Review*, *Panorama*, *Solidarity*, *Literature East and West*, and other journals; wrote prefaces to several books on Philippine Literature. He was consultant to the Asia Society Publications Director (1960-1972) and the Rockefeller Foundation, Humanities Division, (1956-1966). At Boston College (1956-1999) he served on major university committees.

He was a Stanford Creative Writing Fellow, a Bread Loaf Fellow, received grants from the Ford Foundation. the Rockefeller Foundation, American Council of Learned Studies, and the American Philosophical Society, among others. On retirement from Boston College as Emeritus Professor, he taught in the National Senior Service Corps program.

1

WILL YOU HAPPEN, PAST THE SILENCE, THROUGH THE DARK

First, in a box of old pictures, there was the photo I don't recall seeing: Len against a field, dated 1952. It could not have been taken in the Philippines, since he came in 1953, a month after Nanay, Gabriela Paez Viardo, my grandmother died, so they never met. They would have liked each other. Nanay told stories of the revolution against Spain, the war with the Americans; saying, "Someone should write these stories."

It must have been taken in Ithaca when Len was teaching at Cornell, having finished his dissertation at the University of Wisconsin. He looks so intense. On Veterans Day I found another picture: Len in an army photo with his company. And a box with tightly folded letters, I vaguely recall ever reading; letters from editors of *Southwest Review* asking Len to send them stories from the European front; from University of Wisconsin professors, colleagues; from Robert Penn Warren, on whom he wrote his dissertation for his doctorate at the University of Wisconsin, Madison. Also letters from friends and colleagues at the University of the Philippines, Ateneo de Manila, Philippine Normal University; writers, students and friends he made during his first three-year stay. In 1951, during his creative writing fellowship at Stanford, he had met, among others, Fel Santa Maria, Amador Daguio, my mother Catalina Velasquez Ty, of the Curriculum Division Bureau of Public Schools, taking her postgraduate, who invited him to visit the Philippines. So. Len gave up the Fulbright to London, took an open leave from Cornell, and boarded a cargo ship to Manila.

And letters, to me, starting in 1952. The first were from Ithaca: two postcards of Fall in Upper New York, sent February 9. Dear Linda, "*If your card was meant as a prayer, as I hope…then I am grateful.*" A letter followed November 18: Dear Linda, "*Poetry is the heart of any matter…to touch that sometimes is to find yourself alive…However, even if you don't send me any of your poetry, I hope you will write to me.*" And another dated November 30: Dear Linda, "*Although I am apologizing for the fact that the space between us will prevent you from receiving your Thanksgiving greetings until after New Year, if you were the kind of person that I have imagined you to be…the space will only be the distance between the two hands of one body, and the spirit of the greeting will not have diminished.*" Len.

I realized these letters were the memoir Len was not able to write.

Reading these in 2021, October, some 39 months after Len died on his 95th birthday, July 6, I felt strangely sad and yet glad these had not been lost, though I wondered which Len I am to mourn: the one I knew and married, who took the family back to the Philippines several times, each time going around the world, or the one I am just meeting again…

I copied the letters in an Italian leather notebook Len and I, on a whim, bought years ago at Harvard Square. It became a way of mourning, remembering, wishing.

If I had not found these, might I have stopped grieving? Had I found them earlier, we could have read them together. But Len had developed macular degeneration in the late 80s. For years he had taken a St. Jeremiah parishioner in her 90s to the Retina Associates of Mass General but never realized he had the same condition until in 1989, I went for a checkup with Dr. Felipe Tolentino, who offered to see him without an appointment when Len described a white spot in his right eye: "like a Neanderthal." But Len wanted first to finish the school year at Boston College. By May it was too late. The white spot he described was the central vision he had lost. Laser surgery could not restore the sight.

Yet, sitting on the porch overlooking the Sudbury, Len somehow could detect the flight of birds and lifted his hand toward blue heron, bald eagle, swans and even, once, a cormorant blown inland by a storm. Smaller birds, cardinals, woodpeckers, finches, and mourning doves flew in and out of the hydrangeas, butterfly bushes, and tulips, yucca, and many other plants Len dug into the slope along the Sudbury River that entered Boston Harbor by joining with the Charles.

Friends, colleagues from Boston College, University of the Philippines and Ateneo de Manila enjoyed Len's "river": Edna Manlapaz, Virgie Moreno, NVM and Narita Gonzalez, Fr. James Donelan, Bishop Labayan, Nieves and SV Epistola, the Rod Perezes with Odel and Lisa. Nilda Rimonte and Quito, Frankie Jose, Donn Hart, Greg Brilliantes. Fel and Flora Tolentino and Roland Houle of Restoring Sight International that sought to prevent blindness among the poor and children in the Philippines. Father John Wallace of the Sons of Mary often came for a peaceful retreat by the Sudbury. Fr. Miguel Bernad asked us to pray for him to the statue of Virgin he had blessed. My father, retired from the Manila Railroad, and my mother enjoyed sitting by the river when they visited, so did Ninang Trining and Ninong Benigno Marino. Friends and their children, Joe and Mona Dasbach, Bob and Jo Reiter, Helen and John Heineman, Bill and Katy Daly; Julia Budenz, Emily Lyle and Ching Dadufalza from the Radcliffe years; John and Ruth McAleer who took us to the North End, driving us around Boston when we first came. Ruth introduced me to her obstetrician, Dr. Charles Sullivan who delivered both Gretchen and Tina, twelve years apart. And Dick and Gay Hughes who asked us to move with them each time they upgraded their house. Dick and Len were at the University of Wisconsin, with Al Duhamel and Ed Nehls. Mimi Hirsh and David Montenegro came with their guitar.

After monthly lunches during their retirement, colleagues came over to sit in the porch, reliving Boston College days. The Fitzgeralds and Christopher, the Longos, the Duhamels, Dan McCue who with Len sang in the annual musical at the Methodist church to which neighbors Dave and Julie Rundlett belonged, Ed and Margaret Hirsh to whom Len brought Gretchen in her crib while he taught evening school when I was back in the hospital. After morning Mass friends came over for coffee. Our parish priests, Fathers Hession, Flynn and Morris, came too. Before them, Fr. Doherty.

Guests preferred to sit in the porch, brought their plates from the dining room to face the river. Even in winter, Len loved to sit, sometimes work, in the porch Mario Agostinelli built overlooking the Sudbury, charging only at cost because, "teachers are not paid much." Mario called Len, paisan; and while he was building the porch "for her" Tina greeted him each morning with cookies she had saved.

The Bicentennial in 1996 was Len's last visit to the Philippines. Aside from the conference where he gave a paper, Len happily connected with family and friends. With Fel and Tessie Santa Maria, Virgie Moreno, Amel Bonifacio and Amihan, and Andy Cruz he went to see Sister Teresa/Pin Constantino at the Carmelite Monastery. She was at UP when Len started teaching there in 1956. No one foresaw it would be the last time they would all see each other. Remembering past visits to see Fr. Pacifico Ortiz who married us and who was in the landing at Leyte with General Douglas MacArthur and President Osmeña; this time he went to see Fr. Joseph Galdon, Fr. James Donelan who invited us to Holy Cross when he received an honorary degree at BC's "rival." Fr. William Leonard, chaplain in the American army heading south to liberate Manila, was one of Len's Jesuit friends.

While Fr. Leonard completed two memoirs, Len could not start his own. Alzheimer had intervened, compounding the macular degeneration.

However, Len might have been thinking of those past years, thinking of his brothers and sisters whom he took to Walden Pond, Rhode Island, Maine and other sites in New England when, after he was diagnosed with mild cognitive impairment, he continued to sit by the river, whistling to the birds. He might have had the illness long before his diagnosis. According to the evaluation in 2007, his "overall intellect functioning was estimated to be in the superior range" which could have masked the ravages that had already started and delayed its progression. Len no longer took part in conversations, but from time to time, catching the drift, he would make a remark that indicated he got the essence of the exchange. He was still able to attend meetings of the Friends of the Filipino People at Boone Schirmer's home in Cambridge; meetings protesting martial law when Charito Planas and Raul Manglapuz were in town.

In 1999, the year he retired, Len was able to write a piece for Narita Gonzalez's book, *The Father Delaney We Knew*, about being part "of milling men and boys competing to carry the remains of Father Delaney to be interred at the Jesuit Novitiate in Novaliches" from the UP Chapel of the Holy Sacrifice "where he had taken his stand against bigots and panderers and wannabe politicians rehearsing roles for postgraduate careers." Len called the piece, Concelebration...having walked the miles, one among thousands from Ateneo and UP, where the good priest had lived in self-imposed poverty "for these students...beyond invectives ...beyond the understanding of those who tried so hard to be his enemies."

In 2008, after the diagnosis, Len wrote another "last" piece which Emy Arcellana requested for *Regarding Franz*, recollections from colleagues and friends. "Hired fulltime by UP and part time by Ateneo, I first met Franz and felt somehow, he had replaced my three brothers. Franz had a sense of family beyond even the typical Filipino's 'inclusiveness,' a tradition so clearly radiant in his iconic story, 'The Mats.' He was open to all; a true friend, not merely friendly...He was the first one to welcome me to the UP English Department... "how deeply in many of his stories…I felt a spiritual dimension: in language like the light laying of hands, the delicacy of creation recreated."

We realized Len needed immediate intervention when, driving one night, he could not find the way home. Dr. Tolentino suggested a neurologist at Mass General, Dr. Thomas Byrne who had taken care of Robert Penn Warren in his last years. Len had written the first critical book on Warren, "which pointed the way for all subsequent studies of the poet-novelist" according to Fred Hobson, editor, Southern Literary Studies.

Coincidence? From 2006 to 2017, Dr. Byrne and Len discussed meaning, consciousness/conscience and related matters, and of course, Robert Penn Warren, until the mild cognitive impairment progressed to the severe stage. The last meeting, unable perhaps to keep track of their talk, Len said, "You must have a good doctor, Doctor Byrne. You look so good."

After the diagnosis, Len continued to be part of the Vigil at St. Jeremiah, protesting the Cardinal's closing of the church established in 1948 and its sale to help pay for the sexual abuse cases in the archdiocese. He continued to attend meetings at BC, driving in with John Fitzgerald and other colleagues. He was part of the Iskwelahang Filipino Christmas carolers—with Mabini Castro, Rey Endriga and Bert Abriams, he sang bass. He loved, "Ang Pasko ay Sumapit," and "Drummer Boy," and the Tagalog songs Christi-Anne Castro wrote for the carolers. In the July food festival in Lowell, he was a "kitchen helper" at the Filipino tent where, each year, the line grew longer.

From 2012 to 2018, Len was in Continuing Connections, the Alzheimer program of the Senior Center in Framingham, which Lisa Ushkurnis developed and conducted with the assistance of Jamie Jensen and Debbie Bourque. Every Friday for four/five hours, participants read poems, "talked" about current events, watched movies, played chair volleyball or corn hole, sang, drew and painted, did exercises, had massages, listened to "lectures," petted a therapy dog, went to lunch or had lunch brought in, and took short trips. There were surprise programs and, always, a table filled with home baked goods. And there was the unspoken hope that a cure would be found. In time.

Three months after the third anniversary of Len's passing, by chance I found Len's picture at Cornell, with letters from editors of *Southwest Review* offering to help him get published when World War II was over and suggesting he write books instead of stories; letters from his University of Wisconsin friends and professors; from Robert Penn Warren, the exchange lasting some 13 years; reviews of Len's books, other photos and correspondence with colleagues from different universities, including L.M. Grow with whom Len shared an interest in Philippine literature. These were, I realized, Len's memoirs. After much hesitation I took a working title from Len's letter to me: Will you happen?

And so, I collected, typed and edited the material—letters, articles, and photos. It would not be "lyrical and erudite" as Len would have written, but it is Len's "unmistakable presence."

2

IN THE BEGINNING

… 1923: Fond du Lac, the city at the foot of Lake Winnebago, population largely Germans and Scandinavians who found Wisconsin so like the countries they had left. After St. Joseph Grade School, Fond du Lac high school, the University of Wisconsin, Army, Stanford, Cornell.

1953. Manila. Giving up the Fulbright to London, Len docked at Port Area after a month-long trip on a cargo ship, bringing several white suits a tailor in Syracuse told him were de rigueur for Manila and the Embassy crowd. Teaching at UP, Len never got to wear the formal clothes. He had started wearing barongs.

1956. Back to the States, Boston College, regular returns to the Philippines to teach; on the way, lecturing in Taiwan, Bangkok; writing books, reviews, attending conferences; member of scholarship committees at the US Embassy in Manila to interview applicants for study in the United States. I didn't know this until Josie Bunuan told me, recently, that Len had recommended her for a graduate assistantship to BC after she was rejected for having had a prior scholarship to Australia. Two Boston College presidents asked Len to be chair, then dean, but Len explained he was a teacher not an administrator. As member of many committees at BC—dean search, promotion, policies—Len had friends in the other departments with whom he shared stories of the War. Our families, and those of colleagues from the English department at BC, enjoyed many dinners and visits together. Despite offers from several other universities, Len would not leave Boston College, from where both our daughters graduated.

In between, family trips—summer was often going back to Wisconsin where his brothers and sisters took turns showing us the sights; and Europe—in Munich we looked down from the tour bus and saw someone who looked very much like his father; the Holy land, Santiago de Compostela; Greece, Spain, France, Iran, Turkey, Macau, Singapore, Hong Kong… Each time we went home, we went around the world on Pan Am's special round-the-world fare, visiting up to nine cities free. And as Len and Robert Penn Warren agreed: there was always the grass to be mown, leaves to be raked, until it snowed.

After the reviews of Len's books, after the academic correspondence, I added Len's letters to me, from 1953 to 2002: the closest to what his own memoirs might have been, of those years.

This recollection of Len's life, overlapping at times, is a rumination. The letters show a life lived not in the isolation of academe, but one ever opening into fullness: countless connections that deepened into an inner life which shaped the work, enriched daily existence: perhaps, what continues into eternity, endless time, and timeless space.

Then the obituary Len did not want. Maybe, like the monk in the Trappist monastery in Kentucky where Thomas Merton lived, Len wanted only God to know.

Cecilia Brainard posted the obituary in Facebook and said there were "so many comments I could not keep up". Over 247 at one count…Not including postings in other sites I could not also access since I do not have Facebook. Those I was able to read, showed how much Len and his books on Philippine literature meant to friends and many who knew him through his writing. These brought tears and some peace. I am grateful to all. And to Josh Clemens, photo journalism advisor at American River College, for editing the photos.

3

FOND DU LAC

Leonard Ralph Casper. Len was born in Fond du Lac, Wisconsin on July 6, 1923, the seventh child of Louis Casper whose father George came from Bavaria, and Caroline Eder from Alsace Lorraine. Len had three brothers, Louis, Leo and Larry; four sisters, the twins Ruth and Rose, Rita and Roma.

At the foot of Lake Winnebago, Fond du Lac was surrounded by farms. There were a lot of woodcarvers and carpenters, and Len found in the "cold room" of their old house a crucifix a grandfather had carved and his mother's piano. Caroline had taught him a few pieces as she also helped him with the prayers when he was an altar server at St. Joseph.

His father worked at the railroad, Gurney Refrigeration and American Express. At one time Louis ran a saloon, in the back room of which families were served supper. It was during the Depression, and Caroline made clothes for the children out of flour sacks. One time, some rich women came over with shoes and clothes for the children. Caroline explained that the children did not need them: they lived in their own house and had enough for their needs. Len remembers suppers of gravy and bread, and milk, of ice cream and cakes, but never of being hungry.

Caroline slipped on the ice one winter, cracked her kneecap but somehow crawled her way back to the house. The doctor said she would never walk again, yet she nursed herself back into tending her flower and vegetable garden. In the basement which had an earth floor, Louis kept barrels of sauerkraut from the cabbage Caroline raised. On weekends and evenings, with friends and neighbors, the family played sheep head, a card game accompanied with much slapping on the table.

The children attended grade school at St. Joseph School, went on to the Fond Du Lac High. Len wanted to go to college "and secure newspaper work, work on freelance writing in the meantime, and eventually be on a magazine staff."

Len's interest in writing began during high school where he joined the staff of the high school newspaper, *The Fondy Hi-Eye*. Encouraged by teachers like Mary Konen, with whom he corresponded for years afterwards, he wrote about 20 plays, containing what friends called the special "brand of Casper humor."

Len's one-act play, *Purloined*, won honorable mention in the Student Achievement Issue of the *Scholastic*, later winning first place in the state playwriting contest sponsored by the University of Wisconsin Drama Division. Several of his plays were presented in dramatic groups and all-school assemblies. He wrote an extemporaneous skit for the Latin Class—*Deux Femina Facti*, a Senior Class play. In *The Royal Family* he played the part of Oscar Wilde when he directed it in the Madison production. In his play *Truth and Consequence* he played Abe Lincoln.

In addition to work in the Junior Dramatic Club, the Dramatic Guild, Youth Forum, the *Argus* staff, and being an associate editor of

Hi-Eye, he was in the honor roll and won the Legion Award as "a good student, active in school programs, a good leader."

During High School, Len, Ralph Bertz, Rudy Grebe, Jim Kiryakakis, and John Conley formed the Pentagon. In 2000 John wrote to the group: "Recently, out of the blue, I tried to reconstruct the Pentagon from memory…the one we formed in 1940. Or was it 1939? We started it primarily, I believe, because each of us, in his own way, was motivated by intellectual curiosity. But what ignited it? 2001 will be the 60th anniversary of our graduating class."

"We weren't close neighbors. After school we went our separate directions. I seriously doubt that we were ever all in the same class. I just can't visualize a situation where, say, five of us were standing in the hallway and someone extemporaneously proposed a discussion group and the others all said, 'yeah, let's do it.' On reflection…it could have been one of those off-the-wall-things that often popped out…a collective thought that developed out of some random conversation."

"We did not try to keep the organization secret but neither did we talk about it overtly to classmates. Well, it was our own little clique…The discussions were wide-ranging, sometimes argumentative, often vehement, but never acrimonious. Civilized. We had no limits on subject matter, but I don't remember that the conversation ever got raunchy or off color in any way. I'm sure we didn't talk much about the guff that dominated conversation in other school cliques. We all thought of each other as equals. Respected each other's thoughts and enjoyed the give and take. We did not change any minds (at least none that were admitted to) but we all learned a great deal, perhaps more than regular school hours…"

The group continued to correspond after graduation. Rudy Grebe was a classical pianist. He came to visit us in Saxonville, in 1967, thinking vaguely of moving to Massachusetts. John, an electrical engineer, had worked for GE in the North Shore, married Irene Uchman from North Adams. They often came for the day, from their home in Stratford CT. We enjoyed many lunches in area restaurants.

Len graduated at the 82nd commencement of the FDL High school, Class of 1941. (Transcripts: Fond du Lac High School. Grades As, Bs, 1 C). The Better Man of Fond du Lac Union elected him as one of their regents. The new organization aimed to foster school spirit, make better citizens. Len was not able to join the Pentagon's 60th reunion since he had started, after retiring from BC in 1999, to teach at SOAR in Wellesley, a federal government program of seniors teaching seniors.

After high school Len enrolled at the University of Wisconsin, Madison on the GI Bill. In his first year, World War II broke out.

4

WORLD WAR II: MILITARY SERVICE

In his tongue-in-cheek account: How the Casper Axis Helped Defeat the Berlin-Tokyo-Rome Axis: Len wrote—

"In the late 1941, I was completing my first semester at the University of Wisconsin (Madison)…anticipating teaching English in high school. I stood with other students on the broad landing between floors…in Bascom Hall, at the top of the large hill just off Lake Mendota. FDR's voice came over the loudspeaker…about the attack on Pearl Harbor. I was 18 years old…finished the school year and enrolled for the second year. Tuition was minimal, and I earned my meals working as dishwasher in the Greek restaurant downtown, owned by a relative of one of my four buddies, Jim Kiryakakis."

"Sometime thereafter I was listed as draft-eligible and went with a group to Milwaukee for a general physical, but later back to

Fond du Lac and the family physician. I felt disappointed when he announced that I had a pierced eardrum and so was declared 4F because that little hole prevented a gas mask from being entirely effective. I tried to enlist in the merchant marine but was refused for the same reason. I was not violence-inclined (having no special skills, I was prepared to be a mailman the rest of my life, or a high school English teacher). My slightly older brother Larry who also, thanks to the Depression which we had just survived, had no clear future, had already enlisted and was in training with the 101st Airborne); but I just felt left out as the draft went on and most young men disappeared from the streets...

"Finally, my ear healed and I was accepted in the draft in 1943—just short of my 20th birthday..." (*The rest of the account is lost.*)

Len was inducted into the service May 19, 1943, in Milwaukee, from Fond du Lac County. Also inducted were his three brothers (Louis, Leo and Larry), and a sister, Rita, who served as a nurse. The oldest brother Louie was in the Philippine campaign. At the end of the War, his brother Larry received the Purple Heart with three Oak Clusters, a Silver Star, and a Bronze Star with one Cluster; his brother-in law Joseph Willman received the Purple Heart. Len earned two Bronze Stars, American Theater Ribbon, EAME Theater Ribbon WWII Victory Ribbon, and the Good Conduct Medal.

The Fond du Lac contingent was first sent to Fort Sill, Oklahoma, a field artillery base, for basic training. Some of the sturdier draftees were assigned to the pack artillery: 75 mm howitzers on the back of mules. "I was too skinny. It was kind of exciting, beyond close-order drill, to go out on the range where occasionally we saw buffalo and watch 155mm World War I howitzers fired. During basic training I met a young fellow from somewhere else in Wisconsin who wanted to join the Air Corps...but didn't want to apply alone; so I applied with him and was accepted on the basis of having had two years of college. We were assigned to Wichita Falls airbase in northern Texas, where I and many others were hospitalized with nonfatal dysentery, then sent off to Coe College in Iowa for math and geopolitics and early air flight training. Eventually we were to come out as officers, though all I wanted was to be a gunner, if I could make bombardier. I think all this was "masculinity" setting up models of behavior. I had a few hours of airtime and scared the trainer who flew with me, and until, again, I was briefly hospitalized—this time with pharyngitis; we used to exercise in the gym on one part of the campus, then still wet—in winter—double time in "sweats" back to our barracks. That delay was critical, because the bombers in Europe did not have as many casualties as they anticipated and secretly the invasion of the continent from England was being planned. So we were washed out, back to the field artillery…"

Len saw active service as a grade PFC. Army serial # 36 821 365 Organization Battery A 389, the FA Battalion, 97th Infantry Division, 38th Field Artillery Regiment as Marksman. He was qualified as Marksman Carbine, and his specialty was Cannoneer 864 in June 13, 1944. His battle campaigns were in the Rhineland, Central Europe, Belgium, Czechoslovakia, and the Ruhr Valley. He returned to the U.S. June 24, 1945, receiving his Honorable discharge on 2/12/46 at Camp Chafee, Arkansas, having served in foreign service four months, 6 days, in Continental Service, 2 years, four months and 11 days.

The Fort Bragg Post reported on the First Army campaign in the Ruhr, west of the Rhine. Len was part of the "aggressive patrols," active in the division artillery assault on the German installations. First major combat assignment was "the Battle of the Ruhr Pocket, operating as a unit of the 18th Corps Airborne of the First Army".

On April 17, Dusseldorf surrendered.

There followed a lightning 10-day campaign across the Sieg River in assault boats, 40 miles to Dusseldorf; capturing 21,791 POW, clearing 1000 sq meters; destroyed 109 #5mm guns, 2000 German vehicles, 1000s of small arms, and automatic weapons. Occupied 100s of towns, cities; including Sieburg, home of the Glockner Works Machine Factory; Levarkusener, site of the I.G. Farben Industry chemical factory; Solingen, cutlery manufacturing center,

Drakenderhahe, Schaaran, Dusseldorf. There were definite battles in the above cities; lesser battles along the 40-mile route.

Czechoslovakian Campaign. Defensive mission protected the left flank of the Third Army's spearhead into the Redoubt. Cheb (Eger) was the first major Czech city to fall into American hands. Doing 38 miles in 30 hours, 20,000 POWs were taken. The 97th was the first American division to set up a command post in Czechoslovakia. On May 5 the flag was flown half mast, in memory of President Roosevelt, over the factory at Tachau, the new Trident Headquarters. Prague radio ordered all Nazis to resist the Americans by all available means, but the Nazi resistance disintegrated.

The War ended. May 7. At 0816 message from Supreme Hdqrtrs halted all advance pending Nazi surrender. May 8, a lone German fighter plane strafed command post.

When V-E Day came, 97th command post was the resort town of Konstantinary Laxne. Trident troops rounded up straggling Nazi soldiers, accepting surrender. The 97th was ordered from Czechoslovakia to an assembly area; and General Halsey's command post in Sechof Castel near Bamberg, Germany to wait for redeployment.

Brigadier General M.B. Halsey assumed command of the 97th, guided the division through two phases of training, overseas movement and two major campaigns in the ETO. Their maneuver training was at Fort Leonard Wood, MO; amphibian landing at Camp San Luis Obispo, CA. Prepared for overseas; staging and briefing at Le Havre, France, the 97th moved to the front as one of the most completely trained units sent to the ETO.

The division's success in combat was outstanding from the standpoint of individual valor and initiative, skill and efficiency of individual units. They carried missions with clock-like precision— Ruhr Pocket, Cheb Czechoslovakia campaign; were instrumental in capture of Dusseldorf with very minimum bloodshed.

General Halsey attributed combat success on the overall skill, courage, determination of every member of the division.

*

In a letter (December 2000) to Anthony Simunek, author of a book of the last years of war in Czechoslovakia Len explained: I was only a young private back then—in the 389th field artillery of the 97th Infantry Division, serving as cannoneer…that short period of time before my division was returned to the States in preparation for the invasion of Japan stands out in my mind/feelings…I can still see a Czech youth not much younger than myself waving a huge American flag (or was it some sort of Czech flag?) as we passed down the highway on the road to Pilsen; and it moved me as much as my first view of the Statue of Liberty from the troop ship on our return to America.

Though we had practiced with World War I howitzers (155mm) most of the months of our training, we finally were given new ordnance: howitzers towed by 13-ton personnel carriers on "caterpillar" tracks. We could move faster on those vehicles…We anticipated using this equipment to liberate the Philippines and therefore had amphibious training under Marine supervision near San Diego. But suddenly things began to escalate in Europe, and General Eisenhower must have decided that the war there could be ended quickly with new reinforcements; so by train we moved across the US, then shipped to Cherbourg. We first fought in the Ruhr Valley, then became so mobile, the artillery alone was transferred in the Third Army, under Patton who believed in counter-blitzkrieg.

That's how we ended up outside Pilsen. As a cannoneer I never had access to detailed maps of our movements. But from a "liberated" map…certain place names still sound familiar; beginning with Hof and Eger, Plan, Mies, Ullitz… (I think this is where I saw the young man with the flag) and our final bivouac in bed rolls and pup tents within sight of high smokestacks which rumor said was Pilsen. We stayed just outside a farm somewhere, where a mess camp of hot meals was prepared, until we had orders to return to France for reshipment. I remember our tents in a valley under the shadow of the old castle remnants at Bamberg; then we were out of Czechoslovakia.

I will include in this letter a copy of a short story which I published years ago about those "last days" and which I now include in a 50-year old collection of my poetry...about a young poet in wartime...it records those last days in Czechoslovakia which to me are imperishable...

5

SHORT STORIES: *SOUTHWEST REVIEW*

Len trained during World War II, in Texas, Oklahoma and New Mexico. At Fort Sill, Oklahoma, he came across a copy of the *Southwest Review*, published by the Southern Methodist University, Dallas, and sent a short story to the magazine. A correspondence began, with succeeding editors encouraging Len to continue sending stories from the front.

*

July 16, 1943. Dear Leonard Casper, Btry. E, 29th Bn, 7th Eng. Rgt., Fort Sill, OK: "I want to know more about your story, "Seventh Part." ...Frankly, it is one of the most powerful stories we have ever received. We most certainly want to publish it...It is not our practice to pay for fiction—not even from writers like...Jesse Stuart or Wallace Stegner. However, as a little more substantial appreciation of your story than word, we are going to send you a small honorarium of ten dollars. Far more important...we will get the story to the attention of those who can be of great service to you...Charlie Ferguson of READERS DIGEST and Martha Foley, among others...If you should come to Dallas, I'd like to talk to you... Donald Day.

*

May 18, 1944. Dear Leonard Casper, While I know you won't be at this address, I am returning this manuscript...I hope when you get back from the Army that you make a novel out of Hunter's experiences. In the meantime, if you get a chance to do some more writing, don't forget to send it to us. And also, when you return from the Army, don't forget to get in touch with us, for we want to do everything in our power to help you do something in the field of writing. Cordially, Donald Day. (To Cpl. Leonard Casper).

*

June 9, 1944. Dear Leonard Casper, "Swift Night" we are going to publish and I'm going to raise the ante slightly by sending you $15.00...You do this thing tremendously well...I want you to do more stories on this level and when the war is over, I want you to do a book on the same level...I don't want you to emulate Melville's symbolism...but I do want you to deepen and make more profound and subtle your own symbols...I want you to read Hawthorne along with a 75-page analysis which I did on the *Scarlet Letter*... "The Skin the Cat" I'm sending back...Don't let this keep you from sending on any other Hunter things that you do. Cordially, Donald Day. (To Pvt. Leonard Casper).

*

13 February 1945. Dear Leonard Casper, ...We are going to publish COMPARTMEMT OF TIME. I think it is by all odds the most significant thing which you have done. I think it shows the promise that I saw in the first story which you sent here. I want you to take what I'm saying...purely as encouragement, because you are only beginning to show a sparkle of what you can be some day, and that "being" is going to take a tremendous amount of work and development...When this war is over I want the two of us to get together, to sit and to talk. Then I want to offer you a challenge. Until then...good luck. Cordially, Donald Day, Editor.

*

May 7, 1945: Dear Leonard Casper, Here is a check for your story, "Compartment of Time." ...I think this is a powerful story. I am also very curious about when and how and under what circumstances the story came to you, and curious to know what your conscious explanation of this thing is...this thing which obviously came from the very depths of your subconscious mind...Will you please write and let me know? Sincerely, Donald Day/Please keep me informed as to your whereabouts/This a great story...

*

August 21, 1945. Dear Leonard, ...how about doing something for a change that a lot of people will understand? ...this story is worth publishing, but the SWR has to, in main, publish material which our readers can understand...Moreover, I have always thought that you would do a better book than short stories. You have far more opportunity to bring your rather subtle points to the minds of our mostly un-subtle readers. Let me know how things are going. Cordially, Donald Day. Editor. (Mr. Leonard Casper, 112 Eighth St, Fond du lac, Wisconsin).

*

July 20, 1946. Dear Leonard Casper: We wish to print... "Least Common Denominator" ...We express no regret at all that you are neither Melville nor T. Wilder...One of our readers wrote the following comment on "Least Common Denominator": It is rich in associations, the associations of remembered sights and sounds and smells, the feel of joy and pain. I think Leonard Casper may be more than just a good writer. He might well make a significant contribution to American literature." ...We don't want you to get the idea we are interested only in stories with a Southwestern setting...Could you let us have an autobiographical paragraph or two?... Cordially, Allen Maxwell, Editor.

*

February 21, 1947. Dear Mr. Casper, When I was in New York recently I dropped by the Houghton Mifflin office to talk over the contest...in conjunction with SOUTHWEST REVIEW...The first name mentioned by the Houghton Mifflin people was yours. The editors have been continually impressed by your work in the REVIEW and were especially fervent in their praise of "Least Common Denominator." I think they would be delighted to consider a book manuscript from you for the contest...I really think this would be a fine idea... We have uniformly favorable reports from readers on your "Least Common Denominator." John A. Lomax...said it was one of the strongest stories he has ever read...How about sending us something more? Cordially, Allen Maxwell, Editor.

*

September 28, 1948. Dear Mr. Casper: ...We are vastly enthusiastic about "The Return of the Echo". We were delighted to see "Least Common Denominator" on Martha Foley's "Roll of Honor" in *Best American Short Stories 1948*. The story is...fully entitled to that honor, and we are proud that it appeared in our pages. Cordially, Margaret L. Hartley. Assistant Editor. "Sense of Direction," was included Martha Foley's *Best American Short Stories* and in the O. Henry Awards for 1950. Others were anthologized: *Stanford Short Stories*, 1953; *Stories from Epoch*, 1966; and in *Fiction as Process*, 1968 among others. Original publication was widespread: *Contemporary Fiction*, *Epoch*, *New Mexico Quarterly*, *Perspective*, *Southwest Review*, and *Western Review*, among others.

*

February 9, 1951. Dear Leonard Casper: Yesterday we received a letter from Herschel Brickell...Leonard Casper's "Sense of Direction" has been definitely chosen for the 1951 O. Henry...Mr. Brickell asked us to get him a biographical note on the author...Allen Maxwell and I both enjoyed your discussion of a writer's problems. I wonder if you would be willing to let us use a little of this letter...in the "Editor's Notebook..." We are pleased to know that "Seventh Part" was actually your first published story...Cordially, Margaret L. Hartley. (To Mr. Leonard Casper, 213 N, Mills, Madison 5, Wis).

*

August 12, 1951, Dear Leonard: A letter like yours makes a lot of effort that goes down the drain worth it...The Ph.D. training...is the most valuable I know of...I'm tickled to death on the scholarship to Stanford. It should give you—exactly at the right time—the leavening which should produce a great batch of staff-of-life literature. I am looking forward to reading the novel with keen anticipation...Don't sign up for a publisher...get a topnotch agent...I'll only be too glad to get you one...Best, Donald. *The Reader's Digest*, Editorial Representative: Donald Day.

*

October 1, 1951. Dear Leonard Casper: Isn't it about time that you sent us your annual story? ..."Suzuki" didn't reach us until December...After reading your exceedingly thought-provoking article in the Fall *Antioch Review*, "The Writer as a Calculated Risk"...how gladly we would be part of your face-to-face audience...and hope that you may find us a medium through which you will still want "to project some of the resultant integrated experience into the lives of other communities."...All this amounts to a plea to send us a story...Cordially, Margaret L. Hartley.
PS. We noticed from our SW renewal that your summer address was Stanford. We are wondering whether this meant that you were successful in getting the fellowship you wanted there. We hope so.

*

February 19, 1959. Dear Len Casper: We find "Silent Outcry, Sleep" a very fine story indeed, well up to all the others of yours we have published. We are delighted to have it...Yours is undoubtedly one of the most distinguished stories we have had the opportunity to see for a long time...Congratulations on the arrival of the new member of the family! Congratulations also on the forthcoming publication of the Robert Penn Warren book by the University of Washington Press...Cordially, Margaret Hartley. (To Mr. Leonard Casper, 11 Carver Road, Watertown 72, Mass).

*

In 1971, The Southern Methodist University Press published the collection *A Lion Unannounced, Twelve Stories and a Fable*. "Not only the book as a whole, but individual stories...have received special recognition..." It was one of the first two short fiction manuscripts in the National Council on the Arts program. The jurors--Hortense Calisher, Walker Percy and Louis D. Rubin, Jr.--made the selection "in recognition of the quality of the submitted manuscript and in the earnest hope of encouraging future work" by the author.

*

June 30, 1978. Dear Len: This part of your Warren manuscript is certainly splendid, and we are most happy to have it. It is very strong and written with your usual exceptional skill...I wonder if you are in the Philippines now...and good luck with Linda's novel...My best to you and the family, Margaret. (To Leonard Casper, 54 Simpson Drive, Saxonville, Mass, 01701).

*

December 1, 1983. Dear Leonard Casper: Because you have been one of SW's valued friends and contributors during the time Margaret Hartley and I worked together as an editorial team, I thought you would like to have the enclosed reprint of my memorial tribute to her...Since I will be leaving at the end of the year, taking early service retirement, I wanted to say how much I have enjoyed our association, and your excellent work, during my twelve-year tenure...All best wishes for a happy holiday season and for a productive year ahead. Warm regards, Charlotte. Charlotte T. Whaley. Editor.

6

UNIVERSITY OF WISCONSIN

After the War, Len was back at the University of Wisconsin, Madison, on the GI Bill. He received his MA and Ph.D., while a graduate assistant; completing his Bachelor of Arts June 19, 1948; Master of Arts, June 17, 1949; and Ph.D. June 17, 1953. While working on his dissertation, in 1951 Len went to Stanford, on a creative writing fellowship; the next year started teaching at Cornell. Giving up a Fulbright to London in 1953 he went to the Philippines, teaching full time at UP and part time at Ateneo de Manila, until 1956 when he returned to the States and began teaching at Boston College.

Leonard Ralph Casper's thesis submitted in Partial Fulfillment of the Requirements for the Degree of Bachelor of Arts at the University of Wisconsin, 1948, entitled…"My Soul Doth Magnify Itself". The recommendation of the Committee is that the degree be granted with honors. Sgd: Samuel Rogers, Alison White, Paul Wiley.

Descriptive Titles, University of Wisconsin Graduate Courses: Advanced composition, Advanced novel writing, English drama before Shakespeare. English drama in the time of Shakespeare, Anglo-Saxon, Contemporaries and immediate successors of Chaucer. Intellectual opinion in 19th century England, as reflected in literature, The Romantic Movement, American fiction, The 16th century, Literature in 1660-1745, Literature in 1745-1798, Major developments in contemporary American poetry, Conrad and Henry James, Research in English, Seminar in 29th century American literature, Advanced independent reading, Philosophical ideas in literature, American philosophers, Esthetics, Critique of dialectical materialism.

*

Dissertation: Robert Penn Warren

Having grown up in rural Wisconsin, Len had been drawn to the writings of the Southern Agrarians, specifically to that of Robert Penn Warren, on whom he wrote his dissertation, turning to critical analysis despite advice from SOUTHWEST REVIEW editors to work on a novel on his discharge from the army. The editor Allen Maxwell had written him that Houghton Mifflin would be delighted to get a book ms from him.

Len started writing to RPW while at UWI for his Ph.D. Their correspondence continued during his creative writing fellowship at Stanford, and after he began teaching at Cornell University, while he was at University of the Philippines and Ateneo de Manila, 1953-1956, and after Len had begun teaching at Boston College as an associate professor of English, lasting some 13 years. Warren twice delivered a lecture at BC.

Len's dissertation was published by the University of Washington Press in 1960, *Robert Penn Warren: The Dark and Bloody Ground*. The dust jacket said: "Leonard Casper's 1960 pioneering work, *Robert Penn Warren: The Dark and Bloody Ground*: the first book-length study of Warren, pointed the way for all subsequent studies of the poet-novelist." This first book was published with a grant from the Ford Foundation.

In 1997, Len's second book on RPW, *Robert Penn Warren's Later Novels, Blood-Marriage of Earth and Sky* was part of the Southern Literary Series of Louisiana State University. "Lyrical and erudite, a potent distillation of the nearly forty years meditation on the quintessential man of letters...*The Blood-Marriage of Earth and Sky* is the crowning achievement in the career of an eminent Warren scholar. It will surely further the 'coming closeness' that was Warren's best hope."

*

Letters: Len/RPW: 1952-1965

October 7, 1952. Dear Mr. Warren: Because I remember too clearly an early issue of *The Southern Review* in which Aldous Huxley disemboweled certain degree candidates for pestering him for information, I have hesitated writing to you...

For over a year I have been reading and rereading all that you have published since your days at Vanderbilt and something of the works of your writer-friends there, too. I have taken notes on critical comments about your writing; I have put in a supply of typing paper. Even the most difficult obstacle has been outside: at the insistence of my advisor, Frederick J. Hoffman, at the University of Wisconsin, the graduate committee there finally agreed that a dissertation on "The Loss of Sense of Community, and the Role of the Artist in Robert Penn Warren" would be acceptable to them. From that day on, at any time, I could have written this letter, and I have not.

I was prepared to discuss your works as if you were some unknown person from the streets suddenly intruding upon a stage-scene and speaking what you had to say. Perhaps that is the best way to experience what you have been saying. However, the graduate committee wants to be reassured that the writings I will discuss have had an honest-to-goodness author whose history can be at least shortly told; usually an author's identity is verified by a public reading of an epitaph, but they are going to make an exception. And I am convinced that they are right to this extent—your life cannot be prejudged irrelevant to the fullest experience of your writing: perhaps I have been wrong for that first impulsive wish to think of your words detached from speaker, or that speaker detached from any context. I do know that the context of several books has enriched the meaning of any one book, for me. And so I have to ask who you are, you who intrude with arguments, because I don't know until you answer how much sense the question makes. It's not really that bad, of course I know you from *Twentieth Century Authors* and from Tate's piece on the Fugitives, from Princeton University Library Chronicles. Nevertheless, what I ask you now will still seem elementary, although only your own discretion will limit your answers...

I have hesitated to ask these questions (although I am now at the writing stage of the dissertation where I must begin) because you may be too busy elsewhere to want to look back; I can only suggest that this might not be a backward glance but an examination of the ever-present. But worse than the fact that this is only a suggestion: I cannot even assure you that I will even make use of all the answers that you may give; it will depend as I've explained on whether or not your answers will help open up your writings in any way. That's a chance that I can only hope you will be willing to take. Naturally, whatever instructions you send with the answers—should you answer—will be followed.

Although it has been my turn to be next-to-anonymous, believe that behind these words is a person grateful for the consideration you will have already shown by this point. Sincerely, (3 pages). 252 Goldwin Smith Hall, Cornell University, Ithaca, NY.

*

November 13, 1952. Dear Mr. Casper: I am embarrassed to have delayed so long in answering your letter. Though the delay started because I simply didn't know how to come at some of your questions. This is not to say that I don't think the questions are real questions— just to say that sometimes the person in my position literally doesn't know the honest answer... (*Len asked about: Oxford, the Fugitives, Agrarianism, Distributists, History*) ... again my apologies for the tardiness. I hope you get the dissertation done without too much sweat and too many tears. Of course, I'd be curious to know your views when you are through. Sincerely yours, RPW. (2 pages) 1786 Yale Station, New Haven, CT.

*

January 5, 1953. Dear Mr. Casper: I have just found your letter of December 17...First, about sorting out the authorship of the different sections of the books I have done with Brooks...the difficulty...says something about the sort of collaboration ...By and large we did not parcel out the work, but sat down and talked about the commentaries before writing... so in many instances it is impossible to say who "wrote" what...But our collaboration was continuous and close, a sort of rambling conversation going over some years.

About the dedications: RFW and ARPW are my mother and father (Robert Franklin and Anna Ruth Penn), BCBW is Emma Cinina Brescia who was my wife from 1930 to 1951.../Mark van Doren/William A. Read/Donald Davidson/John Crowe Hanson/Katherine Anne Porter/Joseph Warren Beach and wife Dagmar/Domenico Brescia/Daniel Justin Donohue/Frank Lawrence Owsley/Dixon Wecter...Looking back over this list, it seems that most of my dedications have been made to people of personal friendship, and are not strictly speaking literary. In some cases, of course, there is a great literary debt, etc, but those are the obvious ones. Thanks very much for the checklist. It will be a great convenience...best regards, RPW. (2 pages).

*

February 11, 1953. Dear Mr. Warren, I'm sorry to crowd you with questions even before the old ones have been answered ...what I want now is documentation for certain smaller items already published.

I have tracked down the original sources for 80% of your poems and about 10% of your short stories...but it is important that I also have a record of when and where they first appeared. List of poems and short stories ff.

Other people have given me half-hearted clues...I must have title of periodical, volume, issue number, year, month, and pages...I am embarrassed to have to ask you for these; but not to ask for your help…would be false pride…(2 pages) 252 Goldwin Smith Hall, Cornell University, Ithaca, NY.

*

March 4, 1953. Dear Mr. Casper: I don't think I can be much help about the publication places and dates… I have to depend on memory, for I keep no record of such things. Here's the best I can do… (list)

Why don't you write to Rebert Stallman of English, University of CT, Storrs, CT…he is a demon bibliographer on the side of his critical interests.

The other items you list were all published, but I can't remember where… *Voices* had a thing or two when I was a sophomore, and God, were they awful…

I shall have a complete typescript of the new version of *Brother to Dragons*…this will not be the final one probably…but if you want a look at this version, which is very different from the one in the Kenyon…I'll be glad to let you have a whack at it. I don't want to press it on to you, though.

By the way, if you're around NYC in the next month or so, why don't we have a lunch? Yours, RPW.

*

March 10, 1953. Dear Mr. Warren: I've taken your advice and written both Stallman and COSMOPOLITAN and MADEMOISELLE. Little by little I think I can scrape enough information together to give some semblance of documentation, even if thoroughness now seems out of the question. The DOUBLE-DEALER poem must have been "Pro Sua Vita," which I almost overlooked…

I'm taking this much care not just for the sake of a dissertation. The degree is of extreme immediate value to me, of course. But as I have read and studied your work, I have become more and more convinced that a book of critical attention paid to RPW is in order. If I do not produce that book, I hope that someone else will; but I intend to try. I will certainly welcome the typescript of *Brother to Dragons*, therefore—to make the dissertation as complete as possible and to verify or disprove my conclusions from the rest of your writings...

I don't know if this will make me appear even more presumptuous than usual. However, the intention of what I've just said is to reassure you that all is not for naught, unquote. And prepare for requests within six months. I hope for permission to use all that you have copyrighted...

Whether I will be at Cornell or not next school year, I and other people have not yet decided; but I can be reached through Baxter Hathaway of the Creative Writing Dept., here in any event.

The fact is that I have a few good friends University Press, SMU—perhaps your editorship at *SW Review* made you acquainted with several of the same—and they have already asked for a first look at the ms. Random House has also put in a noncommittal bid; but my promise to SMU holds, and I'm afraid if one rejects, the other surely will also. I have had a novel and a book of poetry rejected too many times to care for wishful thinking. But these are the facts and I'm sure you can be even more unimpressed by them than I...

If you ever received my letters on the sources of several of your books, please ignore it. I have already done what I think is an adequate job of criticism without source comparison, and I leave that to other scholars. The bibliography is my main present interest, and I will see that you get a copy of it by the end of April, at least, when I can add a few more items—just in case this thing isn't published after all and available to everyone. I doubt that I will have to bother you again—unfortunately not even for lunch, I suspect—not even a home-cooked one—deadlines and distances being what they are. There is only one question that bothers me right now: about "those first two novels" that preceded *Night Rider*. If you ever find time, I would still like some clue to their nature and whether all or any parts of them were ever assimilated into later writings. This seems to me much more interesting than source-hunting.

Thank you for the letters of the past, your courtesy, good will, and the information. Sincerely... From Cornell University.

*

March 13, 1953. Dear Mr. Casper: I guess a letter from you has gone astray...it may be in New Haven...Anyway there isn't much to say about sources in print...But I will remark that *At Heaven's Gate* does rely some on Dante's *Inferno*, the sections on crime against nature...Logan Murdoch is a usurer, Serett is a homosexual...the others...main characters, are other types of violators of the natural order...though not the types used by Dante. The book didn't start from this, but before long, while I was trying to see the thematic shape of it, the notion took hold.

As for the unpublished novels, one was a story of a farm family in Kentucky in the time just before the first World War. The other involved a small town, and the school in the town. They were both bad sufferers from the thematic blur. If your project for a book ever develops, I don't mind your looking over the manuscripts if you think it might be profitable...I'm damned glad they weren't published. I don't think that any parts were assimilated into other novels. But the second of the unpublished novels grew out of some of the short stories... "Testament of Flood" and "When the Light Gets Green" and some others.

I'll send you a copy of the poem next week. I hope you like it. The last thing, you know, is the one the heart is set on.

By the way, Pro Sua Vita is not the poem in the *Double Dealer*. Pro Sua Vita appeared in the *New Republic*.

It now seems that our trip to Italy may be postponed for April...We are caught in the toils of designing and rebuilding a house. So...Good luck on the degree. Sincerely yours, RPW

PS. Since I am still writing on the poems and shall be until the page proofs are sealed up, I'd appreciate any notions you have about the poem. It's not too late to profit from comments.

*

April 29, 1953. Dear Mr. Casper: Thank you very much for the carefully considered criticisms you have made of the poems. I am now going over them most prayerfully, and already have joined with your conclusions in some instances. Fortunately, I yet have some time to make revisions...

And I must thank you, too, for the bibliography. It will be useful to me. I wish I could have been more helpful, but I have never kept a list. The only things that now come to mind, things not on your list, are some poems that appeared in *This Quarter* (Paris) about 1929, a story, "Do you Like the Ocean?" in *Woman's Day*, in 1947-48, and a story, "Testament of Flood" in *The Magazine* (Los Angeles) about 1933 or 34. Oh, yes, there were some poems in the *Double Dealer* (New Orleans) about 1922 or 23, and in Harold Vinal's *Voices,* about the same time. I can't remember the titles of the poems involved, and they haven't been reprinted anywhere...

As for the MS of the poem, just keep it till you're through and then chuck it into a furnace or overboard, I shan't need it.

I hope that your Manila project turns out happily. Sincerely yours, RPW.

*

May 11, 1957. Dear Mr. Casper: As for the questions on the card:

Rosanna Phelps is my daughter, aged 4 now, Gabriel Penn my son, aged 2. He, by the way, is named for my maternal grandfather, Gabriel Thomas Telemachus Penn, who appears in "Court-Martial..."

I'm in a swivet about last minute revisions of the play. I'll undertake a proper letter in a few days. Sincerely yours, RPW. Fairfield, CT.

*

July 17, 1957. Dear Mr. Casper: I'm sorry to have caused you the trouble of writing again. But I lost your letter and address and I only hope that you would let me have a repeat. I wish I had copies of the poems in anything like the form that they will be in when the book comes out. They have all appeared in magazines, a big batch in the *Yale Review* for spring, another batch in Encounter for May, a group in Kenyon for winter, and a little group in Botteghe Oscure this spring. But all have been so heavily revised that they will be little use to you.

The book will be available late this month, and Erskine said he is sending you a review copy.

...Last spring a contract was drawn for the dramatic version of *Brother to Dragons*, which I wrote last fall and winter and is slated for Broadway in late October or early November. When copies are made of the text in its revised form—just now being finished—I can send you one if you want it. But not really, I'd rather you based a reaction on a viewing rather than a reading.

Again, I'm sorry I lost your letter. Let me know when you're in NY. Sincerely, RPW. Redding Road, Fairfield CT.

*

August 6, 1957. Dear Mr. Casper: I simply haven't had time to answer your letter—the hurly-burly of the play and a trip away. And today I don't have proper time either, but I will give you a couple of bits of information that might serve your purpose. (1) The English Department of Carnegie Institute of Technology is publishing a symposium on AKM as little book. It you want a copy you might write to William Schutte of the department. It is due out pretty soon I think. Naturally I don't know what's in it. And for that matter, may never. (2) The *Paris Review*...has been running a series of interviews with writers of fiction. Last winter Ralph Ellison interviewed me in a long, informal, in fact ramshackle way, taking a tape, and the editors of the *Review* boiled down our billion words. The issue with the interview will be out in late August. If you want a copy you might write to their American representative, Marion Capron...I hope to recover the original long script, but that may be impossible. If I do, you may have that, for better or worse. But you better proceed to get a magazine...You might find Ralph's questions and remarks of considerable interest.

In a day or two I will try to write a proper letter. Now, I'm off to a run-through for music purposes, and nobody could know less about such matters than I do. Sincerely yours, RPW.

*

September 7, 1957. Dear Mr. Casper: I have written William Morris Agency, asking them to send you a copy of the last (and I trust final) version of AKM, which is called, for convenience in distinguishing it, *Willie Stark His Rise and Fall*. It ought to be there in a few days. If it does not come, let me know. Sincerely yours, RPW.

*

December 20, 1957. Dear Mr. Casper: The manuscript is here but in the Christmas hurly-burly but had no chance to do little more than glance at it, but in what I have seen I am struck by the scrupulousness and generosity. I have, as a matter of fact, read the Brown section—by accident; and I suspect your criticism is right. This subject is somewhat on my mind, or at the back of my mind, because my English publishers have recently proposed to do an edition, and I feel the need of writing an introduction to put the book in some perspective of my present views and feelings. In this, your remarks will be very useful…

I do hope that when you are in New York you will let me know. I'd greatly enjoy a meeting. Meanwhile a Merry Christmas and Happy New Year to you and your household.

Best regards and, again, thanks! Sincerely yours, RPW.

*

February 8, 1958. Dear Mr. Casper: No, the pages don't belong to my manuscript—in fact page 229 in my copy is quite different from the one marked thus in the one you sent me…

The other day Erskine remarked to me that he had read or was then reading, your book, and added that he was very favorably impressed. But he also said something about the inherent difficulty of publishing such a book, and about the fact that the decision would not be his alone. He asked me if I had read it, and I told him that, except for some parts, I had not. And I added that I prefer to be out of any discussion about the book.

I simply haven't got at your book, first because of a very great number of pressing things, and second (I guess) because of a growing disinclination to read reviews, etc. What I have read I have found sympathetic and scrupulous and penetrating, and other fine things. I reckon I'll slip into it someday…

I hope the book of stories fares well, and that the summer gives you the time for other work of a more personal nature than what you have been lately doing. Thanks, and regards, RPW.

*

March 15, 1958. Dear Mr. Casper: Yes, I have learned that Random House will not do your book—though I know that Erskine was greatly impressed by your quality as critic and writer. I imagine that it is the sort of thing which a university press will have to do—and what's wrong with that?...

About your questions:

(1) The title of *At Heaven's Gate* is from Shakespeare, not Lyly, and I wasn't singling out one exclusive reference for it from Shakespeare. It popped into my head.

(2) I had nothing to do with the screenplay of AHG. Robert Rossen did the job all by himself. ...I remember saying to Rossen that the end was entirely different from my intention, and he said, "Son, in an American movie you have to forget there was ever such a thing as irony—it's choose-up-sides. Cowboys-and-Indians, cops-and-robbers." And so it was...—good then, but different from my conception...

You ask about books in process—I'm into a novel and I am punctuating it with a poem now and then when a poem gets urgent enough to interrupt it.

Good luck on the book. Sincerely yours, RPW.

*

August 3, 1958. Dear Mr. Casper: Naturally. I am pleased that the University of Washington is doing your book, and I hope you are. I really had no hopes of Random House doing it, and I didn't think there were sound arguments, aside from commercial considerations, against their doing it, since they are my publishers. With a critical book, I really don't think there's much to choose between university press and commercial house.

As for your questions, yes the novel is about finished, and barring accidents, I will be finished by the end of this month. In first draft, that is. I shall do the rewriting in the winter, aiming for summer publication. We get home in late October and I will have my typist to make clean copies for me to work back from for revision, etc. If you want to see a copy in the winter, say December, that would be possible. In a way it might be good to have some little attention paid to this book...Some already, recently, in print and more to come out. In print, spring Partisan; spring Sewanee, summer Yale. If you want a list of things in print in the winter, I can give it to you...

...My German agents writes me that the German version (the old Piscator version) has just been done at the Ruhr Festepiele with an excellent cast and got a grand applause with public and press. The Piscolo Theater of Milan is interested in doing the French version, too, promisingly.

That's about all the odds and ends I can offer. If you happen to want some German press on the play, I can get it for you from my agent, S. Fischer Verlag.

All good luck and congratulations on the child. Since I delivered my first in the middle of the living room floor, I suggest that you keep your strength up for the occasion. I missed the pleasure on number two by the barest. Sincerely yours, RPW.

PS. I shall be at the above address (La Rocca, Forto Ercole, di Grosseto, Italy) until October 1.

*

September 1, 1958. Dear Mr. Casper: Both of your letters are here now, and I'll try to sort out the questions...

3. When I was in my early teens my intention was to be a naval officer. R.Y. Thomas, the local congressman (this was back in the days of congressional appointments to the academy) got me the Annapolis appointment in 1921, or made it rather, but before anything had been done I got hit in the left eye, by a crazy kind of accident. A clinker thrown over a high hedge happened to fall on my face as I lay on the lawn. The vision was impaired in the left eye and stopped the

Annapolis business. Finally I lost all sight in that eye, and it was removed in the spring of 1934 for fear that the right eye might suffer. As a matter of fact, except for games like tennis with a small fast ball I never experienced much inconvenience of a literal kind. I do wear an artificial eye as you surmise...

5. At Minnesota I taught a number of different courses at different times. History if criticism. Modern drama (Ibsen to Shaw). Techniques of the Novel (taking over Beach's course at his retirement). Freshman English (a war measure). Theory of Poetry, and Poetic Criticism. A general course in six important modern books for sophomores, a mob lecture course, Creative Writing. I had taught as my staple work in Louisiana Shakespeare and Elizabethan non-dramatic literature (a seminar). At Yale I gave the workshop 47, Baker's old course which is the third year of the Drama School course in play writing, and a course in theory and practice of fiction in the English Department—as it was grandly called in the catalogue. I never taught the Jacobeans, but at one time I read them very closely.

6. The Ellison-Walter interview is the only thing of that scale I've ever had...

7. BOA stuff. As far as I recollect now I got the start of this from a reference in Winston Coleman's *Slavery Days in Kentucky*, though I had heard something about the case...read more stuff about slave trade etc. When we were living...on a farm near Newport I worked the Brown U collection...thoroughly, and I prowled the Yale Library...about the riot, etc...I did read odds and ends of slave trade stuff, hearings in Parliament, not much, memoirs of officers in the slave trade patrol...Canot's autobiography...

10. Segregation piece. The Life piece began this way. The husband of my wife's sister, John K. Jessup, is an editor of *Life Magazine*...and a neighbor of ours. One evening after dinner at this house he and I were talking about the integration question in Southern schools, I was blowing off my views, and after a while he asked me if I minded if he took the matter of a piece up with whatever and whoever things got took up with for *Life*. I said no...I seem to

remember...that the magazine went to my agent...to work out terms. I had had the question much on my mind...after what I considered a lot of stupid or malicious misrepresentation of novels, I wanted to get something said in more unequivocal terms...

I believe that about covers the questions. If you'll jog me on my return to Fairfield, I'll get the play stuff to you, and the novel MS and such. Meanwhile, I hope the book and babies prosper in your house. Sincerely, RPW.

*

December 9, 1958. Dear Mr. Casper: Thanks for the card, which we appreciate.

As for the BTD thing, I can send you a copy, but it's still in flux. The producer has just managed to get his other play on (*The Disenchanted*), and since it is a hit, he says he is now ready to proceed with BTD...there will certainly be a good deal of pulling and hauling of the text to come. Do you want to see the one I now have, or wait a bit to see how the cat jumps.

I'm sorry that all did not go with perfect smoothness for Mrs. Casper—the trip back to the hospital, I mean. But I trust all is now well, and that you enter on a new dimension of Christmas. But just wait for two more years and see what you're in for. Thanks, and best regards, RPW.

PS. The report on the production, *Willie Stark* at the Margo Jones Theater, are good. Apparently, Frankel did a fun production...

*

July 25, 1959. Dear Mr. Casper: I am ashamed to look at the date above—but I have been in a great hurly-burly, confusions attendant upon the illness of my wife's mother and...a deadline on a play revision. Then I mislaid your letter. But here at last is something.

You may quote from letters...August 1957...about Annapolis. BUT I have been in error there. I have just found among some old papers the copy of my appointment to Annapolis, and it is dated after my entrance to Vanderbilt. I had remembered it, I guess, as having been received before my accident. In any case the wheels had been in motion before the accident. I may have said previously that the appointment was from our local congressman, R.Y. Thomas…

…I have the distinct recollection of the State Guardsman, and it must have been at the time of the tobacco troubles. Since I find myself in error about the Annapolis thing I am a little more leery of my memory. Anyway, I have always had this image…

…..

…You have permission to quote briefly from *Proud Flesh*.

As for the Teatro Piccolo of Milan, no further word.

New novel, *The Cave*, is out August 20.

New "competitors"—Random House has received a book MS based on a dissertation. I can't remember the author. Erksine has not discussed the matter with me. I don't even know that he has read it. And he probably won't discuss the matter with me. Another one is projected but I doubt that it will come along for some time—even if it ever finished…

The other development is the redoing, this spring and summer, of the play Cass Mastern's *Wedding Ring*, now called *Listen to the Mockingbird*. I am now assured it will have a Broadway production this fall—if a tangle of movie rights can be straightened. I will let you know definitely as soon as the thing is settled. Meanwhile, I'd appreciate your not saying anything about it…

I hope you are enjoying the grass-cutting and will enjoy the leaf-raking in October. It is remarkable how many leaves even one tree has, I have found. Goodbye and warm regards, RPW. PD. New collection of poems for spring.

*

September 21, 1959. Dear Mr. Casper: This is to say that AKM—the final-and-finished, win-lose-or-draw version—will open October 16 at the 74th Street Theater in NYC. If after that date you wish tickets, I should be pleased to offer them to you. Assuming, of course, that the play survives the antipathy of Brooks Atkinson…

Did you get my letter trying to answer your batch of questions?

Best regards, and how do you like raking leaves? RPW.

*

September 28, 1959. Dear Mr. Casper: Thank you for your letter. I—we—know what babysitting problems can be like, but if you can manage to get to NYC during the life of the play, don't forget my proposal. The rehearsals begin to look promising...And the director is clearly lucid and intelligent, to say the least.

...You ask about Floyd Collins. I was in Vanderbilt when the poor booger got stuck in the hole. Many lads went up out of curiosity or, to help dig, but I didn't, this to my shame. I am not talking about my lack of humanitarian impulse, but about the fact that I didn't consider the situation so damned interesting, I guess. I had a head full of John Webster and William Blake and W.B. Yeats and Thomas Hardy, and such, without too much interest in hillbillies stuck in holes. But in the '30-ies I reformed and began to think of the thing for a possible novel, as the germ of one, that is. By the time I was writing on *World Enough and Time* I was close to the idea. In fact toward the end, in the section in italics. On Kentucky, I mention Collins, a little private reference buried there. I thought at the time that it was getting warm for a book. I was thinking hard about it for some time but didn't begin actual writing till the late summer. I guess it was of 1957. It dragged on through the winter, with four chapters done. Then we went to Italy and I got into a fury of writing, and at the Recasa (and during three weeks at Zurich, where I had gone alone to get a busted shoulder fixed) I wrote the rest of the book before August 20. It was a very different version from the present one. I laid it aside to let it cool and went into a burst of poetry-writing for some months. Then back home some friends, including, of course, my editor Albert Erskine, and my agent, Elen Strauss, gave a very thorough criticism. If you should want to see the earlier version and the work done along the way I could provide you with the stuff. But perhaps that wouldn't be up your alley...

Gosh, the folklore and gossip about the Floyd Collins business is a great story, another story...

I'm sorry to hear about the house. I know how it happened. I have had it happen to me. But at least you don't have to rake leaves. As I am about to begin doing. All the best, RPW.

*

March 17, 1962. Dear Mr. Casper: I have been long in answering your kind note, but the spring been total confusion for me.

I don't know precisely how to answer your question. *Wilderness* got started, I suppose, by my reading around over some years, odds and ends of stuff about immigrants in the two armies in the Civil War, and especially about Jews—not by intention, just by accident. As far as Dostoievski is concerned, I wasn't conscious of any relation, but the inner memory is a sly one. Anyway, I hadn't read the Grand Inquisitor scene for many years, and I haven't read JB's *Body* since it came out or a little after that. By the way, my man didn't get the name Adam until quite late—in revision—and so this lets out, I guess, Gurowski. In passing, I'll remark that my Southern—or rather ex-Southern—sutler was originally a Jew. But I switched that other Jew into Blanstein (changing his character) and developed the North Carolinian as the right companion for Mose and Adam...

The name Adam—the name was not the traditional Jewish name. I found that it would have been possible in the mid-19th century only in some very self-conscious, rather literary way, as a backwash of the Napoleonic break-up of the ghetto and the new humanistic learning among many Jews.

I suppose you are right about *Wilderness* as being the sort of tale I had used—the sort of exemplum—in bigger novels. I didn't put it to myself that way, but it makes sense. I just got the growing itch to write the particular story. The general motivation for the itch I am sure you understand...

I am delighted at the prospect of seeing you on April 12 and should love some protracted conversation. Best Regards, RPW.

*

October 4, 1965. Dear Mr. Casper: I recently had the great pleasure of meeting Sister Bernadette, at the College of St. Teresa, in

Winona. She is delightful. In the course of our conversation, I mentioned that I was to be at Boston College in November. As I left, she handed me this item, asking me to give it to you. I don't trust my luck to find it in the confusion of my study when the time comes for my visit; so I send it now... Very truly yours, RPW. **PS**. I didn't know what the enclosed was until just now. What an echo from the past!

*

Loose page: I don't know what you'll make of all this. You kindly say that you will take as final what I say about myself. I don't think one can take as final all of what any man says about himself—for one thing he often doesn't finally know. But I'll add, in the same spirit, that I am often struck by the appalling innocence with which some critics try to relate life events and writing—failure to realize that data, enough data, is damn hard to come by, and grossness and/or academicism is interpreting the relations. This goes, too, for some of the professional psychologists, and goes double, sometimes. Goodbye, best regards, and good luck—sincerely yours, RPW.
PS. you ask...the play BTD would be published...97 (?). The Carnegie Tech book on AKM is called...*AKM: A Symposium*. Carnegie Press.

7

LEN'S BOOKS

Books:
Six Filipino Poets, editor, Benipayo Press, Manila, 1955.

Robert Penn Warren: The Dark and Bloody Ground, University of Washington Press, Seattle, 1960; reprint, Greenwood, 1961.

The Wayward Horizon, Essays on Modern Philippine Literature, Community Press, Manila 1961.

The World of Short Fiction: An International Collection, co-editor, Harper and Row, 1962.

Modern Philippine Short Stories, editor, University of New Mexico Press, Albuquerque, 1962.

The Wounded Diamond: Studies in Modern Philippine Literature, Bookmark, Manila, 1964.

New Writing from the Philippines: A Critique and Anthology, Syracuse University Press, 1966.

A Lion Unannounced: Twelve Stories and a Fable, Southern Methodist University Press, Dallas, 1971.

Firewalkers: Literary Concelebrations 1964-84, New Day, Quezon City, 1987.

In Burning Ambush: Essays 1985-1990, New Day, Quezon City, 1991.

The Opposing Thumb: Decoding Literature of the Marcos Regime, Giraffe, Quezon City, 1995.

Sunsurfers Seen From Afar: Critical Essays 1991-1996, Anvil, Manila, 1996.

The Blood Marriage of Earth and Sky: Robert Penn Warren's Later Novels, Louisiana State University, Baton Rouge, 1997.

The Circular Firing Squad, novella, Giraffe, Quezon City, 1999.

Green Circuits of the Sun: Studies in Philippine and American Literature, Giraffe, Quezon City, 2002.

Robert Penn Warren: The Dark and Bloody Ground

The University of Washington Press released Dr. Casper's study of Robert Penn Warren: *The Dark and Bloody Ground*. Associated with Boston College, where he teaches English, Leonard Casper has taught creative writing at Wisconsin, Cornell, the University of the Philippines and at Boston College. His short stories have appeared in the O. Henry and Martha Foley anthologies of the best short fiction.

The somewhat gory sub-title of this volume of literary criticism is a translation of the Indian name of Robert Penn Warren's native state of Kentucky. This is a full-length study of the writer as poet, critic, playwright, and novelist. With a chronological list of Warren's works, plus notes. University of Washington Press, 1960. *The Latest BOOKS*. Baker and Taylor Co.

*

Still another full-length critical book on an American novelist…is Leonard Casper's **Robert Penn Warren: The Dark and Bloody Ground** (University of Washington Press, $4.75). After an introductory survey of previous criticism of Warren, Casper takes up the main formative influences—the New Criticism, the New Agrarianism, and the theories of literature reflected in Warren's textbooks and articles—before discussing in telling detail the poetry and the fiction. Each novel prior to *The Cave* is considered at length, and *All the King's Men* is seen against the background of Warren's several dramatic versions. Casper's main concern throughout is Warren the thinker as reflected in Warren the artist, but Casper has a sharp eye for identifying many of Warren's literary tricks and devices. Included is a checklist of Warren's works and a selected bibliography of writing about him. *Modern Fiction Studies. Newsletter.* P 376.

*

Leonard Casper, son of Mr. and Mrs. Louis Casper, 112 Eighth Street, has published the first complete study of the works of the Pulitzer Prize winner, Robert Penn Warren.

The book's title, 'Robert Penn Warren: The Dark and Bloody Ground" is derived from the Indian name for Kentucky, Warren's home state, and also suggests Warren's symbol for the human condition. The book was published by the University of Washington Press under a grant from the Ford Foundation.

The social and literary criticism, poetry, plays and fiction of Warren, a writer of importance second perhaps only to Faulkner and Hemingway, are searchingly analyzed, with special attention given those characters who "recapitulate, each in his own way, the author's struggle for an understanding that surpasses peace."

"The Dark and Bloody Ground" grew out of Professor Casper's dissertation at the University of Wisconsin in 1956, and out of seven years correspondence with Warren.

Besides being an associate professor of English at Boston College, Casper is himself a poet, short story writer, and critic. He has nearly completed three other books on which he has been working. (With picture.) *Fond du Lac Chronicle.* November 18, 1960.

*

In this first full-length study of the works of Robert Penn Warren, author Leonard Casper has given a revealing insight into the making of the poet-writer.

More than just a biography of Warren and a critical look at his works, "The Dark and Bloody Ground" is also a study of the Fugitives, that group of Southern writers to which Warren was attracted by his respect for "man's search for identity apart from utility," and the background and surroundings which helped the Fugitives form their works.

In the foreword, Casper, associate professor of English of Boston College, gives an accurate synopsis of the various critics' views of every major Warren work.

"That Warren was so long ignored by literary historians was sometimes an accident," Casper states. "To some, Warren was just an apprentice and to others he was also too old to be a newcomer."

"The unpreparedness of some readers has only confirmed his philosophy that neither popular nor critical opinion is half so important as self-knowledge."

Warren's definition of this "condition" might be seen partly in this statement on segregation: "The problem is not to learn to live with the Negro, it is to learn to live with ourselves.

Warren's poem do not assert: they question, Casper says, and he uses this passage from "Picnic Remembered" to illustrate his point:

> Or is the soul a hawk that, fled
> On glimmering wings past vision's path
> Reflects the last gleam to us here
> Though sun is sunk and darkness near
> --Uncharted truth's high heliograph?

Although the meaning of Warren's poetry at its fullest is not available, Casper admits, the poems themselves insists no more than he on being interpreted solely on their merits as predetermined doctrine. When such terminology is employed, often it occurs short of the poem's climax, therefore not interfering with the theme.

CASPER's criticisms of Warren's works seems fair and shows considerable probing. His criticism of "All the King's Men" is more interpretation than criticism...seems needed.

Evil's threat to man is Warren's main theme in some of his major works, Casper says, "...Warren suggests that suffering can be made meaningful only by recovery of the sense of sin and by man's acceptance of the necessity of evil...It's presence makes his existence possible."

Casper's book is well organized and he covers every phase of Warren's work. Separate chapters are set aside for his early fiction, his poetry and his later works.

Casper covers Warren's period with the Fugitives more than adequately. From Warren's approach to the Fugitives at their Vanderbilt University headquarters...("In a soft whisper a stranger asked to see a poem of Tate's, then in return showed me one of his own, about the purple lilies of Hell.") to Warrens' hand in the founding of the new Agrarianism, Casper gives an accurate view of the Southern poet-writer.

FROM WHAT were the Fugitives fleeing? Rather than face the fact that even in the Old South a large and important middleclass had existed, in addition to slave-holders and poor whites, Casper says even agricultural communities chose to believe the legend of the landed aristocracy and plantation system.

The real question seemed to be, Should Industrialism in the South be encouraged to expand? The Fugitives said, "No." They possessed a bone-deep impulse to preserve the humanities and the human soul against the world's drift to materialism.

Warren's growth as a writer "parallels the crabbed and tacking movement, the drift and compensation of his characters toward self-knowledge."

The individual is the object of all Warren's attention, Casper says, but not as the romantics conceived him, in full-winged flight toward perfection. "Warren compels acceptance of an older image, man with a sense of guilt…"

For the reader who enjoys Warren in particular and the Fugitives in general and wants to know more about them, "Robert Penn Warren: The Dark and Bloody Ground" is well worth reading. Marion Ellis.

*

…it is strange that until now, with the publication of Leonard Casper's **"Robert Penn Warren: The Dark and Bloody Ground"** (University of Washington Press, $4.75) there has been no book on Warren. He has written half a dozen novels, most of them popular; recently a volume of his poetry was given a Pulitzer Prize; with Cleanth Brooks he has written several influential textbooks; and he has tried his hand at drama, Perhaps one reason he has been neglected by the academic critics is that his position in American literature is by no means clearly established: he has been praised and he has been damned and he has been sneered at. But this is exactly why a full-length study could be helpful.

Professor Casper who teaches at Boston College, has gone at the job in a systematic fashion. After a foreword, in which he deals with the critics of Warren and their shortcomings, he discusses Warren as a Southerner, as a New Critic and as an Agrarian. These chapters examine in fair detail Warren's activities as one of the Fugitives, the young poets—John Crowe Ransom, Allen Tate, *et al*—who were at Vanderbilt University in the Twenties. They show us his starting point.

Casper proceeds by writing about Warren's criticism, poetry, biography and fiction, and drama. The topical method has the obvious advantage of showing Warren's progress in each of the forms he has used, but it has the equally obvious disadvantage of obscuring his general development. Casper does allude to parallels between poems, say, and novels, but there is no clear line to follow...

The author deals conscientiously with Warren's critical theories and practice, showing that he has been more flexible than most of the New Critics. The chapter on poetry is full, with detailed comments on many poems. The next chapter which occupies almost half the book, begins with Warren's early biography, "John Brown: The Making of a Martyr," and Casper does not seek to gloss over Warren's prejudices. Thereafter he deals with the short stories and novels. (The body of the book was apparently finished before "The Cave" was published, although there is reference to it in the foreword.) Casper gives a detailed summary of each of the novels, and though these summaries grow a little tedious, they do show that he is a careful reader. All in all, Casper's treatment of the fiction is fair and perceptive. He is not blind to weaknesses, but he has none of the captiousness of which many critics of Warren have been guilty.

In his concluding summary, Casper makes much of the fact that Warren has never been a follower of literary fashions. ...Though comparisons can be dangerous, I should like to know what Casper would have come up with if he had placed Warren side by side with Faulkner. Warren is a difficult writer to assess, but I wish Casper had been bold enough to attempt the task. *Southern Review*, December 17, 1960. P.16. Scholars are Cautious Critics. Granville Hicks

*

Literally, the "dark and bloody ground" is Kentucky, the background of Robert Penn Warren's heritage. Professor Casper astutely traces the Southern roots of Warren's heritage while adroitly avoiding the pitfall of overemphasizing the biographical (though Kentucky as a border state remained in the Union, Warren's favorite grandfather was an ex-Confederate officer). However, Warren used the Southern experience not for purposes of parochial regionalism, but as an available symbol "to test his personal vision: the dialectic course of man's compulsion" to be known (p.10). For though violent action is the immediate narrative sense of the "dark and bloody ground," the conflict of ideas within the individual as he seeks self-identity is the thematic sense: "Violence in the world of Robert Penn Warren's fiction is token for the individual's laboring emergence from and through his circumstances, the struggle of each man for self-consciousness. All life becomes a striving to be born" (p.3).

This full-length study is a much-needed perspective on Warren's writing, not only because of the conflicting critical interpretation of his novels (summarized in the "Foreword"), not only because a major contemporary American writer has been up until now largely neglected by the critics, but more importantly because while Warren has been discussed separately as a poet, as a critic, or as a novelist, he has not been seen whole. Though these three major aspects of Warren's works are treated in separate chapters the interrelationship between the formalistic critical creed and the creative achievement and the inter-relationship between the major themes in the poetry and the novels are shown so that the poetry and criticism help illustrate the novels, the form Warren came too late in his career.

As a critic, Warren is seen in relation to the three critics he is most closely associated with, John Crowe Ransom, Allen Tate and Cleanth Brooks, and with New Criticism as a whole. Warren shares with other New Critics a formalistic approach to literature by which art is separated from utility for literary "meanings do not exist except as theme is tempered by a confluence of formal relations" (p.36). However, Warren's early "attempt to disengage the social and esthetic concerns was doomed to failure, given his conviction that in the soul of society literature is nourished" (p.54). Tempered by his own creative experience as a philosophic poet and novelist, Warren's later criticism requires of a piece of literature that "intensify our awareness of the world…in terms of an idea, a 'view." It is toward a coherent "view" of the world that Warren's poetry and fiction have evolved, using his critical faculties to explore his own vision. Mr. Casper seems to be on questionable ground when he seeks evidence for Warren's philosophic and esthetic development in the kind of readings included in the Brooks and Warren textbooks; the selection of readings in a textbook of modern readings is sometimes limited by the practicalities of permission costs and by the need to be "representative" of "up-to-date" (and even by the need to be rhetorical, as in *Modern Rhetoric*) which might very well modify any rhetorical *rationale* of selection. However, this is a minor flaw in Mr. Casper's thorough analysis of the gradually broadened view of literature Warren arrived at.

As a poet Warren's development is seen as "a journey from the physical to the metaphysical" (p.84). Physical violence (and history as violence) in the early poems, such as "Crusade" and "Kentucky Mountain Farm" is used for melodramatic effects and wasteland imagery. *Proud Flesh* (1939), and the prose-verse dramatic version of *All the King's Men*, and "The Ballad of Billie Potts" (1944) illustrate Warren's attempt to illuminate history and experience through chorus and commentary (a technique used in his first two novels published during this period). It is *Brother to Dragons* (1953) which completes the development: "The importance of *Brother to Dragons* in Warren's cannon lies in the clarity of its comment on those terms of the human paradox which need redefining—complicity and innocence, necessity and freedom" (p.79). These are defined by the paradoxes:

> The recognition of complicity is the beginning of innocence.
> The recognition of necessity is the beginning of freedom.
> The recognition of the direction of fulfillment is the death of the self
> And the death of the self is the beginning of selfhood.

The close relationship between the development of thought in Warren's poetry and in his fiction is shown: the early fiction through *World Enough and Time* (1950) shows the gradual apprehension of the ideas presented in *Brother to Dragons*. In *All the King's Men* (1946) the epigraph from Dante underscores Warren's theme: "The curse of man is his identity, which is his separateness and therefore his incompleteness" (p.128). However, the birth trauma (and of the self) celebrated in the nursery rhyme of the title is irrevocable. Humpty Dumpty cannot be put together again. *World Enough and Time* looks forward to the redefinition of the human paradox in *Brother to Dragons* Jerry Beaumont says, "There must be a way whereby the flesh becomes word. Whereby loneliness becomes communion without contamination. Whereby contamination becomes purity without exile." The answer is hidden in the double irony of this "historical" novel: there is never world enough and time for factual proof of faith; yet all that is needed is the simple act of faith that comes from understanding of facts, but facts in themselves become a trap by which the "historical" (and the reader) becomes blind to the truth. *Band of Angels* (1955) extends the definition of the human paradox: "Man inherits the conditions of evil (necessity) yet is capable of choosing otherwise (freedom)…Without choice there is no identity" (p.160). Manty Starr achieves self-realization and the peace of understanding as she reviews her life and its significance.

To Warren action, whether personal or historical, becomes the metaphor of human guilt, for action inevitably causes evil and suffering; yet life without experience is ignorance, not innocence, for complicity is the beginning of innocence. Professor Casper has achieved a major redefinition of Robert Penn Warren's development as a poet and novelist. Of course the danger of any such perspective while the author is still alive is that his next novel may necessitate a qualification of that perspective (even as I write this review of Warren's latest novel, *Wilderness* is being reviewed). *The Cave* (1959) published while Mr. Casper's book was in preparation for publication, is only briefly noted in the "Foreword," but *The Cave* reinforces Mr. Casper's contention that Warren's basic theme is the search for self-identity. *The Cave* illustrates the second part of the human paradox that the recognition of the direction of fulfillment is the death of the self and that the death of the self is the beginning of selfhood: as Mr. Bingham says near the end of the novel of the crowd that gathered at the mouth of the cave, they had sought "to break out of the dark mystery which was themselves." Charles G. Hoffman. University of Rhode Island.

CRITICISM, a Quarterly for Literature and the Arts, Vol IV, No. 3, Summer 1962. p.267. *Robert Penn Warren: The Dark and Bloody Ground* by Leonard Casper. Seattle. University of Washington Press, 1960. Pp. xix + 212. $4.75.

*

When he retired from the Yale English department in 1956 to devote himself entirely to writing, Robert Penn Warren has reached a goal that in academic literary circles is regarded as virtually impossible of attainment. His Vanderbilt colleagues of the 'twenties, however, should not have been surprised; such men as John Crowe Ransom, Allen Tate, Donald Davidson, Andrew Lytle, and Cleanth Brooks (none of whom have been able to give themselves to full-time writing) had early marked "Red" Warren an unusual talent and a compelling power. From those early days when the thin, awkward Kentucky boy drew protective sponsorship on the Vanderbilt campus, he has indeed, in line with many predictions, made major achievements in literature.

Though his career by no means seems near conclusion (he is fifty-five and just last year published his sixth novel, *The Cave*), it has been defined with enough consistency for Leonard Casper to survey its large lineaments with some certainty. In his recently published volume *Robert Penn Warren: The Dark and Bloody Ground*, Mr. Casper views with understanding the world Warren creates and details Warren's progress toward the full realization of that world in each genre he has essayed. Author of six novels, three volumes of poetry, two volumes of short stories, collection of critical essays, several dramas, histories, and biographies, and seven textbooks, Warren has won prizes, Literary Guild contracts, and Pulitzer award. Two of his novels have been made into movies. All his work has met with unusual financial success. Yet he is not really a well-known writer outside the literary world. Nor, despite his obvious largeness of scope, his philosophic depth, and his excellence of technique, has he been given a place of high honor by critics of fiction. Mr. Casper would account for this oversight by the general critical incomprehension of an important element in Warren's work, an element that provides the title for the recent volume: Warren's world is a world of violence, a "dark and bloody ground." On its most literal level, this phrase is the Indian name for Warren's native state of Kentucky. Yet, in a deepening pyramid of meaning, the troubled land can be seen to be the South, America, the modern world, and finally the human condition itself. In Warren's work, violence is a necessity; it is, as Mr. Casper writes, "token for the individual's laboring emergence from and through his circumstances, the struggle of each man for self-consciousness."

From Warren's earliest Fugitive poems, his biography of John Brown, his early novels *Night Rider* and *At Heaven's Gate* through his more fully realized works—some of the *Selected Poems, All the King's Men, World Enough and Time,* and *Band of Angels*—he has been striving to know his own vision; for, as Mr. Casper rightly indicates, writing is for Warren a cognitive process. Thus the struggle for identity on the part of the creative artist is related, in Warren's mind, to the same struggle in all men. It is the struggle to acknowledge and confess sin— the sin of existing, the sin of separateness—and through that confession, to move on toward expiation and redemption. In a sense, as Mr. Casper makes clear, Warren's reading of *The Rime of the Ancient Mariner* is of critical importance in the interpretation of his own work.

Mr. Casper speaks of his own book as a "map" of Warren. It should be a valuable guide to the student of Warren's work, as well as to the reader who knows little of him, or perhaps, who understands little of the Southern temperament. Its "narrative briefs" are accurate and helpful, its commentaries clear, its bibliographies full. One could wish it less gnomic in insight and more conveniently expository in style, as one could desire perhaps a wider perspective than the merely modern one it provides for viewing Warren's world. But, despite these shortcomings, *Robert Penn Warren: The Dark and Bloody Ground* is a sympathetic and intelligent interpretation of an important writer who has been hugely influential on all fronts of American letters. Louise Cowan. NMQ XXX:3. BOOKS. Pp.318-320.

The Blood Marriage of Earth and Sky: Robert Penn Warren's Later Novels

English's Casper examines great American author's later works.

Three-time Pulitzer Prize winner Robert Penn Warren (1905-89) was one of America's most prolific men of letters, and its first poet laureate, but critics have often neglected his later works and focused more on his poetry or better-known fiction, says Prof. Leonard Casper (English).

Casper offers a fresh appraisal of this overlooked period of Warren's career in his new book *The Blood Marriage of Earth and Sky: Robert Penn Warren's Later Novels.* The book examines five novels written by Warren between 1959 and 1977 that Casper says build upon themes central to Warren's poetry and earlier novels, including his acclaimed 1946 book *All the King's Men.*

Those themes include a sense that all things are connected and a vision of the past as an ever-present force, says Casper, who broke ground 38 years ago with his critical analysis *Robert Penn Warren: The Dark and Bloody Ground,* and considers his latest book the crowning achievement of his career as a Warren scholar.

"Through experiments with multiple narrators, stories within a story, and characters who seek to balance the need for self-knowledge and for community, Warren enacted his own yearning for elusive wholeness," said Casper.

The 1959 novel *The Cave* is the story of the rescue of a man trapped in an underground cavern, told in part from the vantage of the man in the cave, and in part from that of family members trying to save him. "A community is drawn together to rescue the fellow in the cave," said Casper, but what they're really involved in is rescuing themselves."

In the 1964 novel, *Flood*, former residents return to a small town that is about to be flooded for a reservoir. "They are going to salvage all they can, but they are really there to dig into their past, said Casper, observing that in Warren's view of the world, "nothing is ever lost,"

"It's as if Warren uses a Hubbell telescope to look into a past which is not so far away, refining the mirrors to look into inner space, not outer space" said Casper, who also offers his perspective on Warren's *Wilderness, Meet Me in the Green Glen,* and *A Place to Come To.*

An agrarian by philosophy, Warren regarded men as stewards of the land, defended the individual against concentration of power in industry or government, and saw the extended family as the basis for the community, according to Casper.

But if Warren described himself as "a yearner" and wrote of the inter connectedness between all things, Casper said he remained an atheist in private life who could not accept the notion of a divine plan for the nature—even as he seemed to argue for one in his writings.

Casper drew the title for his book from an early Warren poem, "Red-Tailed Hawk and Pyre of Youth," in which a soaring hawk "served as a sort of eye of God" for the young poet.

"He was a yearner. He wanted to believe," said Casper. "But he was not sure there were any absolutes. He sees an interrelation between all things, even inanimate things" Some of his poems are about the movement of mountains. He talks about life forces, about the migration of animals and birds, with a yearning. He says, "I'd like to think we're moving toward something, that there is a design for the universe—but I don't know. I don't know." *Boston College Chronicle.* Vol. 7. November 25, 1998. Mark Sullivan.

*

"I can think of no other work on Robert Penn Warren that gathers up so much of what this important author has been about for a half century...No other existing study of Warrens reveals his

largeness and humanity. It is ethical criticism of a very high order."
James H. Justus, AUTHOR OF *The Achievement of Robert Penn Warren.*

Leonard Casper focuses on Warren's five later novels published between 1959 and 1977. Customarily neglected by critics, these novels, Casper shows, sustained and expanded the philosophical and formal themes central to Warren's poetry and early novels, and therefore are essential to comprehending Warren's total vision, a vision that continued to be put to the test in the later novels. Through experiment with multiple narrators, stories within a story, and characters who seek to balance the needs for self-knowledge and for community, Warren enacted his own yearning for elusive wholeness.

While emphasizing the metaphysical intersection of flesh and spirit that links the novels, Casper also gives a rigorously detailed reading of each text—*The Cave, Wilderness, Flood, Meet Me in the Green Glen,* and *A Place To Come To.*

*

Dust Jacket: Leonard Casper's 1960 pioneering work, *Robert Penn Warren: The Dark and Bloody Ground,* the first book-length study of Warren, pointed the way for all subsequent studies of the poet-novelist. Now Casper presents the complement to that seminal book: a potent distillation of nearly forty years meditation on the quintessential man of letters.

While emphasizing the metaphysical intersection of flesh and spirit that links the novels, Casper also gives significant detailed reading of each text—*The Cave, Wilderness, Flood, Meet Me in the Green Glen,* and *A Place to Come To.* In doing so, he redefines and defends the purposes and methods of the original New Criticism, which, he maintains, was often mispracticed by lesser critics or misunderstood by later practitioners of narrower, ideological criticism. Indeed, he views Warren as not only the best model of New Criticism critics but also a novelist who poses the self-same dilemma that concerns postmodernists—existential man in agitated search for an abiding essence—but whose compass search for the "true north" is unsurpassed in scope. Warren's skeptical method of inquiry prevented him from ever embracing, as do many postmodernists, moral relativity as final; he always allowed for a plurality of answers. Seeking among the intimate details evidence of things unseen.

Lyrical and erudite, *The Blood Marriage of Earth and Sky* is the crowning achievement in the career of an eminent Warren scholar. It will surely further the "coming closerness" that was Warren's best hope.

LEONARD CASPER is the author of thirteen previous books and numerous essays, stories and poems. He is professor emeritus of English at Boston College. *Southern Literary Studies*. Fred Hobson, Editor. THE BLOOD-MARRIAGE OF EARTH AND SKY: Robert Penn Warren's Later Novels. Leonard Casper. Louisiana State University Press. July. 128 pages, $25.00.

*

"Casper's critical practice emulates precisely those qualities he values in Warren: He *respects* rather than merely finds *uses* for it. The reader of this compact volume will discover finely crafted meditations on a pivotal figure in modern American literature. That Casper now focuses on the novels written at the time of Warren's most sustained poetic output is not surprising, for even as a critic of fiction Casper is intensely attuned to language. What a tribute to Warren—to have been taken so seriously by so writerly a reader!" Roger Jiang Bresnahan, Michigan State University.

*

At once closely reasoned and Laurentian in its lyricism, Casper's study compels readers to readjust their point of view regarding Warren as a writer, significantly in his later novels. Warren was more than a man of letters, more than an 'entrenched' philosopher. He was the eternal pilgrim recognizing no absolutes, as revealed in his barrage of questions and distinctions (and Casper's too)." Thomas A. Gullason. University of Rhode Island.

The World of Short Fiction

The World of Short Fiction. An International Collection, Thomas A. Gullason, Leonard Casper. Harper & Brothers. 1962.

...has a truly international flavor, with many of the most important and provocative authors of America, England, France, Italy, Germany, Russia, South Africa, and China represented by at least two—and in some cases three—stories. All of the stories are integrated on the bases of related themes and techniques, and all deal with vital stimulating ideas. Eight-hundred-word, critical, up-to-date biographies on each of the authors are included along with ten essay-excerpts from one author's comment on another.

THE WORLD OF SHORT FICTION should prove invigorating and informative fare as a text Introduction to Literature, Comparative Literature, and Freshman English courses, because it not only presents the best writing from many countries for study (translations are highly readable and, at the same time, careful readings of each author's works), but also, with the inclusion of the essay-excerpts and the biographies, helps develop the critical faculties of students. The stories will also serve as excellent models for creative writing courses, because they represent the greatest possible variety of themes and forms, techniques and styles. 548 Pages. $3.75.

THOMAS A. GULLASON (Ph.D. University of Wisconsin) is Associate Professor of English at the University of Rhode Island. Previously, Professor Gullason taught at Heidelberg College and the University of Wisconsin. He has published many articles in such journals as *American Literature, Nineteenth Century Fiction* and *Modern Fiction Studies,* and has been a book reviewer for the *New York Times* and the *American Quarterly.* At present he is collecting the short stories of Stephen Crane.

LEONARD R. CASPER (Ph.D. University of Wisconsin) is Associate Professor of English at Boston College. He taught previously at the University of Wisconsin, Cornell University, and the

University of the Philippines. Professor Casper's other works include ROBERT PENN WARREN: *The Dark and Bloody Ground* and MODERN PHILIINE SHORT STORIES, as well as many short stories, poem, and articles. A Stanford Fellow in Creative WRITING (1951-1952) and Bread Loaf scholar, he is contributing editor and reviewer on several literary journals.

Modern Philippine Short Stories

MODERN PHILIPPINE SHORT STORIES. Edited by Leonard Casper. University of New Mexico Press, Albuquerque. 1962. 235 PAGES.

Dust Jacket: If you have yet to discover the pure gold of English written in the Philippines, treasure is in store for you. A Filipino literary renaissance has been sensed by coterie of experts from Edward O'Brien's enthusiastic tribute in the *Best Short Stories* of 1932 through the full-length printing of Nick Joaquin's "The Woman Who Had Two Navels" by *Partisan Review* in 1953. Yet these sixteen stories are not caviar to the general or just for the *avant-garde*—they will grip any reader.

Stories such as Dagiuio's "Wedding Dance," Arguilla's "How My Brother Brought Home A Wife," Gonzalez' "Lupo and the River" and Diaz' "Death in a Sawmill" depict the exotic primitivism of rural island life. Others (Arcellana's "Divide By Two") are urban, suburban, and down-to-earth. Some, like Nuyda's "Pulse of the Land" contrast Western character and values with those of the Orient.

Here is no regional writing in the any cultist sense—like all true artists these nine are intensely individual—yet if one factor unites them, it is pervasive, quiet realism—a discipline that has been called "a struggle for poise in the very act of seizing experience." Biographical sketches tell of the authors in war as guerrillas, members of the underground, and in the Huk uprisings. But war is of little importance in these sixteen stories. Rather a recognition of external verities—love and life and death.

English was introduced to the Philippines a scant sixty years ago, it is the language of the new Constitution, upper level texts, and of six-seventh of the newspapers but it remains minor. Schools are taught in a national language based on one of the nine native tongues, Tagalog, spoken by two-thirds of the people (80% farmers and fishermen) of the 7083 islands. Yet, English is incontestably the literary language. Five of these authors have studied in the U.S. on Rockefeller grants, one on a Guggenheim. The discipline of creating in English has lent to them depth, self-discovery, universality as surely as to Conrad.

The book's introduction is a survey of Philippine literature by the editor—himself a widely published short story writer and literary critic. His stories have appeared in the O. Henry and Foley annuals, his prose and verse in many magazines here and abroad.

Leonard Casper is a world authority on literature of the Philippines. In 1962, a Fulbright lecturer in Filipino-American studies at Ateneo de Manila and the University of the Philippines, he taught there previously from 1953 to 1956; Editor of *Six Filipino Poets* (Manila, 1953) he has served as contributing foreign editor of *Panorama*, a Manila Monthly, and as guest editor of the *Literary Review's* special Philippine number, summer, 1960. He is the author of articles on culture of the Philippines in the *American Oxford Encyclopedia*, in the *Saturday Review, Journal of Asian Studies,* and *South Atlantic Quarterly*. His opinions are extensively quoted in reviews of Philippine books.

After serving three years as a combat artilleryman in World War II, Casper received three degrees at the University of Wisconsin, where he later taught. He has been a member of the faculty at Cornell and is presently with Boston College as an associate professor of creative writing and contemporary American literature. He was a Stanford Fellow in creative writing in 1951-52, and Bread Loaf Scholar in 1961.

In the fields of general literature and literary scholarship, Dr. Casper was co-editor of the recent *World of Short Fiction* and author of the critical volume, *Robert Penn Warren: The Dark and Bloody Ground* (1960) which he wrote on a grant from the Ford Foundation.

*

"Modern Philippine Short Stories, edited by Leonard Casper. (University of New Mexico Press. 235 pp. $4.50), a collection of tales originally written in English, avoids the costume-and-local-color clichés in portraying life in a unique culture. Donald Keene, author of "Visit Japan," recently returned from a stay in the Philippines. By Donald Keene.

The kind of well-meaning American who asks sundry Asians, "Why don't you stick to your pretty native costumes?" may well object to a collection of stories in English by Filipino writers. This imperialism in reverse, which suggests that an Asian writer who writes in a European language is somehow betraying his people, has a superficial ring of liberalism, but the implication that an outsider knows better than a Filipino or an Indian author which language he should employ can hardly fail to be offensive. Whatever course Philippine literature may take in the future, we are certainly fortunate that there are now Filipinos who can speak to us beautifully in our own language, without risking the terrible hazards of translation.

The nine authors represented in in "Modern Philippine Short Stories" write English with conviction and technical mastery. Their success should not, however, be likened to that of Joseph Conrad; they are not writing in a deliberately chosen foreign language, but the language in which their stories express themselves most naturally. They may, it is true, speak Tagalog, Visayan or some other Philippine language at home, but their education has been almost entirely in English, and their literary tastes were formed by English poetry and prose. Some authors write in both English and Tagalog, but, though stories in the vernacular are financially more profitable, many Filipinos feel that they cannot express themselves fully except in the language of their education.

The stories of this collection, though in English, were written for a Filipino audience. Unlike most stories intended by Asian authors for an American or European audience, they are therefore free from a self-consciousness of parading in pretty native costumes. One does not find the grandfather hoary with the wisdom of the East, the city-bred youth who rediscovers in a village the traditional values of his people, or the shy young girl who achieves maturity as she feels the first stirrings of a man-child within her. These figures are not necessarily spurious, but their repeated presence in Western-oriented collections of Asian stories tends to color all Asia with a uniform golden glow when it should delight us instead with their variety.

Certainly, no country in Asia has a more distinct culture than the Philippines, with its Malay, Spanish and American heritage. The different elements have blended amazingly well; it is one country, for example, where American influence has clearly meant more than gadgets, jazz, and chewing gum. Rizal, the national hero, wrote two remarkable novels in Spanish, the authors of the present demonstrate that English is equally the birthright of the educated Filipino.

All the stories edited by Leonard Casper with an informative introduction are of high quality. Those by Nick Joaquin are especially remarkable. Joaquin is known among Filipino writers for his absorption with the Spanish heritage, which survives today mainly in the Catholicism that is the religion of most Filipinos. No doubt the Filipino character has been sharply differentiated from that of other peoples of Asia by this influence. Joaquin's story, "The Summer Solstice" depicts the weird amalgamation of the Catholic feast of St. John and an indigenous pagan midsummer celebration. Under the spell of the orgy a respectable upper-class matron is transformed into a pagan votary. When the feast ends, her persisting frenzy is expressed in terms of Spanish romanticism, as she commands her placid husband to prove his love by kissing her feet...

Most of the other stories in the collection describe life in the villages. This choice no doubt reflects in part on the editor's preferences, but Filipino writers apparently cannot forget that four-fifths of their people live in the countryside. Their concern may strike us as laudable when contrasted, say, with the overwhelming interest of Japanese authors in urban life, but it is nonetheless true that the lives of simple farmers and fishermen tend to lack variety. A story about an adolescent boy in a village usually resembles others on the same theme. "Wedding Dance" by Amador Daguio, achieves real poignance in the account of a farmer who leaves the wife he loves because she is barren; but we may be moved even more by the greater complexities of "A Warm Hand," by N.V.M. Gonzalez, the most influential of modern Filipino writers, or "Two Brothers," by Rony V. Diaz, a writer of exceptional power.

Each of the nine writers deserves greater attention than I have given here, but the collection a whole is of even more importance than the individual excellences. It is an admirable testimony to the emergence of another important branch of English literature. *Saturday Review*, October 6, 1962. Native Voice in Foreign Tongue.

*

MODERN PHILIPPINE SHORT STORIES, edited by Leonard Casper. Albuquerque: University of New Mexico Press, 1962. 237 pp. $4.50

Extremely well edited by the principal American student of Philippine literature, this collection reprints sixteen short stories written in English, mainly in the 1950s, by nine Filipino authors, most of whom are professors of English or government writers: Amador Daguio, Nick Joaquin, Bienvenido Santos, N.V.M. Gonzalez, Rony Diaz, Edith L. Tiempo, Francisco Arcellana, Hermel Nuyda, and Manuel Arguilla, who was executed by the Japanese in 1944.

The complex cultural tensions within these multi-lingual, quasi-colonial intellectuals, and what it has meant for them to write in English, a minority language now declining in the Philippines, rather than in one of the nine major native languages, are delicate and very interesting questions, and they are discussed sensitively by Mr. Casper in his introduction (as well as in his books and articles elsewhere). He also prefaces each story with a critical biography of its author—

accounts which are very good stories in themselves, as he tells them. Finally. He appends a glossary of dialect words, mostly Tagalog nouns, which crop up in these tales.

In general, these are sophisticated stories about unsophisticated people. They deal mainly with rural folk (who make up eighty percent of the population of the archipelago), but they are written for a mall urban audience and for readers abroad, such as ourselves. Americans will be surprised to learn that most of these pieces appeared first in Sunday supplements in Manila newspapers. There being nothing of popular formula or slick treatment about them. It is painful to think of them wrapped around garbage on Monday morning. If anything, they tend to have a little-magazine or university-review character, perhaps because many of these authors have studied creative writing in the United States on Rockefeller and Guggenheim grants—at the Writers Workshop in Iowa City, in Wallace Stegner's classes at Stanford, at Bread Loaf and elsewhere. Some of these writers have been published previously in the *Sewanee* and *Partisan Reviews,* in *Poetry, Wake, Story, Prairie Schooner,* and *Pacific Spectator.*

Because these stories are of different kinds, and because they vary in quality, it is impossible here to generalize accurately and fairly about their nine authors' talents, their individual voices and differing visions of the world. These stores are especially fresh and moving when they portray simple people in back-country *barrios,* but they are mainly valuable to us not for their exotic subject matter, but, like any good modern fiction, for their disciplined craft, and sensitive delineation of human nature.

Certain foreign touches in these stories might be cited without being captious or patronizing. A subtly un-English diction, for example, now and again reminds the reader of the presence of a narrator making an effort to find the words. There is also, it seems, to this reviewer, rather a good deal of poetic descriptions of landscape and weather, and of dreamy obscurity when dealing with subjective states of mind. This will strike some Anglo-Saxon readers as fancy affectations, at least they would be that in young American writers.

Perhaps they are Filipino traits—as, for example, is the withholding of explanation, the leaving unsaid, in some of these stories, which the editor declares to be typical "Malayan understatement."

Mr. Casper who teaches creative writing at Boston College, is himself a short story writer and poet. Married to a Harvard-trained Filipina author, he has lectured at various universities in the Philippines, and has produced other books, and some very well-written articles, on Filipino language and letters. He is the author of *Robert Penn Warren: The Dark and Bloody Ground* and is probably best known to readers of this journal as the co-editor of *The World of Short Fiction*. James B. Stronks. University of Illinois at Chicago Circle. STUDIES IN SHORT FICTION. Page 180-181.

*

NEW BOOK OUT.
U.S. PROFESSOR PROMOTING WORKS OF FILIPINO WRITERS. By Rodolfo San Diego. (*With picture of Gretchen and Len and Linda Casper*)

An American professor who has been promoting abroad works of Filipino writers in English returned recently to this country to enable him to know more about Philippine literature and to do research.

Dr. Leonard Casper, associate professor of American literature and creative writing in Boston College, rejoins the faculty of the U.P. College of Arts and Sciences as Fulbright-Smith Mundt lecturer. At the state university, Professor Casper is now teaching creative writing and in the following term he will handle courses in contemporary American literature and Philippine literature in English.

According to a letter from the publishers, a new book entitled, *Modern Philippine Short Stories*, edited by Casper under the imprint of the University of New Mexico has been published and will be ready for distribution in the U.S. this month. The works of the following Filipino writers are included in the new book: Manuel Arguilla, N.V.M. Gonzalez, Bienvenido N. Santos, Nick Joaquin, Amador Daguio, Rony V. Diaz, Francisco Arcellana, Hermel Nuyda, and Edith Tiempo.

The editor wrote in the preface of the new book: If you have yet to discover the pure gold of English written in the Philippines, treasure is in store for you."

Professor Casper said that Philippine literature, at least in English, has developed so importantly that there is real serious study of it in college level.

Casper comes back to this country with his wife, the former Belinda Ty of Malabon, Rizal. The couple have a three-year old daughter named Gretchen. Mrs. Casper is a graduate of the U.P. College of Law as valedictorian of her class in 1955. She received her master of laws (international law) degree from Harvard University in 1957.

A former G.I. and student of Wallace Stegner, Casper came here in 1953 and was with the U.P. faculty since until he returned to the U.S in 1956. He has been promoting works by Filipino writers.

While at Boston College, he edited a book entitled *Six Filipino Poets*. In 1960 he published *Robert Penn Warren: The Dark and Bloody Ground* under a Ford Foundation grant.

In 1961 he published *The Wayward Horizon: Essays on Modern Philippine Literature* and co-edited *The World of Short Fiction: An International Collection* (Summer 1960).

He edited the special Philippine issue of Fairleigh Dickinson University's *The Literary Review*, the first U.S. issue devoted exclusively to Philippine literature. This especial number grew out of a meeting with General Romulo some two years back.

Casper also wrote articles on Philippine literature and culture in *South Atlantic Quarterly*, *Antioch Review*, etc. and in the forthcoming *American Oxford Encyclopedia*. He plans to be executive editor of an anthology of Philippine literature in all languages and through Philippine history, for the Asia Society of New York.

He was appointed especial reviewer of Philippine books for the new Asian section of *Books Abroad* (in Oklahoma).

New Writing from the Philippines

Framingham – *New Writing from the Philippines*, the seventh book authored by Framingham resident, Dr. Leonard Casper of 54 Simpson Drive Dr. has been published by Syracuse University Press and will be released on June 12, the Independence Day of the Republic of the Philippines.

The short history of the Philippines, a survey of its literature, a critique of its modern writing in English, and a representative anthology is found in the single volume of the distinguished writer and critic.

The commentary is fresh, authoritative and imaginative and his analyses of the literature produced by more than 30 authors are written with sensitivity and perception.

Literary quality and inaccessibility to an American audience guided Casper's choices for the anthology, which includes an essay, eight short stories, several poems and a play, Nick Joaquin's Portrait of the Artist as Filipino. The selection shows a wide range of theme and style.

"Zita" by Arturo B. Rotor is a moving story about a young girl's initiation into womanhood. A fatherless, diffident Indian boy is the subject of Anthony Morli's "Dada." Bienvenido N. Santos explores the feelings of a Filipino living in Chicago, in "The Day the Dancers Came."

Combining history, literary criticism and literature, New Writing from the Philippines conveys the delicate yet virile quality of the Philippine people and the bittersweet flavor of their culture.

It contains nearly 40 selections written over the past three decades. The contributors are from such diverse fields as journalism, politics, education and medicine.

Dr. Casper's U.S. book publication include *Modern Philippine Short Stories, Robert Penn Warren: The Dark and Bloody Ground*, and *The World of Short Fiction*. His three books published in Manila were *Six*

Filipino Poets, The Wayward Horizon, and *The Wounded Diamond.* The latter two are collections of critical essays.

In 1960 he guest-edited the special issue of the *International Literary Review*, the first magazine in America devoted exclusively to Philippine literature. In addition, he has guest edited special Philippine issues of *Literature East and West*, and has published articles on contemporary Philippine and American literature in such periodicals as *Journal of Asian Studies, Saturday Review. South Atlantic Quarterly* and *Antioch Review.* His poems and short stories have appeared in various "little" magazines, as well as in the *O. Henry* and *Foley* annuals.

A professor of creative writing and contemporary American literature at Boston College, Dr. Casper has also taught at Wisconsin, Cornell. Rhode Island and Northwestern. In 1962-63 he was Fulbright lecturer at Ateneo de Manila, as well as at the University of the Philippines, on whose faculty he has previously served in 1953 to 1956. He holds three degrees from the University of Wisconsin and has been a Stanford Fellow in creative writing and a Bread Loaf Scholar.

Residents of Framingham since 1960, the Caspers are parents of a seven year-old daughter, Gretchen, a student at Brook Water School. Social and Personal. *Framingham News.* June 4, 1966. p.5. Framingham Author Writes History of the Philippines.

*

NEW WRITING FROM THE PHILIPPINES: A Critique and Anthology. By Leonard Casper. Syracuse University Press. 411pp. $7.95. By Helen Cort.

What sort of writing from a small country—or any country—is more significant: that which be written only in that place, or that which could have been written anywhere in the world, with simple changes of names?

Philippine writing has much to offer a world in which long underdeveloped countries are surging upward, struggling with their own identity and their place in the big picture.

"As heir of multiple cultures, as one of the most westernized of all Asian countries, as the oldest of the new republics and independent nations, the Philippines is able to provide from its own experience models of the possibilities of synthesis." By such diverse talents

LEONARD CASPER, professor of creative writing at Boston College who, probably knows more about Philippine literature than anyone living, has put together another marvelous book. His critiques of more than 30 modern writers in English are dazzling: often we must take his judgment on faith because the works discussed are so hard to come by in America.

The selections in the anthology are so full of life and death and the details which make these real for us, that the reader wishes more pieces could have been included. Although professors complain of the dearth of new writing, Mr. Casper has found such a wealth of material to choose from that Nina Estrada's love sonnets are not even mentioned.

Jose Rizal, the 19th century Philippine national hero who spoke 22 languages and traveled, studied and wrote in several countries, produced two great novels which are hardly read outside the Philippines, perhaps because his devotees "too frequently insist that Rizal be read exclusively as propagandist, not as artist."

HIS BURDEN— "to startle into image the Philippine presence, beyond all question of human worth"—is carried today by such diverse talents as N.V.M. Gonzalez, whose deceptively simple "folk" stories epitomize the rural culture, and Nick Joaquin, whose sophisticated exiles and city-dwellers wrestle with neuroses induced by a past of "four hundred years in the convent and fifty in Hollywood," as the Spanish and American colonial experience of the Philippines has been described.

Here are pygmy Negritos, restless Ilocanos, Moslems, Chinese and Indian storekeepers, fishermen and farmers, pious spinsters with their rosaries, night club entertainers—an array as colorful and delicious as the tropical fruits and fantastic fish in the Quiapo market.

AND HERE ARE loneliness, avarice, lust, sacrifice, love, fear, shame, great dignity—and a little laughter, perhaps not enough to be typical.

You will not soon forget the old revolutionary in Wilfrido Nolledo's "Rice Wine," who discovers his daughter has been selling her body to buy him rice, or the tortured, stammering Indian boy facing his gross uncle in "Dada" by Anthony Morli.

Paradoxically, as Leonard Casper says of Manuel Arguilla and could say of most of the authors represented in this collection, "when one seizes a particular firmly, he holds a universe in his hand." Helen Cort was a Peace Corps staff wife in the Philippines. *Boston Herald*, July 3, 1966. p.19. The Philippines: An Anthology of Literature.

*

Leonard Casper. NEW WRITING FROM THE PHILIPPINES: A CRITIQUE AND ANTHOLOGY. Syracuse University Press. 1966. 411pp. $7.95.

Here is a work of beauty and significance, designed to surprise with joy the newcomer to Philippine writing and to reward the knowledgeable with another example of Leonard Casper's critical abilities.

New Writing from the Philippines focusing on literature produced in original English, is a natural result of Professor Casper's long-continuing relation as "witness and agent to a literature in formation" and of his intimate understanding of "a people in search of completion."

The "Anthology" of selections from a score of Filipino writers who have produced in the last three decades is preceded by an article by Carlos P. Romulo, himself once a professor of English literature, who comments on the rapport "between the work of the imagination and the sources if its images which exist external to it, in the very context of life, or reality, in the appearances and qualities of the social fact."

Professor Casper prefaces his two valuable critical chapters with an initial chapter on the writer's milieu--"the Philippine experience," a term which sums up "those socioeconomic conditions which, historically, have both provoked and prevented the search for cultural continuity, and, more especially, the climate of the Philippine imagination itself, including the unremitting reputation of Jose Rizal's nineteenth century novels." The dominant theme is the tension between stability and change.

The confrontation of folk culture and urban commerce, "the uneasy co-existence of traditional folk pattern and the impulse toward social mobility," is reflected in the first group of writers assessed by Professor Casper. He then turns to presumably more complex authors who are and who write about people of many pasts, of conflicting allegiance, of fragmented selves seeking for wholeness of self and society.

The intelligent ordering of material in the author's critique and anthology is supported by helpful notes and lists, and the index contains useful glosses on words of special acculturation. Carl. D. Bennett/ St. Andrews Presbyterian College. STATE UNIVERSITY COLLEGE. New Paltz, New York 12561.

*

Casper, Leonard: *New Writing from the Philippines: A Critique and Anthology*. (Syracuse University Press, 1966) 411 pp. $7.95.

The appearance of an anthology in literature is a rare event, so in fact, that the reviewer greets it with unmixed delight and is tempted to bestow on it unqualified praise. Every year hundreds of short stories, poems, novels, and dramas are produced by Filipino writers in the vernaculars and in English and published in local periodicals, but it is good year when more than three or four slender volumes of reprints appear. Of course, a great portion of this production has little intrinsic value and deserve relegation to obscurity, but there is also much that is fine literature and which speaks eloquently to Filipino ideals and aspirations. Such superior productions are worthy of wide dissemination in the Philippines and abroad, and it is a pity the majority of them become lost for all intents and purposes, practically unknown to the Philippine public for whom it could be a source of pride and spiritual nourishment.

The appearance of this book fills a great need: it presents stories, poems and a drama from twenty of the best writers of the past thirty years on a wide range of themes and in a wide range of styles. These are all items which would otherwise remain unknown in America though a number of them have appeared in books issued in the Philippines. The coverage of this book is representative of what has been done in English in the last thirty years, though there are, to be sure, high-ranking writers and no end of works of lasting value which had been left out. On the whole no important type of production or theme is left unrepresented and works from older and younger members of this generation are included. The selection deserved highest praise from the point of view of taste. There is nothing that is junk, and a good proportion is without doubt of first rank.

The selections occupy slightly more than half of the space in the book. The other half is devoted to critique and factual background. There is full bibliography of Philippine writers in English, a glossary of terms commonly met with in Philippine writings, and a list of writers represented in this volume with an outline of their lives. This is the first time so much information on Philippine literature has been gathered in one place. One could only wish similar biographical information on all the writers discussed could have been provided.

As a history of Philippine literature in English of the past thirty years, this book falls short of success. The author identifies various themes and styles...but the attempts to mark out the schools, tendencies, or types of writing are superficial ...In the selections presented one can recognize features in common to all, different from anything that can be found in American or European literature...it is still a book well worth having, for it contains a selection of some of the finest English writings produced in the Philippines in recent times. John U. Wolff. Cornell University.

*

New Writing from the Philippines: a Critique and Anthology. Leonard Casper.

"It is difficult to imagine the reader who will sample the selection of short stories, poetry, and drama without experiencing a sense of discovery."

"*New Writing from the Philippines* is a valuable and illuminating volume on two main counts. First, Professor Casper's integrity and broad knowledge are evident throughout. Secondly, and most significantly, the literature is allotted space to speak eloquently—as it does—for itself." *Saturday Review*. $7.95 New Letters, University of Missouri, December 1972.

Firewalkers: Literary Concelebrations

Firewalkers: Literary Concelebrations 1964-1984. Quezon City. Phil. 1987. 188 pages.

Leonard Casper has carved out a niche as the foremost American critic and literary historian of Philippine literature...*Firewalkers*, twenty essays on contemporary Philippine writers and their work. The emphasis is on writers (and critics) in English, though one essay also deals with various Philippine publications in the vernaculars.

Casper advocates and exemplifies serious, tireless study and consideration of these writers. The readers of his essays will find apt and informed analysis of values, themes, and goals of such distinguished figures of the postwar scene as Ninotchka Rosca, Nick Joaquin, Severino Montano, and Kerima Polotan. He knows many, perhaps all, of the writers he discusses and speaks from a direct and intimate involvement in their aspirations. In the preface he casually mentions the family library, "which eventually held over a thousand titles"; few collections of Filipiniana could compete. He builds, thus on a firm foundation. Residence and study enable him to assess works in their appropriate milieu; years as an English professor add a further dimension to his thoughtful and sympathetic criticism.

One example of an essay that is stimulating in its original perspective is entitled "*Kami/Tayo*: A Theoretical Division of Philippine Literature." Here Casper relates two Tagalog pronouns, both meaning "we" but not in any way *synonyms*—the first of them excludes the second person or "you," whereas the second includes the person or persons addressed—to two types of writing *kami* (exclusive) for the literature of utility and exploitation and the like, and *tayo* (inclusive) for that of expansiveness, participatory discovery...This leads him to categorize various works, and we sense a preference for the *tayo* writers. *Firewalkers* is a useful guide. Edgar C. Knowlton, Jr. Honolulu. *World Literature Today*. Summer 1988.

A Lion Unannounced: Twelve Stories and A Fable

A Lion Unannounced: Twelve Stories and A Fable. Southern Methodist University Press, Dallas. 1971.

"The Themes of these stories are of the briefness and surprises of life, of the hard grudging giving and giving-up of love among those whose lives are hard, of death and its effect on the still-living; of the love-hate relationships of sons and fathers, mothers and sons, daughters and fathers, brothers and sisters, wives and husbands. The stories all have to do with new people in a new land who come to be old, worn, used people realizing the hardness of what is really an old and tough land, and the unkept promises of their lives. The various small tragedies of these lives are handled with a lyric sense by the writer. There is originality in the technique of telling: the omniscient point of view allows glimpses into many consciousness, always behind it is the author's voice, and Casper's is the voice of a loving, caring storyteller." Marshall Terry, Author of *Old Liberty* and *Tom Northway*.

*

THE STORIES included in **A Lion Unannounced** are interrelated in theme, tone and style; together they make a united work which asks the question, "Who is my brother?"

The theme is universalized from the particulars of the other stories in the fable called, "Face Like an Ikon," which centrally placed in the book to indicates its relationship to the rest. Set in a half-mythic country identified as "the Baltic: then," "Face Like an Ikon" is the only one not located in America. The twelve that surround it concern what might be a single immigrant family whose blood-network becomes in various American states—in Illinois for "The Fifth Wall" and "Silent Outcry, Sleep," in Kansas for "The Balancing Act," in Arizona for "Deep Country Part," in Texas for "A Nest of Boxes," in Wisconsin for "The Tumbler" and the title story "A Lion Unannounced," in Arkansas for "Sense of Direction," and "Drink to Private Gods," in Hawaii for "Aflame, in Flower," in Washington for "Hard in These Fastnesses," in New Mexico for "Least Common Denominator."

Whatever the central characters—the girl-in-spite of herself, the unborn, the lover-antagonist, the spinster-mother—they are in the process of erosion that takes place during their lives in the hardness and toughness of the land, scoured down to a resistant, irreducible self. And in each the theme-question is illuminated from some new angle.

Recurring images appear from story to story, further weaving them together. For one, there is the image of the bird, which as it reappears begins to suggest the possibilities of ascension. Typically, it is the family sense that provides the core of self and the courage to reascend.

A Lion Unannounced is one of the first two short fiction manuscripts in the National Council on the Arts Selection program…the jurors made the selection "in recognition of the quality of the submitted manuscript and in the earnest hope of encouraging future work" by the author.

Not only the book as a whole, but individual stories included in it have received special recognition. "A Sense of Direction," first published in the *Southwest Review* in 1950, was reprinted both in the Martha Foley *Best American Short Stories* volume and in the *Prize Stories:*

O. *Henry Awards* volume that year. Others have been anthologized in *Stanford Short Stories 1953*, *Stories from Epoch* (1966) and *Fiction as Process* (1968). Original publication was widespread: in *Contemporary Fiction, Epoch, New Mexico Quarterly, Perspective, Southwest Review,* and *Western Review.*

Although he has been publishing stories and poems for almost three decades, his books before the present one have all been "academic." Dustjacket.

Leonard Casper is America's best gift to Philippine literary criticism. He is also an ideal critic of Philippine literature. It is rather ironic that one of the most knowledgeable and understanding critics of Philippine literature is not a Filipino. But if there is such a thing as spiritual citizenship, Casper has earned it with the Philippines. His profound knowledge and understanding of Philippine literature in English and his contributions to the proper appreciations of it will always make him one of the most important figures in Philippine letters.

Casper did not bring a new strategy or start a new school of criticism. His importance as a critic is in his humanity. He is informed and informing, candid but just. He has the gift of losing himself in the worlds and myths he criticizes and then coming out of them with revelations that reflect his own experiences but also somehow mirrors ours. *The Philippine Times* April 1978, Professor David V. Quemada.

The Legacy of Leonard Casper
by
Paulino Lim, Jr.

Leonard Casper in the early 50s gave up a London Fulbright to teach at U.P. and Ateneo. He began writing essays on Philippine life and culture that helped Filipinos "discover that they have a world-literature." (1) He also provided the criteria by which to distinguish among the good, the best and the ephemeral.

The essays defined the country's character and psychology reflected in the literature written in English. The Filipino writers were influenced by Spanish, British and American English. The Spanish influence colored their English to be flowery and sentimental, the British crisp and Orwellian, and the American had either Hemingway or Faulkner copycats before they found their own voice.

Casper recalled that "literature in the Philippines has a lengthy history of didacticism, descending from colonial powers and of polemicism, rising from protests against those powers . . . the continuing presence of American military and escalating multinational corporate interests can be decried as alien to Philippine self-definition and -determination." (2) Jose Rizal's *Noli Me Tangere* is an example of a didactic novel designed to expose social injustice. It set the tone for the Filipinos' 'literature of protest' that has been maintained against American and Japanese Occupation forces, and against the ruthless dictatorship of Ferdinand Marcos. Rizal was executed on charges of treason. The dictator protesters ended up behind bars. (3)

At a time when social media can allegedly whitewash Marcos's corrupt dictatorship and get his son elected president, it is worth remembering and re-reading the poems, stories of the jailed protesters. What the son will do remains to be seen. And it will depend upon the writers' integrity and loyalty to either the ruling party or the country.

The link between history and literature, between facts and the writer's imagination, animates Casper's literary criticism. He compares Jose Garcia Villa's infatuation with linguistic inventions to geometric Cuban paintings. He defines the developing themes of writers, like Nick Joaquin's Filipinizing of foreign cultures and the unresolved tensions between the sacred and the profane in the short story "Summer Solstice," and novel *The Woman Who Had Two Navels*. He describes what drives F. Sionil Jose initially is his need to find his father, in order to complete his own self-image. Franz Arcellana's incantatory repetitions echo the rhythms of the pasyon or of litanies longing to reconcile joyful/sorrowful mysteries. NVM Gonzalez praises the fertile work-ethic of the kaingero above the preciousness of the intelligentsia. He pinpoints Ben Santos's portraiture that makes him justly famous, his ability to record the heartbeat of his character.

Dear to me is his essay entitled, "The Four-Chambered Heart of Paulino Lim Jr." I have published a quartet of didactic novels set against the Marcos Dictatorship that I call "The Philippine Quartet," a modest tribute to Lawrence Durrell whose "Alexandria Quartet " I read as an undergraduate. Casper was the speaker at a conference that I organized when I was a student at Santo Tomas in the 60s. I was impressed by his warmth, humor, and knowledge of literature.

Among the women writers he comments on include Edith Tiempo (poetry and fiction), Linda Ty Casper (true-fiction and trilogy of events occurring one hundred years ago), Cecilia Manguerra Brainard (*Song of Yvonne*), Jessica Hagedorn (*Dogeaters*), Ninotchka Rosca (*Twice Blessed*). A more complete listing is found in *Green Circuits*.

This memoir, that his wife Linda Ty Casper has gathered from his writings before Alzheimer's intervened, solidifies one of Leonard Casper's achievements as the foremost American critic of Philippine World Literature. Paulino Lim, Jr., Author and Professor Emeritus of English at California State University, Long Beach.

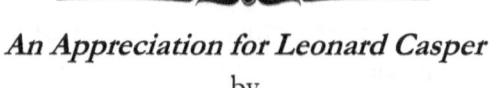

An Appreciation for Leonard Casper
by
L.M. Grow

Leonard Casper was a rare combination of outstanding, multifaceted scholar and quintessential kind and thoughtful human being. His academic range was enormous, yet his depth of insight into single works was virtually unparalleled, and his works resonate today as much as they did when they were originally published. His early (1966) book *New Writing from the Philippines: A Critique and Anthology* already showcased his versatility. Its very subdivision titles speak to its clear contextualization: "Stability and Change: Folk Culture and City Commerce: Confrontations"; "A People of Many Pasts and Complex Parts" (individual author analyses); "Anthology" (single poems and short stories by salient authors). These subtitles are arranged from wider to narrower focus. His penchant for inclusiveness also encompasses "Selected Bibliography of Philippine Literature in English," "Checklist of Philippine Literature Published in the United States, 1930-65," and "Glossary/Index." All these features facilitate its suitability for use as a scholarly resource or as a textbook. As recently as 2021 I confidently recommended that Professor Charlie Wei, who was in the process of starting a Philippine Studies program at his university in Guilin, China, acquire this book as a foundational resource.

In terms of editing, Dr. Casper's remarkable range included an issue of vernacular works (1969), and throughout his critical corpus appear vernacular terms that enrich both texture and pinpoint accuracy in his exfoliations of meaning. He did excellent work in his many published essays and books about American literature as well. His many talents even extended to creative writing. His late career novel *The Circular Firing Squad* (1999) exemplifies the longevity of his creative writing career, and his earlier service as director of several creative writing programs and his participation as fellow in residence in others attest to the esteem in which he was held.

With all his many accomplishments, his kindness, concern for others, and collegiality never wavered. In my case, if he saw a text in a different light from the way I did, he never took a corrective stance; though, being a generation ahead of me and by the mid-1970's a renowned authority, he could well have. Instead he couched his response, in print and directly via letter, as evidence that the text was panoplied enough to support multiple interpretational possibilities. When he sent me copies of his own books, he appended a greeting of "with admiration" or even "with fond admiration," thus shifting the focus from himself to the book's recipient. He even interceded on my behalf in a way that eased greatly the obstacles to my research and scholarly publications for the rest of my career. At my teaching only college, those few of us who engaged in the activity were often looked at askance and with the suspicion that we were shorting our teaching preparations in order to do so. On one occasion, my department head told me, "I don't see what value any of this has," especially referencing a field that she hadn't even heard of---Philippine literature. Shortly thereafter, her office phone rang. Len asked to speak to me. Her comment was, "There's a real professor from Boston College who wants to speak with you." I invited her to stay while Len and I talked about his plan to have my book on the epistolary criticism of Manuel A. Viray published in the United States as a two-part journal entry, simultaneous with its Philippine appearance as a book. Len had already contacted the journal's editor and received approval for the project. Thereafter, those of us who felt impelled to advance human knowledge as well as teach to the best of our abilities had little less resistance to overcome. Faculty were able to recertify by submitting copies of their publications instead of taking graduate courses they should have been teaching instead. After my retirement a mathematics professor discovered a new prime number, and the college proudly announced his find. These occurrences and developments illustrate the reach and strength of the positive influence that Leonard Casper always seemed to exude.

Perhaps the most striking example of Len's ability to synthesize apparently disparate elements into a coherent cultural landscape appears in another late career book: *Green Circuits of the Sun* (2002). The chapter entitled "Directions to the Grail" casts a light tint of Christian Humanism, in the tradition of the late Fr. Miguel Bernad but far more expansive, over what would seem to be the most anomalous undertaking imaginable: integrating a non-Filipino with no Filipino family connections who had not even set foot in the country into a congruent rendering of Philippine culture, a congruence reflecting not just the respective position but also the value to the culture shared by all who have participated in it.

As always throughout Len's writings, the virtues of humility and brotherhood and the absence of even a trace of egotism are evident in his note on the first page of *Green Circuits*: "For Lynn, co-laborer in the same vineyard. Len."

As I have said only once before, Adios po, my old friend. L.M. Grow, Author, Emeritus Senior Professor at Broward College, and Literary Critic whose career specialty was Philippine Literature.

8

LETTERS: UNIVERSITY OF WISCONSIN/UNIVERSITY OF RHODE ISLAND/UNIVERSITY OF SOUTH CAROLINA

Len taught at Cornell *after the Creative Writing Fellowship at Stanford 1951, taking an open leave of absence to accept a Fulbright to London. In August 1949, he requested to be absolved from the obligations of the Fulbright grant and, in 1953, went to the Philippines where he taught at the UP and Ateneo, until 1956 when, married, he returned to the US and began teaching at Boston College; returning several times after, to teach at UP, Ateneo and other colleges, on Fulbright and other grants. He retired in 1999 and began teaching at the SOARS program in Wellesley: seniors teaching seniors.*

Fulbright

HAVE RECEIVED ASSURANCE FROM THE DEPARTMENT OF STATE THAT YOUR AWARD LETTER ON THE WAY. WODLINGER. Western Union August 2, 1949, 2pm. New York, NY 2, 1259p Leonard Casper 112 Eighth Street Fond du Lac WI.

*

On August 3, 1949, Len asked to be absolved of the Fulbright award. Institute of International Education, 2 West 45 St. New York 19, N.Y.

Dear Mr. Wodlinger: ...I have requested to be absolved from obligations of the Fulbright award because, while attempting to explain to friends why I was relinquishing a position...on the staff of the University of Wisconsin, for an opportunity to study abroad, I realized how wrong such a choice was.

In the first place, conditions have changed since the original application. At that time I saw no farther than a Master's degree and considered a year in the United Kingdom primarily for the prestige which it would offer in seeking some (indefinite) future job. Now, having attained the Masters, I prefer progress toward a Ph.D., toward practice teaching, and toward appropriate employment on the level of that higher degree. In view of the fact that my specialties will now become creative writing, American literature and international contemporary literature, it would seem that a whole year to British contemporary literature alone ...is not concentration of effort. In short, I will be further along toward an intelligible goal by remaining in America.

My interest in England has not changed; only clarified. Please proceed as if a grant had not been awarded to me. Sincerely...

Correspondence with University of Wisconsin professors: Helen C. White, chair; Frederick Hoffman; classmates, Sr. Bernetta Quinn; Robert Peters, Thomas A. Gullason, professor at the University of Rhode Island, with whom Len co-edited The World of Short Fiction, Harper and Row, 1962, 1971; *Charles Hoffman, professor at URI.*

*

112 Eighth St. Fond du Lac, WI, August 17, 1949.

Dear Miss White: You will be happy to learn that the Fulbright Committee and the Institute of International Education awarded me a scholarship at St. Catherine's College, Cambridge University. However, before the final notification was made, I withdrew from the competition. Because of your kindness in recommending me, both in writing and by word, I feel I owe you an explanation of my actions.

The decision was difficult, and in either case, cannot be wholly correct. Several matters arose that demanded consideration; at various times, each one seemed the most important one, but their rank no longer significant; what is, is the fact that they were all important...

I make no excuse...and admit its speciousness. At the time of its conception, it seemed thoroughly standard and acceptable...a means of entering England, and I was growing weary at Wisconsin.

As I have told Mr. Wodlinger of the Institute, my interest in England has not changed, it has merely clarified. I have had to see it in a perspective of precedence: if I expect to teach, in this order of preference or some combination thereof, creative writing, American literature...

Furthermore, there was a family financial situation to ponder, not final but possible; not present but imminent, not disastrous but considerable, against the prestige which a year in England would afford, had to be weighed the less spectacular but perhaps more practical experience of a graduate assistantship at Wisconsin. For some time, it had seemed wise to plan each semester as if it might be the last, and to make the most of it.

These are some of the reasons for my refusal of the award—which was most generous, by the way, and most tempting. Someone who deserves it more and who can benefit others and himself more by it, has the scholarship now.

Unfortunately, reason alone doesn't make one happy, and I am neither proud nor completely satisfied with my decision. However, when I saw that the award was becoming probable, it was necessary to review the facts, to insist on being honest, and then to decide what was honest.

I think my greatest regret in having to refuse the Fulbright scholarship lay in the knowledge that it would be a sort of betrayal of those who had recommended me. I hope that you will forgive me for being honest so late. Sincerely...

*
Helen C. White

The University of Wisconsin, December 12, 1955. Mr. Leonard Casper, Department of English, University of the Philippines, Quezon City, Philippines.

Dear Leonard: It is great pleasure, indeed, to hear from you again, and I am delighted to have that very impressive record of publication added to my own very vivid memory of the distinctions of your writing in my own course.

I shall, of course, put your letter in our file for consideration when we take up the problem of instructors for next year. I am afraid we shall not have any opening good enough for you. After all, you are ready to try for an assistant professorship...

Fortunately, I have just received a letter from Mr. James E. Miller, the acting chairman of the English Department of the University of Nebraska, Lincoln, Nebraska, requesting a recommendation for someone in the creative writing field who would work for two years with Professor Wimberly, the editor of *Prairie Schooner* and then succeed him as editor when he retires. Rank and salary would depend on the qualifications of the individual...

I have written a very strong recommendation of you to him...If you are interested, I should be glad to send on your record and this publication list, but I shall hold them until I hear from you. And, of course, I shall keep you in mind when openings come our way.

Again, it is a great pleasure to hear from you and to know that things are coming along so well.

With every good personal wish, I am/Very sincerely yours...Helen C. White, Chairman.

*
Sister Bernetta Quinn

Dear Leonard, It was good to get your letter after the years. Christmas belongs to you in a very special sense, in my memory. I recall how discouraged I would become at the UW students...Your Stanford experience, in the simple village at Christmas Eve, was a star of hope to me, a proof that just as you yourself felt, if good exists, and it does, it must have a reason for being...

I am spending Christmas with our Sisters Carol, Janet, Bernadine, and the parents of the last named, in Our Lady of the Valley parish, here at Langley, S.C. about seventy miles from Columbia. Tomorrow, I go to the MLA, where I may see you, though like myself you may not have much interest in that convention.

As I sat in Midnight Mass I realized that the Child had come to me earlier in the day. Shortly after I arrived, I went with Sister Bernadine to bring a few last holiday remembrances to the Jones family...part of the extreme poverty of the rural South, which in some ways is not poverty at all. The couple of shacks were incredible: at the end of a muddy trail full of holes, and at the center of junk illimitable...it would take a short story to communicate the experience. No embarrassment or shyness, high culture and real cordiality, no apologies to speak of for the debris inside or outside the houses. And in the midst of the debris was a Christmas tree...in the kitchen, apple-lemon cake was baking, if you could find the oven; the children took me to see all their treasures, and we named a turkey in a pen Ruby and a cat Isaiah...I can't convey the event, it was so very special. We loved each other. And the Child was in my spontaneous efforts to give them every possible joy of my presence, and in their response, so unmistakable. I have been in the academic ambience of USC for 3 1/2 years with no welcome, and here in ten minutes I was at the center of the lives of persons who were "gentle" in Chaucer's sense. You are a poet. You will understand.

I am glad Linda's writing has been so successful and that the children continue to enrich your lives...My own days are mostly struggle, mostly uphill except during the larger expanses when they are downhill. I do not know how to proceed any more than the Webster heroine ("My soul is like a ship...") but He has always shown the way.

Have a blessed year. I, too, I guess, know "a kind of peace, as weary as anywhere," but good enough. No, my life is much more rather than less weary, but it goes on, somehow. And let us hope what seems failure is not entirely so. Love to all, Sister Bernetta. 1704 Gamewell Drive, Columbia, South Carolina, 29206, Christmas Day, 1972.

*

Sister Bernetta visited us in 1967. Len took her on day trips. She wanted particularly to see Thoreau's hut on Walden Pond, Concord. It was hard for her to walk uphill and down, the trail unmarked, but Gretchen helped her. She loved the view of the river from the house.

Len and I later were residents of the Rockefeller Foundation Bellagio Center in Italy. Len wrote The Opposing Thumb, Decoding Literature of the Marcos Regime, *during his residency in 1994, the month enabling him to work no longer intermittently with teaching. There were many activities, though not distractions but enrichments at the Center. A close camaraderie developed among the writers, poets, musicians, historians, artists, residents from other disciplines; and the library, music room, halls and meeting rooms were space for varied forums. Len loved to sing in impromptu musicals, to walk the grounds of the huge estate down to Lake Como. And the dining room never closed. Though often, after the sumptuous dinners, Pasquale Pesce, the director would lead those willing and able to walk down to Bellagio, to a place with three floors: Heaven, Earth, Hell; and Len brought back stories of pasta dinners, desserts and of course, wine. I needed a cane to walk then so stayed in the Villa Serbelloni. Other times Gianna Celli, assistant director, took me down to the Lake where bocce was played by residents, and one could see the gates and cemeteries of the towns along the shore. She was generous with offers to take me to places inaccessible with my cane.*

*

Robert Peters

Dear Len: DO write me at home. I don't go to campus all that often, and I would not want your letters delayed a minute longer than necessary. You probably think this is bullshit. Sorry I don't type better. Here's my theory: my correspondence is so vast (I'm not boasting) that I feel if I don't proofread and correct typos, not only will the recipient feel that that I have written his/her in white heat, and thus they have the whole flush of my enthusiasm for them, as my brain races along faster than my fingers do...the latter tripping as they attempt to keep up. I promise though I will try to be more careful when I write to you.

I've been on campus since 6 a.m. And this is the last day of classes, until nearly October. My Poetry and War class has been reading Ginsberg's Plutonium Odes, along with v.nam war poets, Dickey's firebombing, Bly's tooth mother, WW poets. All Quiet on the Western Front, Whitman...A terrific class...from my point of view. Oh, yes, I shamelessly have them read LUDWIG, since he was a thoroughly pacific king. My apologies for not sending the book on to you...I will make amends by throwing in a Countess as well, although you may hate the latter. Why don't you review it? Reviewers seem not to want to touch it—they find it so disturbing, and feel, I gather, that I was revealing more of my inner self than is healthy. Curious the ignorance out there—which assumes that poet/fiction writer does play the negative capability riff, and that true skill is to inhabit the skin of some person not yourself, etc. I don't need to give you this speech.

I disown you utterly for abandoning poetry and that rat race. I'm sure that getting fiction placed is far more difficult...but it's rough for poets, too, until you get a toehold, and when you look at all the mess around, rarely, in the more prestigious ones, do poets without some on-going reputation get published. I think their thinking goes like this: if I publish a James Merrill or Galway Kinnell poem libraries will have to order the magazine, etc. If I publish Joe Pig Puzzle they may even return the mag...I'm about to advice the library here to cancel orders for Antioch, Sewanee, Kenyon, Hudson, etc...where nothing, nothing of any consequence in poetry is happening. Maybe also Poetry magazine...although as bad as it has been around so long it should have shelf space, although nobody reads it.

I'm sending Linda's list over and asking them to order. They should. Also, I am enclosing a list of my stuff still in print and will greatly appreciate your seeing it ordered. You might use as ammo the fact that I will be in Boston and environs reading and performing and talking this November. Will want to see you and family then, no matter how briefly. Who is in charge of such events at BC? I'm not pressuring you here, Leonard...

I'm going back to Wisconsin to be a writer in residence at a retreat in the Northwest woods of Wisconsin, at some camp. Hope they have a lake to plunge into. First I perform my Blood Countess on a rooftop in Minneapolis at night. I had hoped to have time to dash over to Eagle River to see relatives—but since my daughter will be flying in from Geneva, I don't want to miss her...and Jeff and Akemi are coming the day or so after I get home. Last trip back to E. Rover was not all that rewarding...depressing stories on nephews and nieces...and value systems (booze, snowmobiling, killing animals, etc.) depress me. And yet nature itself is so incredibly moving. I guess I'm a thorough California addict by now. Just toting up years the other day, and I have taught in the UC system for 26 years! Of course, you've been at BC longer than that.

Thanks much for the photo—I see the same LC there I used to know so well, and to love. Your collar gives you the look of a semi-frocked Jesuit...but it IS you. My hair looks very similar, in fact, except that I have it clipped truck-driver short, so as to intimidate les gens around me. I can't allow my image to go about seeming to be an over-sized cuddly panda. I prefer the image of critic red in tooth and claw to prevail. Robert Peters.

*

Dear Len, thanks for writing back so soon, and for bringing me up to date. I might say that I have written 5 novels, none apparently publishable. So that effort (which was major at one time) has been a failure, that and trying to write science scripts for public television. I got fired from the latter job. I still fantasize that I can write anything I set my mind to. I have written CRUNCHING GRAVEL, an autobio, of my life in N. Wis in 1936 when I was 12 and go to high school. I take that subculture poverty farm life throughout the seasons. An agent has been working to sell it, and anytime now I should hear what might be good news. I never count on these things though until they actually occur. B. (Robert Peters.) 4 June 87. 9431 Krepp Dr. Huntington Beach.

*

Thomas Gullason

Dear Pal, Believe it or not (not by Ripley but by Poor Tom Turlygood) the day I found your missive on my porch—it was like a missile to me—I was ready to write to you pronto. But as that sometime poet said somewhere, way does indeed lead to way, and here I am at this late date responding to my old Pal, down up the road apiece.

...You remember how, many moons ago, I just dropped in on you people unannounced (it was only because I liked you people, period) and you diplomatically tolerated my behavior. Then one day, I woke and for more than a decade now I always called...JUST SEND ME A NOTE NOT A MISSILE...before a less than grand entrance. So why don't you let me know in advance that you are forsaking the Big World for my little joint so that I can be here waiting with open arms and good fellowship.

After that long-winded introduction, where are we Len? I'm not sure where I am. Sometimes I feel like that fellow from Hawthorne's story who disappeared for 25 years and returned and was way out of step. Then I feel like Rip Van Winkle, snoozing things away. I am sort of bewildered, depressed, angered by the affairs of State and the World, and even by my local yokel world, that is, my professors who profess so much about so little. Gee, you must think I am like Diogenes, and what I really need is a fresh bath...

I know that when I see people like you I perk up, and I enjoy the fun of it all. It's hard being funny here, and relaxed. They tell you can't go home again, but I wish I could start things all over. I hope it's not because I am getting older, but our Wisconsin Days were Fresh Air Fund Days for me. Boy, I wish I could get some fresh air. Or is the air stale everywhere, Len, and I just don't know it.

...the other week I was browsing through some of the journals, and I saw that piece co-authored with Gretchen. Boy, you must be proud. That's great. How is Gretchen doing? What are her plans? She seems on her way onward and upward. And how about our fireball, Tina?... I hope you are all making it big, whatever you are doing.

I thought of Tina the other day, when I was cursing the great good luck Mr. Uptight...I think he has mountains out of molehills—namely, studying navels...

This summer I really splurged my time—writing or rewriting 4 stories (when I should be finishing my critical work). But I could interest no one on the top level, though I at least received a personal letter from an editor, who wanted to see something else. But no go. But then I read Atlantic and Harper's and I find the stories are about drugs, "relationships," and navels. And what do I deal with? Things that must be pretty musty Victorianisms...

At least we can have some benefits. As Willy says it, I honestly do feel it all keeps my pores open. Much more than do my colleagues and what resembles Academia...

My very best to my pals up the road a bit. Yours sincerely, Tom. URI Kingston, RI 02881. 26 November 1981.

*

Frederic Hoffman

Dear Leonard,

...Tell Ed Nehls that I consider his "Composite Biography" of DHL one of *really great* achievements of modern literary scholarship, and that I speak often with great pride of having a in very small share in his career. If he's able will you ask him to write to me. God help him in his distress. People suffer too much in this profession... (Ed Nehls was one of the UW Alums who went on to teach at Boston College: Richard E. Hughes, P. Albert Duhamel, Ed Nehls, and Len.)

I was amused by your having sent your Christmas card to Buffalo. I did almost go there, and may still, but they've never concluded the deal, and in my case I go to Austin, Texas, a week from tomorrow... to lecture and (presumably) to discuss "terms." Somehow, I feel that there will be other opportunities; and the East seems the proper place for me to go. But I shall go where there is the best possibility of decent friends and colleagues, regardless of geography or prestige.

Love to Linda and your daughter (mine is 15 2/3 years old and stunningly beautiful…)

As ever, Fred Hoffman. 2- 8-64. University of California, Riverside.

PS. In 2 weeks I shall send you a copy of my latest book, published by the Princeton U.P.

PS. 2 If you have really *first-rate* graduates, UCR has a PhD (and an MA) program, plus six REA (?) fellowships and others. I do hope you'll think of us.

Note: Fred Hoffman was Len's professor at UW. He invited Len to join the faculty at UC Riverside.

*

Dear Len:

…A change of location and career at age 55 (especially in view of health problems) may appear a crackpot move—but I've never felt better; and my doctor (the most cautious person since the Prime Minister who plucked this flower from that nettle—Neville Chamberlain) has finally broken down and said, It's impossible but it's true—you're well.

I hope to dig in, do much writing, graduate teaching, and the kind of seminar cum coffee—extension I had in Madison—in short, I want very much to be myself and at my best. UW-Madison deserves my best.

I'm glad you're getting things published, hope you'll let me know when the Philippine study will be read. How about your own poetry, and fiction? …This crazy profession is full of (in almost equal amounts) of the best and the worst!)

Love to Linda, and your child (children?) As ever, Fred. 4/14/65. University of California, Riverside.

*

Dear Len:

I've just today had a chance to see your review of *The Mortal No Thought*. I am deeply grateful to you for your expressed admiration; it was quite a shot in the arm. I hope I can live up to your speculative… of the last paragraph.

Hope all goes well with you and yours. As ever, Fred. October 2, 1965.

*

Dear Leonard:

Circumstances have made a trip east before fall semester difficult, if not impossible. I'm grateful to you for your invitation, and I hope you'll have wonderfully relaxing month. I may go to Europe for two weeks or so in September, but the plans for that trip are still—surprising because of imminence—not final. As ever, Fred. 8-27-67
PS. I much regret not seeing you again and failing to meet Linda and Gretchen for the first time.

*

Dear Mr. and Mrs. Casper,

I don't know if you have heard as yet of my husband's death on Christmas Eve. If not, I am sorry that I must tell you so suddenly…

The card that is enclosed was the last he wrote and was unmailed. I would like you to know how fond he was of you. He showed me your book of Philippine stories, which particularly interested me since I had lived in Malaysia for two years and have friends in the Philippines.

Sincerely, Mary Hoffman (1987).

*

Charles Hoffmann

Dear Len and Linda,

…We are destined to meet at Logan, you on your way to the Philippines, we on our way to England… For the moment we are hiding out in Newport…

I hope you have not been haunting the bookstores for our book because the University of Georgia Press decided to postpone publication from the fall list to spring, probably in March...

I am now officially retired from URI on a disability pension because my hearing difficulty, so you can call me emeritus, whether merited or not. I did miss teaching last year, not at all the feuds and factions that the English department is heir to wherever it locates itself, whether in Kingston or Madison Wisconsin and Boston Mass (or Cambridge, Mass) ...

The Hoffmans continue to spin quality yarns which are examined and sent back by the best magazines in the country. We congratulate (and envy) Linda on her growing list of published stories. Tess and I are trying to combine her interest in photography with my writing so that we can break new ground if not fill new holes. Love, Charlie and Tess. December 19, 1987.

9

LEN IN ACADEME

Len was graduate assistant at UW. On graduating he went to Stanford University for a Creative Writing Fellowship, then taught at Cornell for a year, asking for an open leave of absence. In 1953 he took a freighter and went to the Philippines on the invitation of Filipino awardees at Stanford, Amador Daguio, Fel Santa Maria, and others. From 1953 to 1956 he taught at the University of the Philippines, Ateneo de Manila University, and in other colleges in the Philippines as a Fulbright lecturer.

Len started teaching at Boston College in 1956. In 1961 he was named Heights Man of the Year. His creative writing students won prizes in the Atlantic Monthly Contests. The stories were published in the *Stylus*, Volume 75 Nos. 1-4, 1961-62; and bound in a book with a picture of Len, John Hawkes and Ralph Ellison at the Writer's

Conference held at BC, 1960. "These stories and poems, as well as last year's prizes, were written by students under the direction and encouragement of Dr. Leonard Casper. It is partly due to his skill at cauterizing the conceited sentimentality of young and immature writers and pointing out their cherished absurdities that they did so well..."

During the years, as the young writers published books, they would send copies to Len for his library. When the anti-Catholic coalition disrupted Boston College, Len spoke against the divisiveness. P. Albert Duhamel wrote, "I must also say, rather often, how I have been shamed by your integrity...you have defended the 'truth,' when a Chekhov character would have taken refuge in the attitude—well, it won't make a difference in the end."

Letters: Philippines

Len taught at the University of the Philippines and Ateneo de Manila, Philippine Normal College from 1953, until 1956, returning several times. His last visit was 1996 when he presented a paper at the Bicentennial of the Philippine Revolution in Manila. During those years, he corresponded with students, colleagues, writers, administrators and friends. The letters form a personal memory of those years.

*

Andres Cristobal Cruz

Writers Working Together...The Workshop was organized through the initiation of Leonard Casper and Francisco Arcellana. Casper, now teaching at the University of the Philippines, is a well-published American poet and short story writer. His work has appeared in the leading literary magazines and anthologies in the United States. His presence and interest perhaps had something to do with the "seriousness" and "sincerity" of the discussion of an author's story during the workshop. Arcellana heads a sort of "school of writing" in UP, "a name with fame" in Philippine poetry, shirt story and criticism in English. Among those who contributed to the workshop discussion were Carlos A. Angeles, J. Cupiendo Tuvera, N.V.M. Gonzalez, Lourdes C. Paez, Clemente M. Roxas, F. Sionil Jose, Vicente Rivera, Jr. Rony V. Diaz, Godofredo M. Roperos and others. *Counterpoint Magazine* 10/6/53.

*

Dear Len,

    Salamat. Narito ang permission...

    1964 won the Republic Cultural Heritage Award for my books, PANAHON NG AKING PAG-IBIG and WHITE WALL, both collections of selected Tondo stories...Appeared with other Filipino poets in BELOIT POETRY JOURNAL.

    Other spectaculars: got me 3 boys and a girl, the bunso. So,

    Mabuhay ka, yeba, at kumusta kay Linda at sa mga bata. Fondly, Andres Cristobal Cruz. May 5, 1965.

*

Hermel A. Nuyda

Dear mr. casper:

    The honor is mine and, considering that 'pulse of the land' was purposed to promote better understanding of filipinos by their brother americans some of whom, in their impressions of the people, have sorely missed the filipino's true character and have, to a great extent contributed to our people's nationalistic upsurge some three years after the story was published, publishing the story in America would in a way, however insignificant such may be, be good for both our countries, the story, really, is food for american thought. May we thank you for what you plan to do. like the old woman in the story, we would frown at the mention of royalties. The indebtedness is ours. And we are deeply grateful that we have friends in America who, unlike the americans in the story, have not wasted the hospitality which the filipinos have always had for the stranger whatever the cost...

...a guilty conscience, personally...for having written the 'pulse' knowing that not all americans deserve crucifixion.

...afraid there is not much to say on that autobiographical sketch. perhaps: forty; married to evelyn rollins suntay, American; three children—robert, tiny and jella; lawyer; taught social sciences for six years; assisted the senate president for two years; technical assistant of the senate committee on commerce and industry for the last six years; drafted the Philippine government reorganization act of 1954 and major economic laws of the Philippines among which are the laws implementing the revised trade agreement between the united states and the republic of the Philippines, and economic control measures; published some twenty short stories in the local magazines; intends to do some novels on the political life of the country as medium; bakes wonderfully and collects butterflies avidly...

may we thank you for everything and should you ever return, be unlike Ben Santos and do drop in.

very sincerely yours, Hermel A. Nuyda. August 6, 1957.

*

Rony V. Diaz

Dear Len:

...I am comfortably settled here in Bloomington

...I am working on two stories right now. One is a fairly long story called Mestiza and the other is a fifteen-or twenty-page story about my trip to the US, which I call tentatively The Airports of the World. I started work on the Mestiza five months ago but I got stuck in a technical problem. I wanted this story to contain two distinct and contradictory themes and to develop these themes on the same temporal level, but I feel that my solutions are inadequate. I shall send them to you for criticism as soon as I finish them.

You are welcome to all my stories and I am happy that you think some of them are good enough for an anthology. If there is anything else that I can do to help out please let me know...

I plan to go East during the Thanksgiving break. I'll visit you then. Give my best wishes to Belinda. Sincerely, Rony. October 21, 1959.

*

Dear Len –

I shrink in shame...I forgot all about it. When I got you first letter I was buried in books on logging, sawmills. Tides, typhoons, tropical forests, etc.

...The authorization statements are enclosed. (Permission is hereby granted to Leonard Casper. And to the University of New Mexico Press to include the above story (stories) in an anthology of Filipino short stories...("Death in a Sawmill" and "Two Brothers")...

About myself. I'm afraid it won't be coherent but since you promised to do the smelting I'll ramble through...

The rest I think you know...Rony V. Diaz. October 9, 1960.

*

Edith and Edilberto Tiempo

Dear Len,

We were asked by NVM to send you copies of the last issue of Sands and Coral for an anthology you are contemplating. I think two out of the four stories in this issue are worth looking at, "Darkness at the Top End of the Line" and "The Funeral."

How are things with you? Ed and I are fine. We now have two children. The younger, the boy, was born in the States (1958) and U.S. Immigration insisted he was an American citizen! Rowena is in the fourth grade and tall for her age. Do write to us again.

Our love...Sincerely yours, Edith, July 25, 1960.

*

Dear Len,

I am sending...stories of mine, of Ed, and of Jose Montebon, Jr...I thought you might be interested in reading the other stories, although you just asked for mine...

I'll be interested in knowing which story you think I did better, "The Chambers of the Sea" or "The Dimensions of Fear..."

We think of you and the work you are doing. It is wonderful somebody like you is doing this for Filipino writers...As ever. Edith Tiempo. August 1, 1960.

*

Dear Len and Linda,

A thousand pardons for what happened to the first set of forms...my sis-in-law packed up most of her small personal effects and sent them home...we greatly suspect that's where those forms are...

Anyway, I didn't have your address and couldn't tell you the predicament, just hoped you'd write again, which you have...Ed is writing to Len separately, something about information concerning some Foundation grants he wishes to apply for...

Both Ed and I are teaching half-time this summer...so you can see we'll have time for a little writing. I finished the novel I started in the Philippines...There needs to be a clean copy, then the revision, so it's not really done. It's a relief though to get it all written down at last.

...in six weeks' time we will be moving again, to Kalamazoo...this peregrination...seems just now rather extended and at times traumatic...

Alan Swallow is putting out my volume of poetry this year...As ever, Edith. June 14, 1965.

*

Dear Len,

I wrote you a letter weeks ago in care of Franz Arcellana, only to be told that you had gone back to the States. We had wanted you to be one of the six University lecturers during the year...two or three other lectures to smaller groups composed of the English staff and English majors and those taking literature courses...We had thought you were staying for a year, and so we were also inviting you to be a visiting lecturer at the Writer's workshop in April.

The next time you plan on visiting the Philippines, please write us a note about it. It's rather unfair that you should stay only in the Manila area...

I was happy about your review of the *Dalton Pass* stories in *Solidarity*. In the Varsitarian report about your lecture there was this statement that might have been a misquotation: Among the Tayo writers he cited Edilberto K. Tiempo, whose work, *To Be Free*, he regards as the best Filipino novel written."

...Do you have a review of *To Be Free?* ...I'm interested in your opinion especially because you were quite harsh on my first two novels. Frankly, Len, I couldn't read any edition of *Watch in the Night (Cry Slaughter)*, I have been embarrassed by that novel...

But *Dalton Pass* and *To Be Free* I have been able to reread.

I am now working on another story collection, reworking old, published stories that I think can salvaged...Very sincerely, Ed (Tiempo). January 26, 1974.

*

Rodolfo Paras-Perez

Dear Len,

Paris, at least for the present gives me a sense of peace—or perhaps--release...Anyway, now that I feel more at ease—I could let you into my module shop and show the capsule-making process...Then, I think, you could perhaps give me more suggestions, as you have already so generously done. I am grateful for that... "Technically", I want the first line or the first two lines to contain all words that I'll use throughout...

I do not know how relevant these jottings and sidenotes are for evaluating the "modules: as "poetry." But I do hope you can indicate directions and points of refinements which I have not explored in the 'form'...

So long...many thanks and especial good wishes to you all. Sincerely, Rod. 4 November 1967.

*

Dear Len and Linda

Three of my files—at least the ones which are more organized...are on the way to you, the xeroxed copies...

About some unfinished matters, I am leaving to you which I mentioned previously: I expect a refund from the BIR—for 1969 and the 1970, both of which I addressed under your care. I hope you do not mind...again, thanks.

I enjoyed our evening with you—very much so, I have meant to write you but the amount of packing and paperwork, ruled out anything, including the sense of day and of night.

There are moreover other projects which will always link me to the United State: we (my colleagues at the Fogg) have already started plans for an exhibition in Ingres and Delacroix slated for 1973-74. It is something to look forward to. Also, it will be a good isolation against many things happening in the Philippines which appear none too happy. Best to all. Rod. 1 September 1970.

*

Dear Len and Linda

...So many things going on, exhibitions, writing commitments and, of course, demonstrations which are now regarded by the activists as the cure-all formula for almost anything. You must have heard of the suspension of the writ on this end: rallies...

My one-man show at the Luz Gallery is now over...It was quite well received...built around the modular concept...I am also participating in a group show currently at the Galerie Bleue in Makati, called Nudes '71...

Soon I expect to retreat a bit from the creative front and finish my researches: one on Castaneda and the other on Carlos Francisco...I do want to go back to the States as soon as possible...I feel very much stranded now—isolated...If you hear something for me—an opening in my line—do let me know...As you can see this self-exile project is something of an obsession for me now: it is the only alternative at the moment.

I am enclosing a letter to the IRS. Please post it for me...best wishes for you all—merci mille fois for the many abala—I do appreciate everything deeply...Rod. 27 Oct '71.

*

Dear Len and Linda

...Recent events strongly indicate that artists in the Philippines are at this point in history indeed without any place in society. Propagandists, yes. This in spite of the Cultural Center.

Joya told me he could still spare one-print of the etching you like ($40) ...a friend of his is leaving New York who will buy art supplies for him...

Thank you for the many things you so warmly did for us. I hope I can thank you more properly someday but meanwhile I can simply give you my warmest regards...fond good wishes. Rod. 26 January 1971.

*

Alex G. Hufana

Dear Len:

...Some two envelopes I sent you came back...such are the idiosyncrasies of the mail...

Regarding Wayward, I haven't yet polished the foreword...I have the page proofs of the whole book...I have finished the proofreading...I have finished the whole Poro Point Anthology...the date of concluding the whole work, November 30, 1960...there's nothing heroic, however, in the portrayal of the book...if I were to be heroic about this country infested with so many heroes...all we lack is a willing, up-to-date publisher...I've lined up a writing program of my life. If it's not so assuming, here it is:

> Sickle Season (Finished)
> Poro Point Anthology (finished...)
> Qualifications and Qualms (all notes and outlines...)
> Epic of the Folk (research done)
> Epic of the Clown...

Ambition. Ambitions. Hence, I need all the time. What is this Filipino culture they're talking about after all? Will the above not be my contribution to the so-called Filipino nationhood? I wish I had the time. Poor head of mine...thick and whatever it is. The flesh should keep up...Alex. December 15, 1960.

*

Dear Len:

Wayward Horizon will soon be through the press before I'll go out of the country...and if the Rockefeller would be kind enough to make me a fellow this year...

...When you ask me what special field you would like to push me in the Rockefeller, I would judge it would be as a poet, an epic poet...capable of invading the drama, the verse drama...Again if the trip will come through I'll be elbowing with the California Pinoys again and make them the portraits for The Roots of Driftwood...In the end, however, I rely on your confidence by way of persuading Compton and Rockefeller...the simplicity of Berkeley attracts me...together with the complexity of San Francisco and Los Angeles...Alex. January 11, 1961.

*

Dear Len:

...I'm happy at things happening to you. That you're going to do a sequel to *Wayward Horizon* is one of the brightest things you can do for the cultural nationhood on the far side of the earth...well and good that it will be tied up with the Benipayo-Bookmark system...

...Just keep the Iloco drama for a while until I hear from Guggenheim...

...It does not matter really where you will be assigned—Ateneo or UP, as long as you will be there, opening the awareness of people who should be aware about Fil-American writing. Off campus lectures might be just the activities...the wider the audience reached the better the transmission...then our Middle Ages will be over...

It's only that you mentioned it that I know about the details of the Asia Society project...if the Asia Society will by necessity insist on untarnished reputation no writer who thinks of doing justice to his part of writing can himself remain clean...your estimate of Villa is dispassionate, not less cutting than the estimate of Salvador Lopez...Villa is not bitter any more towards anybody.

Maybe next year I will call on Ivor Winters...get a word from him about my poems; perhaps I'll have a chance to hobnob with a powerful prejudice...Alex. November 15, 1961.

*

Dear Len:

...It is my wish if New Directions bit any of my work at all for its magniloquent World Poets Series that it should be *Journey to Judgment*, though only part I, which has been a labor to me...Besides the original typescript given to the publisher, I have my own correction copy and another copy, which you may want to place before New Directions instead of Sickle Season and Poro Point...

A Miss Susan Conheim of the Asia Society...has written me twice about my contributions to the Beloit journal. Haven't written back (I should tell you that three books of mine are coming out: a revised version of my MA thesis, which Diliman Review is putting out...under the title, *An Introduction to the Plays in Iloco of Mena Pecson Crisologo; Curtain Raisers, Five Plays*, which the UP is putting on bidding; and *Memento Mori*...)

Do write. And my best. I look forward to reading Linda's novel. Alex. November 13, 1963.

*

Dear Len:

...A long while indeed that we haven't heard from each other, and I rejoice at the news about LIT E/W which I had no idea of till then (I can't even guess at which poem was in there...)

Nothing new on me in 2 years; I'm writing miserably for lack of time, the misery extends to resentment against committee work that engages me like sin though necessary. Guerrilla writing on the Islam epic I've been underloaded to undertake is my chief pain.

...That little item in the special Free Press issue (on Philippine Christianization) about Syracuse and its efforts to build a Filipiniana attracted me no end. I have done some garbage, proofs of Curtain-Raisers worked like hell in my numerous alterations...I wonder if they may lend to some researcher's curiosity (if you say Go then I may ask the Univ College to send them to Syracuse...)

I shall be glad for any news. In faith always, Alex. UP. May 5, 1965.

*

Dear Len:

Many thanks for the permission for the dedication...

I'm even now taking up Bert Florentino on his word that I write Rockefeller for publication money...Glum this early, so we think of ourselves—which is good for brushing up on the comic lot. How many cavans of rice does a Phil ha. average, indeed!...

I'm expecting surprises, Nov 9 and what it promises for political creatures is one of these. My edge over the animals in such a zoo is that I've not neglected the human who if he must perish and his specie renew must do so in writing.

Syracuse's collection may someday do a social good for the Filipino...which reminds me...of the collection of the late Prof Hilario...some precious thing must be stowed away in there—something that may go into some gaps in literary history...As faithfully, Alex. Oct 22, 1965.

*

Dear Len:

Franz (A) told me you were here on sabbatical...

Welcome.

I can't begin to appreciate what you're doing for Phil. lit. without saying yes, in part, to your proposition.

In part, because I shall not be able to do anything on Iloco fiction, much as I want to. At least not as soon as your deadline...I can't trust my memory of stories I read in the Bannawag...before the War and after (the start of the 25-year period you're asking for) ...

All we can do is not even eclectic, but to be apocryphal...

Perhaps in poetry I could do some evaluation. I have some representative texts to work with...if you agree you may reassign me to this specific thing...I would not mind it being "labor of love..."

Thanks for including me in your "Philippine Literature: The Unexplored Potential..." Majul spared me a copy...

Do write, will you? Cordially, Alex. July 17, 1968.

*

Dear Len:

You must excuse me for not doing that assignment on Iloco poetry. The tentative lines I did could not hang together....

...What you said in the The Asia Society magazine and in other connections is becoming manifest, the Filipinos tend to do their studies in areas of least resistance...

I may still be here when you get back. Boston is close by and by your leave I shall be bothering you for personal information.

With all best wishes. The snow is falling outside—what a sight! Alex. Forest Hills, NY. Dec. 14, 1968.

*

Dear Len:

...let me know if it is convenient to see you. My sponsors are going to send me to Boston...Yes, I'm graduating this month with the M.S.L.S...

What do I wish to see you for? ...to consult with you on the wisdom of trying for a publisher while I flourish here. Maybe you can see draft of *ORATORIOS, A Poet's Progress Abroad*...23 oratorios drafted to satisfaction, each 6 pages...Fragments of Part III...Does the proposition have promise?... Regards now. Alex G. Hufana. 15 Oct. 1969.

*

Dear Len:

I don't think you got my first letter addressed to Boston

University. Frankie Sionil gave me your house address which I somehow misplaced...

How are you? And Linda? And Pipit? The last issue of Solidarity has your write-up...and I'm clipping it for use at the Cultural Center of the Philippine Library...

The next time you come to Manila we may be able to show you the beginnings of cultural safekeeping. Regards, Alex G. Hufana. 25 Oct 1969.

*

Dear Len:

Thanks for your letter with the invitation to do the scenery...I'll call you from whatever hotel (JDR) arranged for me...

I will be seeing...Asia Society...after I talk with you on how to crash American publishing...that can wait till I can write prose which seems to be the only marketable thing...

I'm bringing alone the typed part of Oratorio...if Syracuse wants the ms, they can have it, including 3 batches of letters...the need is over for these, including their prejudices...deposit them with you for transmittal...

At the Cultural Center of the Philippine Library, I'll be collecting the effects of others—with the goal of scholarship that future students may undertake. For this I need your holographs, yours and Linda's...See you. Cordially, Alex. Oct 28, 1969.

*

Dear Len, Linda and Gretchen,

Thanks for the reception. I can't stress this well enough...

Len there are some more revisions of certain pages in the ms of Oratorio which you have. I'll send them in with the rest, from California...

Maybe you want to know of the group I met at luncheon at the Boston Council for International Visitors. Credential-wise, a Mr. Peter Davison was outstanding—Director of the Atlantic Monthly Press, poet and editor...Regards, Alex. Nov.11, 1969.

*

Dear Len:

Much travel has dulled Jack-of-all Trades. I haven't touched ORATORIOS although I have jotted down some notes...Then Los Angeles proffered us difficulties...not those of Bulosan who didn't have any children to transfer to the public school nearby...I can now appreciate the rigmaroles pertaining to being a stranger, that things officially called Alien.

I should be writing Mrs. Crown—if could only be sure myself about the ORATORIOS...I see that I had succumbed to the faddish in most of the sections, if not to the all-too-easy...

Linda's ms and yours should be the first archival acquisitions of the Cultural Center Library. Later, may I have your diaries and letters?... if I'm not asking too much and too soon.

Do write. With all the best, Cordially, Alex. 23 January 1970.

*

Dear Len,

...Did you get the 3rd class envelope of stuff for Syracuse? I sent it in LA.—sifted or sorted...the innocuous remainder I gave to Berkeley...

Short-term employments are hard to come by here...I'll try Yale—when I have rendered service to my Manila patrons in 4 years...Yale's Southeast Asia collection offers me the possibility...I think I can contribute to the building of Philippine items...anything to solidify signs of Philippine Studies.

The ORATORIOS rehashed I might be able to send you before I take my family home in June...You may think it rife for Random House, who knows, Cordially, Alex. 8 April/70.

*

Dear Len,

I'm glad you have the ORATORIOS. Do anything you can with the ms...I respited from this spilling Rabelaisian portion doing eight paintings for some Flips (I got the term from NVM who got it from students...it seems the term means familiar Filipinos abroad)...

About Special Collections I tried to induce NVM to donate his drafts…But he is wise, withholding his discardables…You have done much already for Syracuse…

I should do some painting to commemorate the birth of your second child in my own birth month. Some corner in Diliman could afford me the chance, and when you and the family come for a visit, who knows you may like the painting to keep beside that marvelous Perez print on your wall.

All thanks to Linda for the Oberammergau clipping. I should rehash a section of the Hitler epic to integrate some of the information furnished. I'm making some notes now. Cordially, Alex. May 26, 1970.

*

Dear Len:

A friend of my sister's…is returning with his family to his Calif home, I'm giving him this letter and a Printed Matter envelope, which will be sent to you…

…the Pamana magazine and *The Wife of Lot* are sample copies…they could be disposed to Syracuse U when you're through looking them over. Personally I would revise the…poems further…I've counted out the feasibility of entering it in in the 1971 Palanca…

You'll also notice that I've reprinted your two reviews from Literature EAST AND WEST, to put up a model for subsequent book reviews in Pamana…You remember "Salidom-ay"? It's another dance drama, the crude version of which I sent on to you in 1959. The rewriting is due to appear in the Aug 14th issue of *Now* magazine…

There are some cultural jitters here, but they may be of interest to you when they're featured in the Sept. issue of *Pamana*…

Do write. When are you coming over? I may be able to show you the CCP Library, or what will become of it in the usual span of time that libraries take to develop.

Our best always. Cordially, Alex. July 21, 1971.

*

N.V.M. Gonzalez

Dear Len,

Congratulations, congratulations indeed. Do send me the Free Press forms for the release of copyright. I can take care of Daguio, Nick Joaquin, Arguilla, Arcellana, Nuyda...Don't hesitate to give instructions.

Succeeded with Bookmark and Benipayo to have a cooperative venture on a big scale...a program to release fifteen books in the next eighteen months. Fantastic? Maybe.

I would like therefore to inquire if New Mexico Press would consider our issuing the book you are editing for them...they called my dare to get 15 titles this year, and I'm in awful trouble...

...Perhaps you can edit a pamphlet series, say POETS OF THE PHILIPPINES...all this is by way of telling you that things are changing and for the better...

...I'll send you for comment a full list of projected titles...Please send by next mail a photo of yours, and a fairly complete biographical date, to date. Regards to the family, NVM Gonzalez. March 11, 1960.

*

Dear Len:

...I am presenting SILENT OUTCRY SLEEP as one of the titles for our editorial conference...So Linda's and your anthology is out...

But Maneng Viray is happy doing the anthology with you...

I am waiting for the release forms for the New Mexico book...will LR people be satisfied with Benipayo's copyright release?...

Great changes here, but I don't know where we're going?...

Congratulations on the associate-ship! Out here I'm due for a 15 peso raise...Congratulations to Linda also. Yrs, NVM Gonzalez. April 18, 1960.

*

Dear Len:

...I am sending all the permissions by airmail...If you are in correspondence with Nuyda, also send him a separate form to be sent direct to you, explaining my difficulty. (I have been having the darndest time with Nuyda. Can't seem to get him.) ...

I am trying to convince myself that I should get a Saxon Memorial grant...if you have any suggestions, please jot them down for me...

An anthropological material might not be contemporary enough as cover design for the book of stories. How about a design based on the tuba container and the coconut shell bowl? NVM. November 21, 1960.

*

Dear Len:

I have delayed this to allow you to have a fuller view of how the Yabes issue has developed...the Yabes defense...as an academy, the UP, through him as editor, had the right to publish material that could be read as subversive in character, on the ground that it was especially for intellectual...the defense could not hold...since the...magazine and its materials were and are even now available to the most unpolitically sophisticated freshman...

I will write you about what I can find in the next two weeks...Yrs, NVM Gonzalez, July 1, 1961.

*

Dear Len and Linda:

...Linda, keep an eye on an envelope from Bookmark. Eddie Makabenta has good news that I cannot rob him the pleasure of passing on to you...congratulations for the Asia Mag story.

...Swallow will, come May 1964, make a SELECTED STORIES. I hope you can help me make up my mind about what to include...am listing my preferences...

There will be royalties coming...from SIX FILIPINO POETS. Instruct me what to do as regards doling out shares.

Narita sends her best. Ibarra wore his first soutane June 16. Yrs, NVM. 24 June 63.

*

My dear Len and Linda:

I made out a memo for the President re my case. He attached this to Len's memo to him...So this struggle is now on official terms.

Fel and I are still working on our book.

...I've begun something myself...I can do plenty if I just abandon myself to it...If Guggen fails, I'll have to try another—just so to be able to get out of this mess...Our love to Gretchen, Yrs, NVM June 6, 1963.

*

Dear Len:

I am excited about the progress you have made in the hurried month it took to reestablish yourself there. As regards letting more people know about our work...when I see Florentino—he is working on *Seven Hills Away*—I'll inform him of your needs...

...there's the Oxford deal...perhaps; and I'm taking it if I come not so much for my writing but for future use in the powerplay here on the campus...

I'm doing what I can about the World Lit book. Two sections are now being stenciled, your introduction for the entirety and my section introduction and notes...my problem is to get into the pedagogical tone...which a mind dulled by the day's grind can't seem to produce...I've to cure myself of self-pity...More's the pity since many teachers have heard about our work and they're waiting, literally, with bated breath, I hear...

There are fifty copies of the New Mexico book at Bookmark...somebody has to shove this sort of thing down somebody's throat!...

You'll be coming back when things have settled down—say in five years. But heaven knows what these guys will be up to...Our love to Gretchen and Linda. Yrs., NVM. July21, 1963.

*

Dear Len:

No further word from Guggenheim, but I'm going to Italy, maybe with Narita and Lakshmi. There is a place on Lake Como...outside the reach of politicians and educators...It may be November—I can't stay longer without feeling the rot...It will be eleven months first—to work on the big thing—and then Oxford...the RF man came...and whom they succeeded in not being able to look me up, finally managed. Of course, they had...gotten what big chunks they wanted. Mine are only leavings, but I'll make the most of it and maybe the Holy Ghost will take care of the rest...Warmest regards, NVM, August 15. 1963.

Your memorandum re my "case" went to the Board and won the issue once and for all. It has become part of the official record...

*

My dear Len:

...A letter just came from Donald Keene... "Perhaps Casper will feel inspired to produce a second volume." Can the Univ. of New Mexico consider this?...

Have you received *Look, Stranger?* I suspect my Catholic associations have made the liberal press notice...sour, they have not even touched my book...

Linda's proofs are becoming thicker and thicker... Our love to you all, NVM. Oct. 3, 1963.

*

My dear Len:

Now that all that pall and gloom has lifted, it is possible perhaps to talk about literary matters. Actually, I have been carrying your letter with me for weeks, transferring it from my breast pocket to my wallet...

How did you west coast lectures turn out? I'm sending you copies of Florentino's "propaganda" material. The booklet is being sent by Bookmark and other offices to interested parties, and this kind of "circulation" might help a bit.

...We have not received final word from Rockfound. I am not worried about this delay...we have to make Lakshmi stronger for this trip, or strong for leaving behind...

But don't push the lectures unless there is evident enthusiasm, please...I'll adjust itineraries to whatever you think is profitable...So much for all this...With our very bests. Yrs., NVM. November 4, 1963.

*

Dear Len:

...There are prospects for visiting Germany, France and England...I've recommended your MPSS for translation into German...there is a possibility of a visiting writing professorship at Hayward...for nine months at a handsome rate...

Before we leave, I'll package the stuff for Asia Society for you...we are through with the 4th year Lit. book...Your share of the earnings need not be as small as you stipulated...

Please pump some markets for me that you can think of...Yrs., NVM. 6 February 1964.

*

My dear Len:

So this is Rome...one may walk to the Vatican City...I have a desk at the American Academy, fifteen minutes from the Monastery...It just worked out this good...

...In a few more days I'll be better organized and can do more work...Manila is in a terrible lethargy, the atmosphere of moral bankruptcy/so heavy it affects everything, even machines... After Stonehill and the smuggling business, I do not know what else can follow; but it will. Yrs., NVM. April 10, 1964.

*

Dear Len:

It was good of you to write despite pressures at BC that you describe and I am not unheartened indeed by your confidential news about the Book 1V...when I have the biog. and critical material done on the MSS. I have, I'll send this over...I'm sorry to hear about Guerrero...there has been a shake-up somewhere.

...It will be great if you, Linda and Gretchen can come see us this summer. The flat is large. Plenty of room...there's a family plan fare...can a few articles do the trick?...

...The big book, *Marching Orders*, is being difficult; I've half a dozen problems to do every day.

Outside of helping me get a house, the Amer. Ac has been of little academic help...only wish the fellows were warmer...Our very bests. NVM. 27 May 64.

*

Dear Len and Linda-

The book of PI stories in German translation is being edited here...

...We're in the middle of the Black Forest—45 minutes out of Stuttgart and will move to Bonn tomorrow...Our bests, always, NVM. JULY 10, 64.

*

Dear Len and Linda:

...While at Herrenalb, in the Black Forest, I wrote you a hurried letter about sending to Horst Erdmann Verlag...a copy of Linda's book of short stories. The firm is well on its way to doing the Philippine anthology...but I have a feeling their selections are inadequate...

There's card here from Swallow that SELECTED STORIES will go in the fall list with your introduction...Is Linda's novel finished? The Cologne publisher I met might be interested...

The German reaction to our stories is that it's much closer to their own than that of any Asian literature...As usual there will be delays because of sheer indifference from Manila...Very sincerely, NVM. July 16, 1964.

*

Dear Linda and Len:

...If my agent can only place three stories, we'll have the transportation money to proceed to Boston...and I haven't written much from all this worrying! The book I have in mind is taking shape in the most material way—scenes, etc.—but I may have to cut it in two—always short of the vision. With our very bests and love to Gretchen, Yrs., NVM. August 23, 1964. The British Council has an invitation.

*

Dear Len –

I helped Bookmark launch your Reconnaissance Award and we could only get the *Times,* the *Free Press* and the *Chronicle* to publicize the Award and the book… (all politics, you know.)

My plan to publish the Palanca stories and plays…failed as Palanca wants a penalty clause in our contract…

Please forget about the reprinting of reviews from *Books Abroad*…since UP started a similar project, I'm giving it up.

Golden Argosy? I have forgotten this plan. I don't even remember what it's supposed to contain.

I'll try to get a copy of *Lit Appr* for you…

Re the Syracuse MS collection—I have a ton of papers-…The problem is to ship them.

The US embassy *Exchange* will devote an issue on the state of the F arts in the Phi; *Phil Studies* will devote a # to poetry, fiction and drama soon.

How did you like *The Wounded Diamond?*…

I hope you find another excuse to come back here again (for a few more years. To say the least, Eddie and I and friends over here are missing you all -- Our best to you & Linda & Gretchen. Oct. 30, 1964.

*

Dear Len:

Now as regards BC prospects, you've done the most, so let it be if nothing breaks at the moment…We had a wonderful time at the Villa Serbelloni, in the Lake Como area. And in London, do you know the short story is practically dead there?

Now and then I receive papers from Manila. FP carries an announcement of the Reconnaissance Award.

...Greg B has left the ss editorship...Joe Ayala is now in charge. I have been trying to get Brilliantes to stick it out, he's a last stand of sorts...a good bet is Jimmy Abad, he should get encouraged too. Our bests, always. Yrs., NVM. 12 Nov 1964.

*

Dear Len:

Do tell me more about Bonnie Crown's agenting...

The other day we airmailed a package for Gretchen. Don't mind the racket she makes. I've a story about a flamenco dancer to write one of these days. Regards, NVM. 10 April 1965. Rome.

*

Dear Len:

Your *Wounded Diamond* has not been much reviewed here...And I wonder how much interest there will be in the Reconnaissance Award. I tried to plug it in the weekly page I do for the *Weekly Nation*...

Best to you all. I like Gretchen's cover. Sincerely, NVM Sept. 23/65. Diliman.

*

Dear Len:

Many thanks for the review. A fresh breath of fresh air, this...

We could plan on having you for whatever year once your plans...you could come as critic or writer in residence. If Rockfound approves of the idea (they furnish funds for transport) then there is no problem...

Also, I'm acting as literary consultant for the *Weekly Nation*...

I should be ready with the ms next year, can you think of a way of my going there with it in my valise?...I do know I must make the ms early, teaching, editing, committee work and all...

So. Do write. Our very bests, NVM. 19 October 1965.

*

Dear Len:

...am sending you a copy of Heritage I, which contains an unsigned review of Linda's Transparent Sun...I've decided to contribute as regularly as possible out of a sense of participation, for as long as this is possible.

Are you still anxious to plan on coming?... My own plans are hazy...

Do write when you can, and best to Gretchen and Linda. Yrs., NVM, July 24/67.

*

My dear Len:

...Your verse play got in, and I'm just waiting for the printing contract to come in then go to press... (If Linda has a story, do send it pronto) ... I've put a stake into a sabbatical come summer 1967 or 68...to coincide with work on the book...

We're all well. The review on the Selected Stories didn't bring in the sales. We've to try another tack—perhaps a Univ of Michigan Press imprint or something. Yrs., NVM. Feb 10. 1968.

*

Dear Len:

Meanwhile the book is getting made – the novel, I mean. Did your Syracuse book sell well enough to make them smile kindly if offered a volume of short stories by me?

I'm plugging for the use of both the Syracuse and the New Mexico anthology in SF State and here. There seems to be a demand, and no textbooks are readily available...

I wish we were close by and can join you at Thanksgiving. Yrs., NVM. Nov. 24, 1969.

*

Dear Len:

Shortly after your letter arrived, Ben managed to have me interested in filing an application for a Guggenheim (secret, lang ano!)...You'll receive a copy for the project proposal, as I have taken the liberty of naming you as one of my references...The issue of what to do with English will never be resolved for us until someone does some work once and for all in Filipino and, with the utmost artistic control, establish how far he can seek nourishment and support from his own culture, such as it is and in the somewhat scary direction...that it is taking...My faith in the country is not being worn thin...The demos are my proof that henceforth the ideals will be that much more identifiable, much more vocalized. Under Bagatsing, Manila traffic has improved immensely; the Miranda bombing is being solved...

Am using your Syracuse book again...a million thanks for any boost... NVM. 1/29/72.

*

Dear Len:

Unless my recollection of the whole business is wrong, Vision and Form... was not directly financed by Bookmark, but was composed for them...

...happy to hear Gretchen's getting a Guitar Master...I've just nearly finished...with a guitar I'm making as a wedding present for Mike and his bride. Ibarra arrives tonight from Rome, will received his Holy Orders here at San Francisco...Also we've been grandparents – Selma's first. Write soon, NVM. 11 July 1973.

*

Dear Len:

...I've dispatched the form saying how important it is that you do what you are planning to do as "the one critic that can explain how our writers' vision articulates with the true life of the modern Filipino." I think the committee will read that most carefully...Napakamarami ang marurunong sa atin...

Your former student...Roger Bresnahan has arranged to have an article on me in Asiaweek...a longer piece in Virginia Quarterly Review...

Thanks for the encyclopedia entry.

Linda, let me send your best pieces to Short Story International...some non-profit obviously.

Well, the best of luck, Len. Yrs., NVM. Am looking forward to reading the article you and Gretchen collaborated on. Must be a great feeling working with the next generation. November 15, 1982.

*

Dear Len:

Jose Luna Castro, who edits PHILIPPINES Today...just called to ask if I could...ask your permission to reprint in full the essay you wrote on me for Salem Press...PT will be unable to provide an honorarium.

Will be writing you soon about a number for Literary Review.

...oh yes, the wedding!... do extend my congratulations to the bride and groom. It seems not long ago Gretchen was that little...Sincerely, NVM. January 31, 1984.

*

"The View from Lake Como"

One risks going into superlatives for slim a volume but "The Opposing Thumb" simply calls for it. Len wrote there what probably is the most instructive essay on contemporary Philippine writers...the book is not about decoding Philippine writing of the Marcos period- as much as it is about the Filipino literary imagination, about how it has had to cope with actuality, about how it has had to invent masks and other forms of disguises-to find in literature the enabling gesture that makes for fervor and constancy in our practice of hope. He gives us the lie of the land and it's a geography we need." April 23, 1995

*

Wallace A. Bacon

Dear Mr. Casper,

This summer the Department of the School of Speech is holding a symposium on the work of Robert Penn Warren...

...at my request, he has suggested the names of...people who might be interested in talking about his work. Your own name is at the top of his list, and I am writing to ask whether you can be persuaded to come to Northwestern for a week, beginning July 3...,

We should very much appreciate hearing from you...Sincerely yours, Wallace A. Bacon, Chairman, Department of Interpretation, January 12, 1961.

*

Dear Mr. Casper,

...I am very much pleased to know that you that you will be able to be with us this summer, and I shall write again when I can describe the arrangements for the symposium in the weeks following your lectures...We hope to arrange a series of readings of the work by Warren...the lectures you will provide will be the only formal lectures on Warren from a critical point of view...your book on Warren will be a text for the students...I should be happy to know whether there are any *particular* things you would like the students to read in preparation for your lectures...

Furthermore, I find myself much interested your experience in the Philippines, because I am due in Quezon City on September 1 as a lecturer in English and speech...I am hopeful that your editions of Philippine stories (which I do not know) will provide me with materials to be used. And of course I shall be very glad to have a chance to talk with you about what I may expect in Quezon City!

...let me say again how glad I am that you have accepted the invitation to join us for the week beginning July 3. Cordially, Wallace A. Bacon. January 20, 1961.

*

Dear Len,

Welcome to Evanston! We are looking forward with much pleasure to your lectures...

Will it be all right with you if we schedule two periods on Wednesday...with a coffee period...? This will make up for the missed period on July 4 (Tuesday).

Also, if you and your wife are free on Tuesday for dinner, I should very much like to have you come to my house...and we can have a chance to visit. Cordially, Wallace. July 2, 1961.

*

Dear Linda and Len,

I suddenly find life more hectic than usual...I am looking forward to drawing a long breath once I climb aboard the plane. There are moments when I think I'll never make it...

I am delighted to have the stories and the review of Rizal. How different the two stories are. But in each of them now, I can hear a friend speaking. I shall hope to hear more.

...It has been a rewarding symposium for all of us, and we have back again and again to Len's week of lectures and his book for help. The readings were exciting...

...Not everyone liked him (Warren), and I spent some time trying to suggest that it was not precisely the most important thing in the world whether *they* "liked him," or not. We have had our own search for identity in the class.

Do you remember Brother Dunstan, by any chance? The symposium became something of a revelation for him, and his oral reading stretched and stretched in stature until it didn't look like the old Brother Dunstan at all.

...I'll be thinking of both of you as I head for Manila; meanwhile how grateful I am for having come to know you this summer. More later. Truly, Wallace. August 6, 1961.

*

Carlos P. Romulo

Dear Prof. Casper,

The new schoolyear has begun, and it is with some disappointment that I realize you will not be able to be with us this year...A measure of your success at the U.P. is indicated by the fact that a desire was expressed that you may be allowed another opportunity to work with us here.

I am sure that you have left an indelible impression among your students and that the interest you have stimulated for Philippine literature in the course of your many appearances in the country will find fruition in due course.

...may I congratulate Mrs. Casper for her thoughtful article published in the last issue of U.P. Today, and for a new novel...We are proud of her not only as an alumnus but as a writer and one who, no doubt, has helped to contribute to your profound understanding of our people and literature...Very sincerely, Carlos P. Romulo. July 8, 1963.

*

Dear Dr. Casper,

...You have my permission to reprint my address "Literature and Society" ...

...I am happy to know that you are coming back to the Philippines in 1967 where you are always welcomed. I don't have to tell you are admired and respected on our campus.

Looking forward to greeting you and Mrs. Casper, I am
Sincerely yours, Carlos P. Romulo. April 5, 1965.

*

Pin Constantino/ Sr. Teresa

Dear Len, Linda, Gretchen, darling girl,

How good to hear from you again! It made accepting the undeserved honor easier, pleasanter Otherwise I'd demure...!

...I'm happy that you've so very thoughtfully, generously devised the means. Yes, I know it can keep criticisms solid and respectable and enduringly fruitful...But before I rush out to something else—dear Linda, *The Peninsulars* is a beautifully written story!... what a life-filled history packed full novel it is. I do hope you can get a forum on it...

And I'm still ghost-writing and researching on poultry, rice, corn, steel, milk at the DBP, and after 4:30pm, doing all kinds of extra work—Pius XII Center, SOS Children's Village, education, TV, errands for Fathers, most recently Acting Dir of Research Asian Social Institute (set up by Cardinal S. –grad sch on eco. And socio.) And Saturdays I teach 2 classes at Assumption C. AM and evaluating Eng. major course at St. Joseph C. PM. Sundays I'm at Carmel or CWL or De La Salle curric committee or Congress for Cultural Freedom or home—with my 85 year old mother. Keep us—this dear country—in your prayers. God love you dearly. In Him, Pin. Our Lady's Nativity. Sept. 8/64.

*

Reconnaissance Award...the judge in this first Reconnaissance Award, Miss Josefina D. Constantino, writer and professor of English...

The Reconnaissance Award is the first of its kind in literary criticism. The Award has been made possible by Dr. Leonard Casper, writer, critic and world authority on recent Philippine literature. Bookmark, Inc. was asked to convert the royalties from his book the *Wounded Diamond* into an annual award for the best criticism, by a Filipino, of a work of Philippine Literature...The Reconnaissance Awards are a testimony to the fact that literary criticism in the Philippines can continually claim its due of challenge and esteem.

The winning entry in English...Laura S. Oloroso's "The Aeneas Myth as Symbol in Nick Joaquin's *A Portrait of the Artist as Filipino*...a happy synthesis of the traditional and modern in craftsmanship, sensibility, and critical commitment."

Pedro L. Ricarte's winning award in Pilipino...Isang Pag-aaral ng Makabagong Tulang Tagalog...an attempt to assess modern Pilipino poetry by making a neo poetic-philosophical instrument of analyses: an existentialist reading of some Pilipino poems.

*

Dear Sr. Teresa,

Yesterday, a family named Miranda sent us your autobiographical piece, "From the Agora..." I thank you, but especially I want you to know the effect of your prayers (through the grace of God) ... helped me cope with my disgust with BC's administration...My mind keeps going back to the classroom joy of group discussions...on human diversity vs divisiveness, exemplified by ethnic literature and the resourcefulness of so many persons/characters. And my habitual sense of justice returns to the way that changing administrators (Jesuits, all) so recklessly removed so many of us Catholic-bred...because we reached the age of 70 (I am 77 now) and by law (a law against ageism...) said we in education were expendable. Forget meritocracies: We kept the high standards that our deans only gave lip service to, and therefore were vulnerable to every fund-producing father's complaint against us. I have published 14 books and scores of stories and articles" but BC cares for Mammonism, not meritocracy…I won't itemize the incidents of disrespect which we endured from chairpersons who were apostate Catholics or non-Catholics…

…But bitterness is self-consuming when no one listens; so I have put together 50 years of poetry…my latest unpublished by America and other religious magazines.

…I feel so close to Linda now, more and more (we both have eyes trouble: I, macula degeneration—but seeing Dr. Tolentino…she with glaucoma)…I am an apprentice to her gardening and we just celebrated our 44th anniversary…

I especially thank the Lord for putting persons such as yourself in my life, and of course, in the world…It has to be grace as a gift, because who could deserve all these goodness?

Time now to look for that poem, which I may have sent you once before. Love. Len. 7/18/00.

*

Gilda Cordero Fernando

Dear Dr. C and L –

Am very happy to be included in Literature East and West and happier still that you have written.

Thanks for the nice things you said about me in "Wounded." What I've really been quite bothered by is the Reconnaissance Award…wouldn't that giving a Go signal to the young UP cannibals to cut us up?…for a country that doesn't have enough fiction to feed a locust, is such encouragement wise?…If only there was some way to be completely ignored, I'd be completely content…

Bert Florentino said, "well, the usefulness of criticism for oneself can best be gauged by the answer to the question: Have you ever learned anything from the critics? Personally, I can't deny I have.

It seems half my life I'm trying to prove that I'm really not half as bad as Dr. Casper thinks I am...

The column, on the other hand is real satisfaction. For the first time I feel I am being read...

Linda, Woman & Home is specializing in children's stories and maybe you'd like to do one with historical background for Pipit's age...Please be interested. W & H will pay you many centavos.

Love to you all & specially Gretchen – Gilda. Marcelo sends regards. Eddie Makabenta says Peninsulars is doing very well and Wounded Diamond is far and away a best seller. Dec. 1. 1964.

*

For Dr. Leonard Casper

Permission is hereby granted to use A HARVEST OF HUMBLE FOLK for LITERATURE EAST AND WEST. 1965.

Donato Benipayo, Publisher, *The Butcher, the Baker, The Candlestick Maker*, Benipayo Press, Makati, Rizal

Teodoro M. Locsin, Editor, PHILIPPINES FREE PRESS, Makati, Rizal.

Gilda Cordero-Fernando, Author, 33 Panay Avenue, Q.C.

November 18, 1964.

*

Ricaredo Demetillo

Dear Len,

Here's the biodata you wish: Birth—June 2, 1920...Ricaredo Demetillo is an assistant professor of Humanities at the University of the Philippines. He took his training at Silliman University and the State University of Iowa, in the poetry workshop under Paul Engle and Robert Lowell.

He has published four books of poems and one book of poetry criticism.

In the last two years he has been working on a book of poems...

*

I am still revising and pruning the poems in *Masks and Signatures*. Let us hope, the book can be published this year or early next.

As usual, my class schedule is full, but I always manage to get the time to read and write a little...Cordially, Rick. January 18, 1965.

*

Dear Len-

Here are the forms for permission to publish excerpt from *Barter in Panay*. I own the copyright To Barter, as UP is a government entity and cannot own any copyright.

The best of luck on the project. Cordially yours, Ricaredo Demetillo. May 7, 1965.

*

Arturo B. Rotor

Dear Mr. Casper

By this time, you should have received my written permission to include "Zita" in your anthology...Thank you for your nice letter.

I am aware of course of the role you have played in encouraging Filipino writers in English. I have often wished I could meet you...Alas my interest in literature has to yield priority to the demand of medical practice. Anyway, next time you are in Manila, will give me a ring?...Sincerely yours, Arturo B. Rotor. October 19, 1965.

*

Morton J. Netzorg

Dear Len

...I'm not anywhere as well informed as you are as to the nature and extent of criticism or what passes for criticism in the Philippines today. In my day--and that day is long past—there were few who made an attempt to be critical in the sense of measuring against any standards, but 'do I like it'. Those who were not of this class were basically sortable into a few sub-classes: those whose inquiry was basically 'how can I turn this to my own (off-stage) advantage; and those who sought by writing about writing to gain repute as writers, etc. ...

You call for Philippine writers who are informed and disciplined. This is asking much...Your own criticism, in one opinion, is gaining in magnitude and power and in persuasiveness because it is less and less dependent upon over specificity and more and more rests upon your command and control of the body of work, the full literature.

Not that your attention isn't keenly fixed on the particular piece of work, but that the piece of work isn't considered as unique; rather it has a place in a context, and a part of the value of what you have had to say has been in placing and stating that context...

Let me cease meandering and tell you outright how much I prize your letter. And also let me tell you that here is nothing niggling about the desire to see Wounded Diamond exceeded; even as man stands to be obsoleted by some superior being, any book eventually loses its immediacy and holds part of its place, if it holds any place at all, as part of history or of literary history as much as by its intrinsic merits...Sincerely, Jock (Morton J. Netzorg). Feb 2, 1965.

*

Donn V. Hart

Dear Len,

...your decision on the brochure was correct (re collection of Philippine literature at Syracuse University). I shall take your suggestions...When you write to Carlos Romulo, send me a carbon copy and I can follow your plea with my request. Send me any suggestions for promoting the collection. I am yours to command! Needless to say, and again and again, how grateful I am to you for your magnificent assistance with the collection...

I trust I have not embarrassed you by singing your praises at Syracuse. Frankly, I think if you and Syracuse could have a mutually satisfactory agreement, we could have a great time...We need to revive the "sociological approach to literature" that the sociologists foolishly abandoned in their search for statistical data...such a program needs badly a person of your caliber, imagination, professional attainment, and willingness to work hard...I plead with you to respond to Professor Piskor's request for vitae...Donn. February 5, 1965.

*

Dear Len,

Mr. Ward Morehouse, State Education Department, Albany, New York...wants to assemble a set of solid Manila-published book representing the splendid scope of Filipino culture...

...Could you, would you send Ward, as quickly as possible, titles of collections of poetry, short stories, and novels, that you think are still in print, and represent some of the best of Filipino accomplishments in this area of human endeavor? I shall consider it a favor. You should be used to such requests—it seems all you do for me is favors!

How is your WOUNDED DIAMOND book progressing with Syracuse University Press?

... We have decided to become a little more aggressive on the Filipiniana collection. Oh, I think we shall get some hand-painted colored slides done by Fred Marquand's father when in Manila. A most fascinating coup—if finalized... Ta ta, Donn. January 21, 1966.

*

Dear Len,

I appreciated, and I know Mr. Morehouse does also, your letter regarding some appropriate choices of Philippine belles lettres for his project. I had written him earlier that THE PENINSULARS was a must...

I am delighted at the progress of the WOUNDED DIAMOND. I am confident this book will bring prestige to the Press and more honor to you...Cordially, Donn. February 8, 1966.

*

Daisy H. Avellana

Dear Mr. Casper,

Your letter dated March 7 reached me only today, it took a roundabout way to get here. Bert F mailed it to our office in Pasay, from there someone mailed it to the Pasay post office, then back to Taft, and finally to our new office (Documentary, Incorporated) on Remedios Street...

I am sending my own copy of the PORTRAIT script through a friend who will mail it from Hawaii...Nick says he is very happy about your wanting to use PORTRAIT for your anthology.

...Barangay is filming the play (with my husband directing) and we hope to have it ready for entry in the Venice Film Festival. Please wish us luck—we will need it.

My daughter Ivi sends her regards. Sincerely, Daisy H Avellana. March 26, 1965.

*

Carlos A. Angeles

Dear Len:

I have never thanked you for all the things you have done for me for the simple reason that I did not know where to address my letters—so I am taking this wonderful chance to let you know how much I appreciate your untold kindness since way back.

...Also I am getting older. I still keep up religiously with any poetry book or magazine I can get hold of, but I have not done anything the past six or seven years.

...the book, "A Stun of Jewels" won the Republic Cultural Heritage Award for 1964...the Carlos Palanca Memorial Awards in Literature in September of the same year.

...Alberto Florentino told me that of the 992 copies given to Bookmark...658 copies...were sold in nine months.

...I am aiming for an American publisher...although I don't know if I can swing it...

I have, indeed, grown up and outgrown most of my poems. Your selection...of the poems you intend to include in the new Syracuse University anthology, were written years ago, and appeal less to my vanity now, except for the "The Eye."...

Or perhaps I should read my poems all over again and give myself re-evaluation of each and every poem I have written. Or maybe it is for the better. Then I probably could write again...

Regard to you and yours. All best, Carlos. (Carlos A. Angeles) May5, 1965.

*

Jose Villa

Dear Professor Casper,

I understand you have an essay on my...Selected Poems and New—would it be too much to ask you to send me a copy of it? Thank you very thank you very much.

If you come to New York I should like you to look me up... Salut to you and yours. August 3, 1959. Sincerely yours, J Villa.

*

Dear Mr. Casper

Thank you. I will write to you at more length later.

Melonwatermelon greetings! J.Villa. June 18, 1965.

*

Dear Mr. Casper.

...The story listed as published in Bulosan's mag—is a phony. It's not by me... (it is illiterate)...

I have a list of my book appearances & I can help you there.

I have no list of the poems in mags...Regards, J V. Tuesday. Aug 17/65.

*

Eric Torres

Dear Len,

...got your May 15 letter only this afternoon. Enclosed are the permissions. Father Donelan informed me that you need data re publishing I've done here, in the usual scholarly manner...Am certainly looking forward to returning to Boston and meeting with you...I'm doing a lot of things these days by ear...

Incidentally, did you receive Gilda's gift? Sorry I couldn't mail it to you in s more ceremonious manner, but I hope it got to you, otherwise Gilda will never forgive me...Eric. May 26, 1965.

*

Virgie Moreno

Dear Len,

Your casual publication of the Four B/Sonnets Poem was mortally welcome. You help yourself to any of my works without "pasintabi," since you receive and use them so well, you own them, too.

I have not since spoken about my going or coming from there to here. That night with Linda and you and Gretchen was starry...

Enclosed are 4 poems on the Sun, called Sun Series, with magnificent woodcuts by Rod Perez. Use them if you care...it might be too late to send you one in progress...

Love to Linda and Gretchen and Charles River. Faithfully, Virgie. June 16, 1965.

*

Dear Len,

...I cannot say often enough that I want you to help yourself to all of my poems.

...sheer mad work here prevents me from writing to you longer...John Ciardi and George Bluestone from Seattle came to the conference (UP Writers). Wish you and Linda were here truly.

My new passion is movies, I hope to write a movie script...My nostalgia for last years; brief visit to Boston drowns me. Affectionately, Virgie. August 5, 1965.

*

Anthony Morli

Dear Len.

...I find it extremely difficult to talk about myself...

At the moment, writing the libretto for the opera "El Filibusterismo" and "May Day Eve" based on the story by Nick Joaquin.

Has written the libretto, and words and music of the first contemporary Filipino musical play "Lenny."

Is doing the screenplay of "Lenny" and now very much interested in motion pictures, as film director and writer.

Regards. Sincerely yours, Anthony Morli. 8 June 1965.

*

Oh yes. I was christened Anthony Morli Dharam. I have dropped the Dharam and now use Anthony Morli. My father was British Indian, my mother Filipina.

My works have appeared in Katha #1; Philippine Writer; Philippine Cross Section; Philippine P.E.N. Anthology. Sincerely yours, Anthony Morli. 8 June 1965.

*

Dear Mr. Casper,

I have before me your "New Writing from the Philippines" ... needless to say it is very interesting and well presented.

Incidentally, due to my mother's sudden death on December 8th, 1965...I am here now in Manila since...

May I look forward to hearing from you soon?

With my regards and best wishes for the coming Xmas season. Anthony Morli. November 9, 1966.

*

My dear Mr. Casper;

This is to thank you for my copy of "New Writing from the Philippines" and the check for $20.00...

I am always eager to hear from you and if there is anything I could do for you here in the Philippines, do not hesitate to let me know...

I am hoping to go back to the States when circumstances and opportunity permit...Yours very sincerely, Anthony Morli. Dec. 26. 1966.

*

Alberto Florentino

Dear Len.

...I have been so busy since I returned last Sept, I put out Makiling and Mir-i-nisa (received the copies), Wound Scar, Memory of Fire and Virgie's 2 Plays...I am working on Alcuaz' book of paintings. I am working full time at OB and organizing...another guild similar to Filipiniana Book Guild (which published Twenty Years in the Philippines) which will concentrate on books printed 1900-1945...marketing 5,000 to the public school sector. I am also actively engaged in organizing the Phil. Educ. Theater Assn, am again board director of Pamana; I am trying to earn enough to tide us over during summer...So you can imagine the pace I keep...

...I cannot match Benipayo book selling...

Re advt for East-West books (I'm sorry I asked you to do this in any trade journal at your expense without any idea of how much classified ads cost. If it will cost too much, and I mean this, please refrain from doing so...I have bothered you enough...

Re your suggestion to incorporate with some Filipino publisher...I have hinted the same to Bookmark, Solidaridad. They've been very cold to the idea...

...on top of your financial assistance, I will try to get Bookmark.

...I have definite plans about your book...I would like to make it an editorial design masterpiece.

My best to Linda and Gretchen, did she like Makiling and Mir-i-nisa? Bert. Not dated.

*

Dear Len:

...As I must have told you the Peso Book series is bankrupt...

Literature at the Crossroads (the 3 symposiums by the Congress for Cultural Freedom in 1962 on the novel, poetry, and the theater in the Philippines) is coming out the end of this month. I have without your permission, dedicated the volume to you—do you mind? If you do, send a wire...

New address – Marilag, UP Village. May you think of visiting Manila again. Bert. February 5, 1965.

*

Dear Bert:

At least school is put to bed and I can answer your letter...

I cannot argue with your reasons for pressing EW books...at least I am satisfied that the price is not arbitrary, although it remains to be seen if it is competitive...

Tentatively, I think you should rely on free advertising through reviews that I can manage here, as well as Cellar's listings.

As for copyright, please copyright the book's name...in the Philippines so I can approach a US publisher in future years freely...

Your plans of a second guild with Benesa sound good, such works are apparently most commercial. Judging by Cellar's quick sales of the Fil Book Guild. I only wish you luck with your plans which, ironically make you more than ever the least recognized and rewarded force in serious Philippine publishing. Cordially, Len. June 11, 1967.

*

Dear Len and Linda:

I am sending by airmail several children's books for Gretchen...among them my first children's (junior) book.

I am back in publishing. I resigned from the UP Press after an oppressive six months...I am in no better condition than...when I started publishing in 1962...I still have no subsidy, still no capital, still owe the presses money. (...Bookmark offered to pay off my printing debts and get my books remaindered at 10% of list price...I am left without any stocks or capital. This act of Bookmark is a mixture of cruelty-and-kindness!)

...I think I have to stop my Peso book series. At the time when the minimum wage was P4 and bookpaper tax 5%, it was really never making any money...it's still a record, don't you think, 10 titles in three years, which brought back to stores and library shelves the works of Villa and Joaquin, et al?...

I am brimming with ideas again... (Linda, if I do get your okay to publish your raindrop story will you allow me to get a Filipino artist to do it?)

I junked the anthology of short novels...Too expensive...

How are both coming along? Have you, Len, finished the anthology of Phil literature?...What suggestions do you have in mind? Please write—and forgive me for being so silent but the last six months was a torment and I wrote to no one at all. Yours, Bert. No date.

*

Dear Len

Did you receive my LETTER TO THE WORLD (8pp) which I sent without the proper stamps? It was my reply to PARADE magazine's suggesting to write a letter to Mr. Reagan and Mr. Andropov c/o Parade, but which I addressed to the world...I will reproduce them in quantity and mail them again...I'm caught up in a new topic: research on thermonuclear war and world politics. I am writing more letters to the world (#2, #3), and this might make a small book. I wish I could have an agent, could you recommend one...? I have another project: IMMORTAL WORDS (OR PROSE) which can be a marketable non-book, or made into a calendar or a series of educational posters...I have started with the Bible...the Preamble of the American Declaration of Independence; the Preamble of the Communist Manifesto...

Since I came to New York I have ceased to think like a barrio boy... As early as the 1960s I published the Seven Wonders of the Universe in Focus and later gave to Irving Wallace for his Book of

Lists series, but he has not published it...Eva sends me the more liberal magazines in Manila...

Are you visiting New York with Linda and your girls?... I'd like to see Boston. In fact I will one day send my proposal for research to any of the Universities there. Do send me the application forms...Best wishes...Bert. 15 November 1983.

*

Dear Len –

...I came to the US as guest of the P.E.N. US center...I came to Aspen after the P.E.N. Congress and am now cooking up a wild idea. I am going to publish US fictionists and poets i.e. – print the books in Manila and distribute, promote them in the US... US printing is 10x expensive as Manila prices...

When I was in the East Coast, I had so rigid a schedule I had no time to see you at Boston. Now I am in Aspen-Denver, I want so much to see you for advice on this.

...Again my problems are (1) lack of capital (2) distance of market (3) editorial judgement and adm. work.

Are you by any chance going somewhere near Denver?... I wanted so much to visit you...

I will visit Alan Swallow at Denver. I missed Cellar Bookshop – where is it? I ordered a copy of your latest book and asked them to mail it to me at Manila.

I remember you had a collection of stories...Perhaps...you could let me do your book? My best wishes to you all. Bert. July 24, 1986.

*

Dear Bert,

I think you will find out why Eder does not like to be bothered about examining drafts of articles, particularly those that fall within the "specialty" of us volunteer subeditors.

Brace yourself. But we're both professionals and friends...

...because I personally think so highly about what you pioneered, I think you might add another 1-2000 words on projects which you have initiated in the 80s and 90s, and those like **ETERNITE** as future plans...you are a doer, a person of *accomplishment*...So don't be afraid to expand this essay...

I am grateful that you sent me this draft (which can be perfected so easily) and when you send me its replacement, I can practically guarantee its acceptance in *Pilipinas*...Your obedient servant, (Len) 1/23/00.

*

Dear Bert,

...I know that some of my alterations try to put in their place some persons who maybe your New York coterie-buddies. But I try to be objective.

...I continue to believe in the value of this piece and hope you can/will revise it in good time, at your convenience. Between us, we have no deadline...Len. Feb 19, 2000.

*

Ceres S.C. Alabado

Dear Mr. Casper

We have the honor to invite you to be one of the judges of this year's PAMANA's Children's Story Writing Contest, English Division, Elementary Level...For entries written by adults, and for entries written by students...

We hope you can meet with the other two members of the panel of judges for the final decision on August 30, Friday, at 4:00 o'clock...National Library, T.M. Kalaw Street, Manila.

In appreciation of your cooperation and kindness, we thank you sincerely. Yours truly. Ceres S.C. Alabado. July 29, 1968.

*

Jose M. Lansang, Jr.

Dear Dr. Casper—

I asked Dr. Ordonez to ask you to write an introduction to "Travelling: Poems by—" and he remarked, "Won't his reader's report do?" It would do very well for dust-jacket comments...you could sort of expand the report into a full-pledged Introduction.

Dear Len, Please, do so. I know you can do it and it will not cost you too much work. What you have...is a perspective of Philippine Writing which locates all our writers in their right places. For his part, Elmer was glad I had rearranged the poems in the book according to your well-thought-out arrangement, I did.

I'm hoping also that the book will garner me the Palanca Prize for 1969 but of course there will be competition. Yours very truly, Jun. March 14, 1969.

*

Miguel S. Diaz

Dear Professor Casper,

I am sending you this message to tell you how pleased and grateful I am for the copy of Literature East and West which you have painstakingly sent me, together with the separately bound copies of my stories...

I wish to congratulate you for the superb editing which left the story to itself, a true Filipino farm story...I'm equally flattered by your bold postscript that my story was an excerpt from a novel in progress and which now I have to live up to. Incidentally, I am now at the finishing end of said novel which I wrote in English and later to be translated into Ilocano. I hope one of these days you will help me out towards its publication...

...I reiterate our endless thanks to you for what you have done to us, for the glory you have caused to descend upon us. May God always abide in your ways. Very truly yours, Miguel S. Diaz. 18 September 1970.

*

Emmanuel Lacaba

Dear Caspers,

I suppose that by now you're back in Boston from Europe...

...If you got to read the *Free Press* there, I guess I don't have to tell you the current literary gossip.

...I've submitted *Punch and Judos* to Joaquin; I'm now working on ballet librettos and a musical, *Asiong Salonga* perhaps with Julie Borromeo Aragon at Dance Theater Philippines; she's trying to make me learn ballet, too, since the company is in need of male dancers...But it's a wonderful new world...There's an interesting new course in school, Father Roque Ferrid's Tagalog philosophy, which he teaches on the assumption that each language creates its own philosophy...textbooks in English, French and German, but our lectures and papers are in Pilipino. *Taliba Pilipino*, which borrows from other languages...

...there really is, a Tagalog renaissance on its way to a peak...anyway, hope you're all in the best of health and creativity. Has Linda finished her next novel? My especial regards to little Gretchen. Affectionately, Emman. 22 Sept. '69.

*

Dear Len

This year I am applying at the University of Sao Paolo, to continue writing that essay I showed you...in 1969. However, I hope you forget about that...I asked you to read it after it had been buried among my files for two years...Anyway, I have also grown older (I hope) since then...I am finishing that study, writing it in Tagalog, have called it *Si Bernado Carpio't si Mariang Makiling*, and *Singsing ng Dayang at ang Pagkahulog ni Icaro: Buhay at Paglilini sa Pilipinas*. Does it sound pompous?...

...besides, if there is any lifework for me, it could be only anything that involves fieldwork and living with a variety of people; I don't think I will neglect my poetry & fiction...I am suggesting to Sao Paolo that I look into the possibility of having the documentary replace the research paper as vehicle for research...is my proposal too far out?...Could I cite you as one of my references? I will be eternally grateful.

...do you think I am too ambitious? Somehow, a vision that tries to be as close to Infinity as possible goads one to continue with immediate tasks; it gives one, at least, a reason to go on writing, or to stay alive...

...I have been isolating myself lately, without quite realizing it...I now have a daughter and she is called Miriam Manavi Mithi Mezcaline Mendiola, behold, I bring you tidings of great joy. Wishes of great joy, too, to you and Linda and Gretchen.

It is Saturday midnight in Pateros; outside my screened windows, the darkness of graves: bird cage, bird cage, good night, good morning. Sincerely, Eman. (Lacaba). 28 March 1971.

*

V.F. Porto

Dear Prof Casper,

Dr. M. Ramos, Sr. and I have thought of commissioning you to write for Alemar-Phoenix a book for introductory courses in literature, or *a Critical Anthology of Philippine Literature in English.*

While one of your students in 1956 I liked very much your approach in teaching Eng. 124 (Hart Crane to T.S. Eliot). Our managing editor, Dr (Maximo) Ramos, was the one who suggested this... We could discuss details later. V.F. Porto, Asst Managing Editor, June 7, 1973.

*

Severino Montano

Dear Leonard,

...I was busy dress rehearsing for summer cultural and PNC Reunion performances...

...I have not stopped studying my role, in full detail, visually and auditorily...I have long arias...I say my arias in the way Tchakovski might play or write his symphonies...12 long arias...

...Last night, the last aria on death...caused a strong electric tension, so strong that the Asst. Sec. of Education came up to actually embrace and kiss me…followed by two activist Irish priests who are not in love with the Jesuits. Also. Others followed. …

…I had a session of two hours with Lucretia Kasilag…regarding the production of *Gabriela Silang*.

…I gave her your article. She was happy to find herself agreeing to what you think of *Gabriela Silang*…She said…I just got a letter from him (Casper)…

How is "Gabrielle"? (Gretchen). Certainly, I have not forgotten her. I hope she will be interested in socio psychoanalysis and come back, help the Filipino children grow up emotionally and otherwise. From what I saw, she has a lot on the ball and a special quality that distinguishes her apart from Americans of her age and orientation.

Tell her to write to me…Congratulations for Linda's good Radcliffe luck…Yours ever, Severino (Montano). April 2, 1974.

*

Dear Leonard and Linda,

Robin Prising has written…that Linda reviewed his book in Boston, and asked if I knew you! … Has it been two years since we exchanged letters?

…by the time you get this I shall be touring the Visayas and Mindanao…we board the naval vessel—Presidential ship…accompanied and guarded by a smaller naval ship. We will cover 10 cities.

I retired for good from my job at PNC…I should have done it much earlier and not given my creative years …I am with CEU and UE teaching most of all my disciplines besides directing major productions. A year ago I directed *Madama Butterfly* with two top singers from Milano's *La Scala*. There were several attempts to do *But Not My Sons* for movies…One of my former graduate students is going to do *But Not My Sons* at the Meralco Theatre…with Rosa Rosal…

…I must really take time out to enjoy garden, house and my protegees…

I finished a new play last November *Dayang Raya Elvi Kiram*, circa 1904 to 2000…wrote three major papers, two of Filipino drama, one of the new dramaturgy from People's China that might affect oriental drama eventually.

I am reading my sixth book…*Lobsang Rampa*…what may western literature become if his influence really gets into western psychology and problems of life and patterns of life?

…do let me hear from you…News from you as you know will always be welcome and a joy…As always, yours, Severino. Sept 4, 1975.

*

Dear Len,

…Our tour with *Minda Mora* through the Visayas and Mindanao including Cotobato was most successful in a truly bourgeois manner…only the establishment could afford to see the show…in Cotobato, every inch of ground was guarded by soldiers…the upper Muslim citizens came to cheer the play which I wrote especially to defend their brotherhood!!!

…the Captain (of The RPS Mt. Samat) and his wife invited me to join them in an official trip of the Sulu Seas: Tawi-Tawi, Bungao, Siasi, Jolo, Basilan and all over the Thousand Islands of the dissident fighting area.

…The Sulu Seas are an island paradise, if ever there are any in this lunatic 20th century. And before the ozone in the sun is destroyed by nuclear powers among the industrialized countries I am glad I saw what Edens are like…

You can see why I have just finished another work such as: My Odyssey Over Eden in the Sulu Seas, in the year 1975—a group of poems—24 in number—

I also finished the movie shooting script But Not My Sons and the movie treatment of *Inherit the Earth and Laugh*…

These are the latest news about me…Regards to Linda and the girls. Affectionately, Severino (Montano) January 26, 1976.

*

Greg Brilliantes

Dear Linda and Len,

After too many unemployed orbits in the outer darkness, I've made a reentry and landed this contract to edit "an honest-to-goodness literary quarterly" for the BNFI, which is run by Larry Cruz, formerly of Asia Magazine and the son of Abe Cruz of the old *Mirror*...before I run out of my quota of freshly printed stationery: I'm gathering material for two or three issue, and I've promised the Lord I'll devote an extra half-hour of thanksgiving after communion if you'll send over stuff for the *Review*...anything you would want to see published in a magazine which I envision to look, in format, like a cross between *Evergreen* and *The Paris Review*...maybe a corner for contending controversialists in the arts, as one finds in *Encounter* and *The New York Review of Books*...Baby sends her love. When is your next visit to our Bayang Magiliw?...

Sursum corda and all that. With warmest regards. Greg B. August 28, 1974.

*

Dear Len,

I'd make a vow not to talk about writing but to sit still. Read, listen, learn—until I wrote something that would drive you and NVM ecstatic with critical joy, but I'll break it for you. Fr. Donelan and the Ateneo...

I'd like to touch on The Distance to Andromeda, which NVM described as "a story that is written but once on a generation"...A Wind Over The Earth ("the spears Winklereid gathered on his breast, etc.," remember?), Dr. Lazaro, and perhaps two others—Sunday and the Rain; and perhaps Journey to the Edge of the Sea...Meanwhile may I look forward to a criticism of my volume of short stories from you? Will you write me one before December 20? I'm sure it will help me single out relevant points for our "craft conversation." With all good wishes. Greg. November 27.

*

Dear Linda and Len,

...lack of paper delayed (the January issue) ...lack of New Society harmony, including a PR group's interference with the layouts, has set back the latter (April). So it goes, as Vonnegut would say...I had the contributor's list ready early February but the Director flew off to Nepal and then to Cairo...So it goes.

Thank you for your kind letter, Len. I sure needed the boost. I'm not a Bureau staffer. I edit the REVIEW for a contractor's fee, and...I have to contend with all sorts of New Society crap.

I've just come back from three weeks in Cebu...I'll sleep off the lousy memories, meditate for a week or two, and write you again. As always, GREG. May 12, 1975.

*

Ninotchka Rosca

Dear Mr. Casper,

I hope it is not too late to thank you for the review in *Solidarity*.

...My only objection to the review is the company...Also I am inclined to look at those stories as too immature. I have bitterly regretted their publication ten times over.

I have just finished a volume of short stories—all of them new...under the title *The Monsoon Collection*...If I maybe a little immodest...I believe some of these stories are stylistically interesting while some are of importance—to my country and to Philippine literature.

I also begin working on my novel this year—a little waveringly...since the form is new to me...Alas, the novel will probably never see print until all these things that afflict shall have passed away.

I do not know that it got around that I was planning to write you a letter—but a host of people send you their regards: Amelia Bonifacio, Alberto Florentino (from whom I got your address), Ric Demetillo who just got out of the hospital, Rod Paras-Perez, Gilda Cordero Fernando, Nick Joaquin who maintains his silence. There are others—if I listed down their names it would add nine more pages—and they are all asking, in one great chorus, when you are going to visit this unhappy country again...They send all their wishes for the continued health of your family, as I do. Again, my thanks. Ninotchka Rosca. January 27, 1975.

*

Jack Larkin

Dear Len,

...As of my last letter, I asked you to select some of the current fiction and work up a joint review. Could you please let me know what books you are doing?... Also, is your daughter Gretchen doing any of the items you suggested?...

Also can you do the following, if you have not done so? Leopoldo Yabes, *Philippine Short Stories, 1941-1955, Parts I & II*. Quezon City, UP Press, 1981.

Thanks. Jack Larkin. Oct. 27, 1982.

*

Jimmy Abad/ Gemino Abad

Dear Professor Casper and Linda,

I'm applying for a Fulbright Award...and would like to mention your name...as an authority in Philippine Literature in English whom I would consult while there...

My research is on "Filipino Poetry in English: 1910 to 1980. May I have your advice here...I wonder if Berkeley would be a good place to visit...

My research is an offshoot of *In Another Light* and *A Formal Approach to Lyric Poetry*...I feel it can afford me a working base for a reasonably accurate account of the achievement of Filipino writers in English...

I feel there is a distinctively Filipino tradition in Philippine poetry in English...despite the short period of time (1910 say, to 1980) ... a truly remarkable phenomenon worthy of study and analysis...

There are two things I should do while there (should I get the award): first to deepen my knowledge of post-structuralist criticism. Here, again, I need your advice—which University would be good to visit?

The literary scene is pretty alive. Recently, two book-launchings in poetry...It seems to me that the poems in Tagalog move toward mass consciousness and revolution; those in English, toward individualism.

I have a little group of poets—we call ourselves, rather immodestly, the Philippine Literary Arts Council, organized September, 1981...to promote poetry in English, especially through poetry reading at Paco Park and other public places. Rather quixotic—against traffic noise...Yet, we've toured Baguio City, Cebu, Dumaguete; audiences were receptive enough, especially when poems were in plain colloquial English or were comic. We've also put out a first issue of Caracoa (a poetry journal) ...PLAC is the counterpart (but not hostile to) of Galian sa Arte at Tula, a group of poets in Tagalog, of which once I was adviser, with Rio Alma. Truly yours, Jimmy Abad. 22 March 1983.

*

Michael Cullinane

Dear Caspers: (Leonard Casper and Linda Ty-Casper)

Forgive the delay in getting all this material to you and to responding to Gretchen's suggestion...that you would be interested in setting up a panel of Filipino writers and literary critics for the August conference. I am very enthusiastic about such a panel and encourage you to proceed with the plan...

As you can see. The general theme of the SEASSI conference is history. A panel on literature that took a historical view (say of English writing from the 1920s to the present) would be ideal, but such an approach is not required and you may wish to focus on some other topic. Even one of present concerns...it's up to you...I would be happy with whatever direction you take...let me know your needs.

...I leave all the decision regarding the content and format of the literature session to you and look forward to hearing from you. I would appreciate your giving me a rough idea of what the panel will look like before the AAS meeting (22-24 March) ...

All the best and stay warm. Sincerely yours, Michael Cullinane. 23 Jan. 1985.

*

Dear Prof Casper:

...I'm delighted that you have had such a great response to your request for papers at the August meeting. Bringing all those people together in one room will be a rich experience for all of us. With this in mind I would like to extend the time...and encourage you to consider five hours.

...why don't we plan for two sessions...the morning session as you suggest can be devoted to more substantial presentations or more formal statements...with the afternoon session for a more open ended discussion, opening the doors to the peanut gallery...At this point, I would be pleased to "authorize" a two session panel and permit you to organize the panel as you see fit. Onward...!

...We will decide on how much is available for SEASSI...at the ASS meeting in Philadelphia in later March...If only we had a mountain of money—all we need is one wing of a B-1 bomber!

Thanks again for all the foot/phone/letter-work. Keep in touch and I'll probably see you in Philadelphia. Sincerely, Mike (Michael Cullinane) March 5, 1985.

*

Isagani R. Cruz

Dear Dr. Casper,

On behalf of the Manila Critics Circle, Inc. I would like to invite you to become an honorary member of the Circle.

We are a group of reviewers and critics dedicated to uplifting and promoting book publishing in the Philippines.

Annually, we give out National Book Award to deserving

writers of books...

You can also uplift our own standards by giving us comments on our choices for the National Book Awards...

Sincerely yours, Isagani R. Cruz. February 4, 1985.

*

Jaime An Lin

Dear Professor Casper,

I am honored to be asked to participate this coming August in the panel discussion of the place of history in modern Philippine literature. I see this as a perfect opportunity to meet some of the authors whose work I admire and am now studying for my doctorate. And of course, this will allow me to see what you think of certain ideas that I want to pursue and develop in my dissertation and to appraise you to my progress so far.

...It was not until I started graduate study in comparative literature at IU, that my interest in Philippine literature, particularly as it relates to world literary traditions, became more focused. I would like to make this a life-long professional pursuit because this is an area that is still relatively unexplored and often neglected by most literary scholars. I am, therefore, very glad and grateful for the opportunity to meet you and Linda and the handful of Filipinos who share this enthusiasm for the subject...

Again, thank you... Yours truly, Jaime. February 24, 1985.

*

Elmer Ordonez

Dear Len,

...Your panel on the place of history in modern Philippine literature promises to be an exciting one and you honor me with an invitation...I am accepting...Elenita and I look forward to seeing you and Linda at Ann Arbor.

My trip to the Philippines entailed participation in a panel of the Philippine Studies Association Conference in UP...I met old friends and colleagues—including Ben Santos...and new faces and writers...

I also did quite a bit of research on alternative writing (both above ground and underground) including protest and revolutionary pieces. I was able to go to the countryside and record previously unrecorded songs and poems of the resistance.

This is the other dimension of Philippine literature that I wish to bring out in the panel. This research is actually part of my project with the Center for Developing Areas Studies, McGill University

Martial law caught us in Penang, Malaysia where I was visiting prof at the university there. On the advice friends we moved to Canada after my stint in Malaysia (abruptly cut with the cancellation of our passports) ...I settled for teaching at the secondary level (Elenita at grade school level). Our careers became secondary to what we felt we could do to help our friends back home. My literary studies (including a sequel to my Conrad book) was put on hold for quite a while. It was only in 1978 when I attended a panel on Phil, literature (Ben Santos, D. Quemada, Rolando Santos...) at the AAS meeting in Chicago that I decided to start again on Phillit. Since then, I have attended and, 1981 participated in panels (1980 in Kalamazoo, 1981 in Honolulu, 1984 in Ann Arbor and with my research now I hope to make a contribution to rounding out our picture of Filipino writing.

We do have a lot to talk about in Ann Arbor, Warm regards to you and Linda...Sincerely, Elmer. March 21. 1985.

*

Boone Schirmer

Dear Len:

I enclose a statement in opposition to the proposed extradition treaty between the Marcos dictatorship and the Reagan Administration.

If this treaty is passed by the U.S. Senate it is possible that President Marcos will attempt to extradite back to Filipino jails outstanding democratic opponents like Charito Planas, Benigno Aquino, Raul Manglapus, Heherson Alvarez.

The Friends of the Filipino People urges you to read the enclosed declaration of opposition to the extradition treaty. If you agree with it, please sign the statement of support and mail as soon as possible to the Alliance for Philippine Concerns...Sincerely yours, Boone Schirmer, Standing Committee, Friends of the Filipino People. February 11, 1982.

PS. If in addition, you would write or call Senators Kennedy and Tsongas with a personal message of opposition to the proposed...that would be very helpful...Dear Len, If you could get any more names to this statement from BC, that would be great. B.

*

Fr. Miguel A. Bernard, S.J.

Dear Len,

It was very good of Linda and yourself to have me and Don Plocke for dinner...

I also enjoyed the drive through the pretty country...John Larkin sends his regards to you.

Best wishes, M.A. Bernad, April 8, 1975.

*

Fr. Joseph A. Galdon. S.J.

Dear Len,

I wanted to thank you specially for the time you spent with us at the Ateneo. Both your lectures were very well rec'd and the participants were delighted. One told me later, "He lectures so well! How can he remember all that?"

If I can get to Boston in January, I will look you up. I would like to walk about B.C...I'm not sure how free I will be.

Joe, July 24 (no year)

*

Dear Fr. Joe Galdon,

...I am delighted that you find my article on Realuyo and the others useful; and absolutely, I would be as pleased as usual if the PS editorial board review it...

Yesterday Linda and I returned from a "routine" visit to Dr. Felipe Tolentino who, thank the Lord, said the macular degeneration in my right eye is responding to treatment...to the extent that I was actually able to, for the first time, to identify all of the top characters in the eyes chart...that doesn't sound like much but I am still euphoric about it, though I draw no conclusions from its happening...

The next project I have assigned myself will be the analysis of the three centennial prize winning novels...so I will continue though retired from BC... (Incidentally, I may be teaching a special kind of course one hour a week this coming spring: retired professors with retired laymen as students...a government-encouraged program headquartered in Wellesley...come March I look forward to the classroom again...

I need no longer live only vicariously in the exploits of Linda and of our professor-daughters...

Linda said she already sent you our Christmas wishes. God loves you, I'm sure. Len, 11/16/00.

*

Robert F. Drinan, S.J.

Dear Leonard:

I enjoyed your article on the Philippines in the *Boston College Biweekly* of January 31.

I was in the Philippines just before Christmas on a human rights mission and wrote the article which I attached...

With warm personal regards, I am...Cordially yours, Bob (Robert F. Drinan, S.J. Professor of Law, Georgetown University Law Center. April 11, 1985.

*

Gloria F. Rodriguez

Dear Len,

This is a quick note to ask you for a biographical sketch...for the back cover of FIREWALKERS...I sent you...two sketches for a possible book cover design...I have already received the galley proofs...they were submitted to the press with the layout.

I missed Linda when she dropped in at our office...in case I miss her altogether tell her thanks a lot for the copy of her book she left for me. Mrs. Vigilia...borrowed it right away, so I haven't had a chance to read it myself.

I will be in Connecticut, visiting my youngest daughter who's just had her first baby...She is Mts. Cynthia Militar...My three daughters who are all in the U.S. (the oldest, Nadine R. Sarreal, is in Texas; the middle, Audrey Ann R. Roco, is in NJ...Best wishes...Sincerely, Gloria. May 12, 1986.

*

Dear Len,

...a preview visit to the ALLIW library in Ateneo. I am impressed! Edna (Manlapaz) besides talking about the program for November 13 for Linda's book launching, also wanted to plant the seed for my future donation of my Giraffe record...to preserve the GFR story of my role in the publishing scene in the Philippines. There's still a lot of fire in me, having worked as librarian for 12 years (8 as librarian of Brent School Baguio and the next 4 in the Reference Department of the University of Connecticut...as head of the Interlibrary Lopan Service 1967-1971, while Ralph was working on his Ph.D. in Microbiology) ...

I am writing this to enclose in the box of books...copies of your and Linda's (TSW)...some extras for your needs...and also a copy I am requesting you to send to Dr. Lynn M. Grow...should reach you...much ahead of when you need your TSW copies for classroom use. It was a long haul, but I made it on both your books...

In haste, but with much affection, Gloria. 7 October 2002.

PS. I can hardly wait to see Linda again, my oldest daughter, writer Nadine, will finally get to meet her.

*

Dear Len,

I thought of asking Ralph to answer your letter...by email, but you said your computer is on the blink...

What is the title of the novel Linda is presently working on?... a phone call from Linda Nietes' sister-in-law for another 15 copies of The Stranded Whale for Phil Expressions, making a total of 38. M Romero of ARKIPELAGO...got 3 copies.

...I renewed my... (Department of Trade & Industry) registration for Giraffe Books...this might be the last time...because of "time constraints" ... (I will be 80 by then...)

Our love to you and Linda and may we all retain our faculties fairly well. Affectionately, Gloria. October 20, 2003.

*

Julian E. Dacanay, Jr. Esq.

Dear Dr. Casper,

First, allow me to extend my warmest greetings, hello, and hope you are in the best of health...I am now working on putting out my first collection of writings...*Selected Writings*. The table of contents is here attached.

My request is, could you write the introduction to this, my first book?

I was one of your students in the early 60s when you conducted your first Ateneo Graduate School Seminar in Creative Writing and I wrote *Tell Me in Darkness, Mud under the Sea*, both stories and the one-act play, *The Executives*. You gave me a grade 1+ and you even asked me if I could give you a copy of *Tell Me in Darkness* so that you could try to get it published abroad.

Tell Me in Darkness was published in the Ateneo Heights, in F. Sionil Jose's *Equinox 1* and in Asuncion David-Maramba's *Contemporary Philippine Literature*...

So here is hoping you would grant me my request and please write me soon. I still work at the SEC and still live in Pasig. Julian E. Dacanay Jr., Esq. November 18, 1986.

*

Roger Bresnahan

Dear Len,

Well, finally you see before you the results of my 6-month sabbatical, plus the work of so many years interrupted by a lot of committee work, etc. As I told Linda, I've split the major interviews into two groups—fiction writers and critics. The volume of fiction writers has been accepted by New Day...

I've enclosed your interview...it's still a very long interview, but...you've got a lot to say that people would like to hear. Please go over it again to make any corrections you wish...please send me a list of your publications on Philippine literature...

This for Linda, I've enclosed my review of *Ten-Thousand Seeds of Tobacco* from Asiaweek...the magazine's style does involve a lot of abbreviation and elliptical expressions. I've learned to live with that in order to do some service for Philippine and Southeast Asian writing...Yours, Roger. 9 December1987.

*

Cecilia Manguerra Brainard

Dear Leonard,

...The final decision regarding my book, *Acapulco at Sunset*...is to publish it without a Foreword. I do want to thank you, very sincerely, for the time you took to read the manuscript, think about it, write about the matter, and get the material back to me right away, despite your busy schedule...

I'll be sure and send you and Linda a review copy...many thanks for extending to me the courtesy of writing the piece.

Sincerely, Cecilia. August 4, 1995.

*

James F. Donelan, S.J.

Dear Len

The Grand Tour rolls on. Sponsored this year by PCIB. The main audience consists of teachers.

I see Gretchen every so often. But my schedule has been hectic. The Grand Tour plus six hours of Juniorate (S.J.) teaching, plus AIM etc. leaves very little time. And Gretchen's location out at that lunar landscape puts us at opposite ends of civilization. From all accounts she is satisfied with her projects and all is well.

Love to Linda & Tina. Jim. Undated.

*

Alfred A. Yuson

Dear Krip,

...Thanks for the TOMAS copy and for your new book; THE WORD ON PARADISE" ESSAYS 1991-2000 on WRITERs AND WRITING, I will treasure it for both its tsismis...and for its equally honest judgments about what had been accomplished beyond barkada-type mutual congratulations...One thing that has made me trust and respect and honor Frankie is that he never bothered to defend himself against my tough review of his first Rosales novel and that he has accepted my admiration for 90% of his writing also with respectful silence. I judge you to be the same caliber of person, essentially, and I am proud to be some kind of a friend, in your estimation...Len. 11/10/01.

*

Dear Susan Garfield:

It is with great pleasure I recommend Alfred Yuson for a residence at the Rockefeller Foundation's Study and Conference Center at Bellagio, Italy...I have read one of his books of poetry...both of his novels...as well as his...stories.

A few years ago I was asked by Skoob...in the Netherlands to write an introduction to his shortened version of GREAT

PHILIPPINE JUNGLE ENERGY CAFÉ, which was to serve as a model, when published in Singapore, for other Southeast Asian authors whose works would then circulate in the part of the world, in regional solidarity...

Although Yuson is...still a young man, I believe he offers one of the most significant direction for the future of Philippine Writing in English... (He will make a wonderful companion for the other Bellagio "residents" as his knowledge and congeniality are everywhere visible in his latest book...

His broad understanding of the interplay of place and ethnic culture is evidence of the propriety of his being the author his projected novel, MORNING LAKE. Its theme, the persistent relevance of all that has been tried and tested in a culture, even as it wants to be open to advances, not to novelty but to dynamic change, is anthropologically an ancient one...

I therefore recommend Yuson as a resident at Bellagio...Sincerely, Leonard Casper. 1/29/03.

*

Paulino Lim, Jr.

Dear Linda and Len,

Enclosed are copies of my play and short story "Nurse Rita." Barbara and I went to Manila for the book launching...We also had a very enjoyable visit to my hometown at the foot of Mayon Volcano.

The play's been rejected by three theater groups in the US. But the text, I believe, stands on its own merit...

Wishing you God's blessings and good health. Sincerely, Paulino. February 18, '08.

*

Dear Linda and Len,

...Since retiring from full-time teaching...I've been involved in the OLLI (Osher Lifelong Learning Institute) program at school. It's fun teaching seniors and Fellow retirees. I've taught Romantic Poetry, Graham Greene, and "Stage Drunk: intoxication as a Dramatic

Device. My next offering is "W. Somerset Maugham."

Barbara extends her best wishes to both of you and family. I'd like to add my prayers. Sincerely yours, Paulino. Oct. 4, 2014.

*

Bienvenido Santos

Dear Len:

I'm grateful to you for your letter, that "reverend" portion which…about time someone like you opened my eyes to the truth: I have been luckier than most…

Did I say anything about the National Artist Award? I do not WANT it, Len. Not from that couple…if offered to me, I will turn it down…You are right, what more do I need?

I'm not going to teach anymore after June 10…you can be sure, I'm going to write my heart out…because it is the only way…I know you will be busy but please, for my own selfish reasons, write to me… I'll be in the Philippines not later than Nov 1…the priority in my life is my health. I spent two days in the hospital week, the usual emergency treatment for chest pains…fortunately everything turned out well…O, Len, you don't know how helpful you have been. Thank you, dear friend. As ever, Ben. May 24, 1983.

*

Dear Len:

Last month during the launching of DISTANCES: IN TIME I autographed a copy (hardcover) for you with the understanding that Ateneo airmails you the copy…it's been more than a month since…I am truly grateful for what you have done and I trust you like the book.

I'll be in Manila again next month. From there I'll fly to SF sometime in March. It's quite boring here in the provinces. I feel like a shuttle-cock going from Naga City to Daraga and back. It's better in Manila though quite expensive…in spite of the devaluation of the peso, prices are quite pretty stiff.

It has quieted a bit down here. We Filipinos are uncomfortable in the role of revolutionists…I can't help feeling so frustrated and angry at all the lies and corruption all over the place, the hiya that used to characterize our culture is just about obliterated...

The *What the Hell For*, etc. novel I started 10 years ago and discarded around 1980...I don't know how long it will take me to finish revising...it used to take me years. I know there's precious little time but I tire easily...So I'm starting another novel. Just found a great title for it (SO MANY DIFFERENT PLACES), culled from a poem by Neruda...Has anything like this happened to you?...

...Every time my chest hurts, I'm reminded of my mortality. (I had good visits with Estrella just before she died!) And I sober up. I take it easy.

Do the same, young man. Remember me to Linda and the daughters. As ever, Ben. Jan. 27, 1984.

*

Undated. From Len.

I am anticipating that you, in turn, will be relating anecdotes about your life and times as an "exile," past and present, along with how these stories came to be written and related circumstances.

These, I say, are just my anticipations. Correct me at once if this doesn't conform with your own intentions...you do the "personal things," I the "impersonal."

For the future—when Bruce first consulted with me, I told him I'd be glad to bring this book (*The Man Who Thought He Looked like Robert Taylor*) to the attention of American scholars interested in the Philippines...then between the two us we could name a dozen Philippine-American newspapers which would run as news the announcement of the book's release...There are hundred of thousands of Filipino immigrants...many will be interested...I should think several thousand books could be moved within two years...I am quite willing to help in bringing the book to the notice of schools and newspapers.

For that reason and simply because I want to do justice to your work, I will put together the best Introduction I can; and try to get you a copy before I send it on to Bruce...

And please keep on writing: "Immigration Blues" is marvelous. Our best to you and Beatriz.

*

Dear Len:

...Two things are keeping me here my latest book, *Dwell in the Wilderness*, a collection of my stories still uncollected...published between 1931-1941, will be launched...I still have to see a doctor for one of those things that perennially plague old guys like me.

I usually stay at the Tropicana, an apartel in Malate where Linda and Gretchen and Mauro Avena dropped by after treating me to lunch; but with too many fires breaking in Manila...

Frankie throws his usual parties...Tess does all the work...he told me he's publishing your review of my works. Frankie knows a lot of people in the world of publishing, and I don't mean just writers, from all over the world...

The format of the panel discussion you describe suits me, an impromptu and relaxed exchange. So, count me in.

Hope you're well and Linda and the girls. As ever, Ben. February 16, 1985.

*

Manuel A. Viray

Dear Linda, Len and Gretchen:

...we have kept thinking how kind and hospitable you were to us. Many, many thanks for the visit but most of all for the opportunity to have been able to talk with you and see you once again after many years: the stay, the books, the conversation.

...I am glad I was able to talk to you because whatever vague plans I had and whatever hesitation was present disappeared when we talked... Linda was most patient and kind to us, and Gretchen was a delight...Our warmest and best to you. Cordially, Maneng. Sept. 15, 1964.

*

Dear Len:

Am sending to you the other working draft—Every time I sit down a letter such as this or talk about the book, I begin to have second doubts. But always your words come back. So, in a sense your counsel and encouragement sustain me...I hope you can decipher some of the corrections, and having done so, if you would be able more or less, to record your reactions and judgements in fairly undisturbed terms...Cordially, Maneng. Sept 16. 1964.

*

Dear Len:

So far I have not received any reply from Manila or the University of Nueva Caceres...

The way it would look now, if I do not receive any replies by the first of November—you remember I set myself a decision for the end of October—I will try to forget the typescript's publication...

I am sending you a Manila Chronicle issue (October 15, 1964), containing a short item, *Wounded Diamond* and the "Reconnaissance Award."

I assume you have the original and also that I sent to you the working script of *After This Exile*. Please confirm this. I am having difficulty remembering whether or not I had sent the working script to you... Cordially, Maneng. October 29, 1964.

*

Dear Len:

Many thanks for The *Wounded Diamond*... first about the jacket design, based on Gretchen's handiwork: it is beautiful and unusual configuration—color and composition. I particularly like the extension...made from the planes in the foreground...there is more concern in these pieces than in your previous ones on the thematic nature of present-day Philippine writing...The rest of the evaluations are the best one can find in the welter of Philippine literary criticism and I do not except Bernad's either...When we were there last year you said that something revelatory: that in your creative writing classes you enjoin your students to write fiction showing characters that reveal they have lived. This matter of characterization is a patent weakness I think in Philippine fiction.

Still nailed to the job...Maneng. February 4, 1965.

*

Dear Len:

...I am happy that Syracuse will issue your revised *Wounded Diamond*. Went through the book...and found how just and perceptive most of the estimates are. What I envy is your skill in placing the proper perspective not only on a writer's ideas or controlling themes but also his "style" ...

I am working on another angle for *After This Exile*. If something concrete comes up, I will write to you again.

Just in case you have Villa's address, give it to me and I will see what I can do about helping obtain his permission which would enable you to include some of his poems...Cordially, Maneng. April 5, 1965.

*

Dear Len:

I received the two copies of *Literature East and West* and I should thank you and congratulate you at the same time. For this work you are doing for Philippine imaginative writing and for including me...Enclosed is a press release, which I hope will be published on Philippine papers.

...Life was not as arduous as this in Manila or in Washington, DC...I suppose that one can only breathe, eat, drink, etc, automatically from day to day under the circumstances, taking care that the disorder and/or decay will not intrude unnecessarily into one's dreams, much less at the process of living.

This is an idea I keep returning to as I fashion in a peremptory way my next piece of writing. April 19, 1965.

*

Dear Linda and Len and Gretchen:

By the time you get this short note we would have been a year in Djakarta.

The real purpose of this note, however, is to thank you for having me appear in the book, *New Writing from the Philippines*. I thought I saw a review somewhere in The Daily Mirror...Thank you also for having my copy sent to me.

...As I write this I remember your lovely house out there and that particularly chilly summer and I become homesick really. Isn't it funny I get homesick for New England but not for Manila... Affectionately, Maneng. September 29, 1966.

*

Dear Linda and Len:

...I retired from the service three years ago. Last posting was in Phnom Penh...where we lost everything. Have made arrangements for all the Filipino nationals to return to the Philippines as soon as possible...my wife followed on the last flight home...The Communists were coming in. My wife and I came in with one suitcase each...Charing died about a year later.

Was able to adjust myself...

...I used to go to UP, talked to one, two friends. Attended "writing workshops." Visited the museums and galleries. Worked my daily schedule on what passes as verse and/or fiction. Frankie Sionil Jose who had run my stories in *Solidarity* had scheduled their publication. Paper, its price, disappeared. Kaput.

...Months later, at an organizational meeting...of the Manila chapter of International PEN, the participants decided to submit a resolution to the President, reminding him of the unpleasantness that go with censorship...that led to the imprisonment of writers...

My younger sister reminded me all my daughters and their families are abroad. You've got to go, she said...

I try to keep up with the trickle of news from the Philippines. Miss the homeland...

So far I have written manuscripts, a collection of variables...*Gaze and Other Verses; Annotations for an Elegy* based on the victims of war in Vietnam; *At Wah-Hing's*; --a memento of writers...in a pre-war restaurant in Manila (specifically Plaza Santa Cruz); *In the*

Sunlit Park—about parents and kids; *Victoria Station*...

Have been debating with myself if I should send out these titles. Have been more hesitant than courageous...My best to you always. Cordially, Maneng. July 15, 1985.

*

Dear Len:

Deeply appreciate your kindness and generosity in giving to me in mid-November...copies of your reviews and criticism—and my "Shawl from Kashmir" ... my sister sent me a copy of my Judas Iscariot story, "First in Haldama."

I wrote those things three, four decades ago...

Because of common problems NVM and I share, we agreed...to do something about the excruciating lack of awareness in this and other countries of Philippine literature in English...

All your papers are fascinating.

...I've sent my chapbook of verse, *Morning Song*, to New Day...Will write again...Cordially Maneng. December 4, 1987.

*

Dear Len:

Thanks a lot for the books you've been sending, and inscribing to me...and your literary concelebrations, which spans two decades, *Firewalkers*.

...some new and valuable information about the nature, status and problems of Philippine writing in English and in the vernaculars...what we probably miss (when we lose contact) is the animated exchange on imaginative writing, estimates and evaluations, theories and approaches, characterization and style instead of the physical presence *per se*.

But to go back, the amazing thing in the *Wounded Stag* is the cover design...

I am delighted that *Firewalkers* is out...Here you remain knowledgeable and astute. I like to believe I have an idea of the criteria which impels the formulation and direction of your judgments...

I returned to the corrected page proof of "The Veronicans at Wa-Hing's," thanks again for asking me to write the article...

My manuscript *Morning Song* is now going the rounds of the university presses in Manila...

Will end here or I will be rambling on senselessly. Cordially, Maneng. August 28. 1988.

*

Dear Len:

Thanks a lot for the copies of J Villa's *Selected Poetry*...I believe I've indicated doing drafts for Broken Rhythm...

Wishing you all a joyous Christmas holiday and wonderful years to come. Cordially, Maneng. December 1990.

*

F. Sionil Jose

Dear Len:
...I am now putting out a new journal...fully financed by the Congress for Cultural Freedom...it will be Philippine-oriented...

I wonder if you can give me a really hard-hitting article on why Filipinos (quality writers...) cannot get published in the United States. AND then I hope you will cite real examples.

...I hope that you can confirm my views. I need not tell you what they are but the editors and publishers I have spoken with have already confirmed them...

I can only offer you peanuts for your work but you will have my undying gratitude...Sincerely, Frankie. August. 26, 1965.

*

Dear Len:

Your "Dominion Over the Horizon" is coming out in the next issue of SOLIDARITY together with the reviews...Your book is in the shop downstairs and it is selling very well...Sincerely, Frankie. 12 September 1966.

*

Dear Len:

Many thanks for your letter...and the review on "The Battle of Bataan."

Has all the stories in Linda's collection appeared already in print?... I would like to use them in SOLIDARITY including the novella...

With regards to your collection of short stories, let me know who your publishers are so that I can place my orders. I would like to be properly stocked if and when you come to Manila so that we can have a reception for you and an autographing session...

If you have any long piece I will welcome it very much. Sincerely, Frankie. 7 August 1970.

*

Dear Len –

...Yes, the chances of *Solidarity* being revived this year are very good...

Of course, I would like to see your name in the same old box...it will have a broader Southeast Asian spectrum, less on the Philippines...But the special issues will not be completely on the subjects concerned...A good one third will be on general topics.

I was looking over my old files and I came across a memoir which I asked you way back to write. I will use it in the forthcoming issues.

...you are very welcome to do reviews for the magazine like you did in the past...As for Gretchen's pieces, do send them over...

Now, for chismis:...

Hello to Linda, and I hope you are well. Frankie. August 2, 1982.

*

Dear Len-

Many thanks for the review which, I hope, can catch up with the issue now in the press...

In the meantime, I hope you can do a sort of memoir; after all you have known us for quite a long time, and it is really interesting what you think of Filipino writers as individuals and not just as writers. We have no Malcolm Cowley, you know. And Franz who got a grant from Rockefeller years ago to do a literary history of the Philippines hasn't done it. And Yabes who has a prodigious memory is happiest doing his anthologies…

With all best wishes, Frankie. July 28, 1983.

*

Hello Linda and Len

I was in Singapore last October and met Burton Raffel and we did talk a bit about you…

Len, is there any long piece you have that has not been published yet? I am getting more literary…will have another special literary issue early next year.

Let me know if there's anything you need from here…

I hope your 1985 will be richer and happier. I told Burton Linda is our most under rated novelist but not by my lights. Frankie. Xmas 84.

*

Dear Len –

I just got your note about the Ben Santos review…it doesn't matter much if it comes out first in Manila; the circulation of SOLIDARITY and AMERASIA do not really cross one another.

I am not at all bothered about the Marcos demos here…nothing compared to the Cory demos—millions, man; Marcos just has a few thousands. All of them mercenaries.

What worries me is that the country is not yet really stable; too many warlords still with guns…

…No problems here now except my overweight. All the best, Frankie. April 30, 1986.

*

Dear Len –

I am preparing a memorial issue for SP Lopez and it will be primarily a literary issue.

Can you give me something for it? Deadline is Sept 30.

I have in mind a piece which you can do with your left foot. Something about Phil lit, writers, critics...

Please remember the caveats which you already know...

I hope you have already received the SOLIDARITY issue with your piece in it. So sorry for the LLLOOONNGGG delay. Walang pera...Affectionately, Frankie. August 15, 1994.

*

Dear Frankie,

Linda and I join in congratulating you on Random House Modern Library's...continuing your Rosales series. I even approve of their consolidating several of the novels which really read better when put together. Also, that strategy may increase the possibility of the Nobel committee having more titles handy and publicly recognized...as we both hope it does.

It is also good to know that you will continue to work on Ricarte. He deserves it...Heroes, as we all know by now, are rarely to be found among famous "leaders."

Giraffe has just brought out my own first longish work—a novella, *The Circular Firing Squad*, about the MIFF 83...I wrote it in 1987 and haven't been able to find an American publisher...So be it...

I am 76 this year...under backdoor pressure...to retire...I hope to continue reviewing Phil lit...

Our love to Tessie as well. Len 3/4/99.

*

Dear Frankie

Wonderful! ...you have long deserved being acknowledged as a National Artist...Congratulations.

Of course, there will be those who envy and carp, but you've been defamed before; and truth will out. I remember how many envied NVM and tried to pull him down to their own mediocre size...Nor will I ever forget that you were one of Linda's foremost boosters when others passed her by...that the centennial Awards would be badly given...

By all means...send me a draft of the novel and I will tell you unsparingly what I think about it, might still need. Not that I am infallible, but I am not involved in literary politics...Len. April 17, 2001.

*

Dear Len – many thanks your note re the Samsons. It's very comforting to be commended by someone who really knows. But don't forget that I also learned a lot from you! Mabuhay ka! Frankie. 11/21/02.

*

Dear Frankie:

...I included your MASS (part of the SAMSONS edition) in my pro bono class on US-Philippine Relations...in Wellesley, (sponsored by the US for senior education) and the middle-aged students raved about it...

But I want to add more of my own response to it...When I first read THE PRETENDERS... sometime in the late fifties and then included my remarks in my 1966 NEW WRITING FROM THE PHILIPPINES (Syracuse U. Press) I hardly did that novel justice. I even recall, after we had been introduced to one another by Father Donelan on Padre Faura, admiring your self-control because my comments seemed not to bother you...I had considered Tony Samson's suicide "defeatist and cowardly and irrational."

How wrongheaded those judgements were, I can say now that I have matured...

I liked MASS even the first time. I like it now for additional reasons, including the way that it helps convey the immense vision which is the Rosales saga...In addition to MASS' satisfying its own requirements as an individual "island", it contributed greatly to the whole "archipelago" configuration...I can understand better now, and find wholly credible, even admirable the nobility of conscience in a man who, having committed both incest and abandonment of his bastard, knows that his (private) self-betrayal is hardly superior to the other (more public) betrayals which you dramatize between sexes and classes and nations…Len. 11/21/02.

*

My dear Linda and Len –

It's been ages since I wrote to you and just now…I came across two of Lenny's…I hope both of you are in good health, and that you have been blessed with more grandchildren…

I…finished the first draft of a new novel, perhaps my very last…I know that even my very good friends will hesitate to tell me to stop writing…I will send you a copy if and when it comes out early next year…

Tessie will be 81 this year and I will be 86 in December. Nick passed away when he was 86, so I'm keeping my fingers crossed…I am diabetic with a heart condition…but I have such a good appetite even when I am flush with fever…

…Retirement should be good for you, Lenny…I hope you have put down your memoirs, particularly a summation of your fixation with our lit and those crummy Filipino writers, their high fallutin language, their bloated egos and the intense private wars with one another, I have always tried to be above such but you know if you are here, it is very difficult to transcend oneself. But I suppose that is the artistic life…and I can imagine how it was in the ancient Greek agora, all that free discussion and the personal barbs in between…

Well, both of you have done more than your share to create that foundation, particularly Linda's underrated work. I gave her name once as a possible National Artist but I am not in the inner council…In any case there's a great deal of quarreling now over the Award—it is in the Supreme Court…

I'm not sure if Tessie and I will ever go to the US AGAIN--…Just the same, I hope you will make it yet to Manila soon. I hope both of you are well. Mabuhay kayo! Affectionately, Frankie. Oct 4, 2010.

10

LETTERS: LEN TO LINDA

1952

Dear Linda,

Today I celebrated Christmas. Your card arrived. And if it was meant as prayer, as I hope—May the profound beauty and joy of Christmas stay with you throughout the year—then I am grateful; and the only way I can say it, is to repeat the very same words to you.

It did, in fact, snow today as it should on Christmas when it can. Not because, it snowed in Bethlehem but because the first fall purifies the air of dust, and the later falls in big flakes, are like wet kapok angels on the eyelashes; and there is such a comfort in being in such a snow as if this were crystal manna, a reminder—but like many of the best reminders, quiet, almost unspoken, a profound beauty and joy, a lasting provocation toward innocence. Len. Ithaca, February 9, 1952. Addressed to Linda Velasquez Ty, 17 Araneta Avenue Malabon, Rizal. Philippines. (Airletter)

*

Dear Linda,

This is just a small cascade, of course; others here are as tall as the one I saw on a color slide last night, from some part of Pampanga, I think, now in Huklandia. But the smallness doesn't make it less cold and pure; and the little ones have their own sound, as they nudge thin layers off thick rocks and drop to the lake.

Niagara Falls is only 150 miles from here, the granddaddy of all these. Len (Postcard, Cornell, Ithaca, NY, November 9, 1952.)

*

Dear Linda,

Of course, by the time you get this, these leaves will have collapsed into fine powder, like old brown cocoons for butterflies. But for a while, the leaves did look like butterflies or flowers. And now there will be snow (it's in the air today); but the white and black will be green again, when the sun comes north next year. Len. (Postcard, November 9. 1952)

*

Dear Linda,

Just tramping around , over these heavy hills or alongside the rushing waters in the gorges, has taught me several things: how much heat and monumental weight it takes to squeeze these volumes of wet earth into fused layers of slate and shale, and how much for rain to make rivers that wear ripple-marks into that stone or gradually rub the stone away until there are sudden deep cuts, fifty or more yards deep in what seemed like everlasting rock; and finally, how little impression my footsteps make on land or water.

Yes, I've written some poetry, Linda, although I'm never quite sure whether it's real poetry or just the beginnings, even when parts of it are published. But even though my footprints are featherweight, I haven't stopped walking, I do respect the possibilities that are in man; even though he may look insignificant next to a waterfall or cliffside, he can appreciate them and they will never know him; and so man should appreciate himself as well. So, I haven't stopped.

That's not completely true, however; I haven't written a poem since last winter. At Stanford I was working on a novel; during June and July, I wrote a few short stories; *now* it is almost entirely critical work for a thesis. But except for the last of these, I hope there was something close to poetry in all these prose, even if the words were not metered or rhymed. Poetry is the heart of any matter.

But the *heart* of hearts, the heart of poetry which you speak of: to touch *that* sometimes and to find *yourself* alive, that must be something! Perhaps you've already managed to do that; but even if you have, I can't say that I envy you. Isn't it strange, Linda, how many people compete with one another, as if there isn't enough success to go around, they seem to feel, and so they want each other's jobs, or clothes, or husbands, or titles, because those are the things that success means to them. But the writers I have known, all young seekers say perhaps what they themselves, full of wondering and wonderment, know a little more about success and can question the fact that they've appeared on page 6 of such and such a magazine or were paid eight dollars a page; to them that isn't necessarily success. The test lies really in what they have written, compared with they *might* have written. And if they are the right poets, they're interested in what *needs* to be said and said well, for this time or that place or *all* place-times; and so they aren't envious when someone else says what they themselves perhaps might never have succeeded in saying. When the heart is touched, it can be heard by all, and then it no longer matters who was the cause, because a new cause is made, sprung in each of them, in the new sound of their new hearts.

However, even if you don't send me any of your poetry, I hope that you will write to me anyway—whatever time is left after law and the other thousand things…Meanwhile, I will try on Tagalog—so far my vocabulary is five words and they don't make much sense together. But perhaps enough footsteps retraced can wear down *this* rock, too. Vaya con Dios, Len Cornell, Ithaca, November 28, 1952.

*

Dear Linda,

Having made a mistake yesterday, I want to straighten it out today. I sent you a card from the UN but only by regular mail, so that it won't arrive until next year. Time is a strange dimension, but so is space; you know. This noon at the UN Assembly building, at a conference on human rights, I realized for the first time how short space is, so short between human minds that distance between continents seems unreal. Delegates from Egypt, Poland, France and India were discussing a Lebanese amendment to a report which the Committee on Human Rights has just spent a whole year in preparing. Actually, however, it seemed more as if all the peoples of the *world* had spent all *history* preparing this document, which enlarged the UN Charter in the direction of facilitating all dependent territories toward the securing of independence.

You know how it is, Linda: a person raised in only one country sometimes thinks that was the original country from which all others came, and of which they are imitations. *Our* history books in America are as nationalistic as those elsewhere; and so, although the books never said so, as a child I had the idea that men like Thomas Jefferson *invented* human rights. Slowly, as I've traveled or exchanged letters, or have been talked to, I've learned that the desire for self-respect and therefore the willingness to respect others is part of the human race, not part of those who live in one place or time. I'm sure that you know these things; I'm not telling you anything new, but I suppose in a sense, I *am* telling *myself*. You see, Linda, I thought I knew what the "universality of man" meant; I believed it: but even something we believe, can be enlarged in our understanding of it, in time, just as a person who loves another can find each year another reason for that love. So at the UN I heard these voices in the five official languages saying words I had heard all my life, and they came alive again for me because they are so much alive for all *these*. The tone of their voices said that. And there was demonstrated what previously I had accepted on faith alone: that humanity will never be driven completely out of humans. And that's quite a bit to learn in a world with daily headlines such as ours.

And so, in another sense, although I am apologizing for the fact that space between us will prevent you from receiving my Thanksgiving greetings until after New Year, still if you are the sort of person that I have imagined you to be from everything your mother has said, the space will be only the distance between two hands of one body, and the spirit of the greetings will not have diminished. Sincerely, Len. Ithaca, November 30, 1952.

1953

Dear Linda Belinda,

Whether you know it or not, or whether you will call it or not, you have sent me a poem. The stillness of one sunset, and summer's conflagration there at Baguio; the night and day sides of yourself. I wonder if you are always as quiet as your letters are. This is what I find so remarkable—quiet follows quiet then suddenly, as if from nowhere an accomplishment presents itself. *It* speaks, and it is all the unused words that *you* have stored; and unless at the moment of accomplishment, one is aware and listens, it is very easy to look through you as if you were just part of the furniture. Am I being fair? Do I know you at all, yet?

What is just as remarkable is that you should be able to imagine and appreciate perhaps certain submerged values in life, and at the same time be seriously studying law as seriously as I know you are. More lawyers should be able to temper their wits and codicils with human quality—and perhaps vice versa.

Well, this is a big talk again; but I won't apologize for meaning what is under the words. So many of your countrymen are talented in so many ways that sometimes during the past year I have given up hope of being useful to them. But, *because* of that fact, were there ever a need, I would feel doubly proud.

There is one piece of work right now that I wish I had a hand in. Amador Daguio is preparing a textbook comparing democracy and communism, for the normal school in Tacloban, where he teaches. We have already exchanged ideas through the mail, and it has been so fruitful just to be forced to think out abstract notions which previously were taken for granted, and to put specific cases before each other, to clarify what is desirable. But even airmail can't replace face-to-face conversations, when ideas are hot, *then* they should be grasped and wrought. Or perhaps it's just because Amador himself is so excited that I feel excited, too, reading about what goes on in his mind.

The other provoking thing is the appearance of more publications with "home talent" in them, in the Philippines. Amador mentions several new anthologies that are in the process; and I know NVM Gonzalez' *Diliman Review* should soon be out. The people will have an opportunity to speak what's on their minds, not what is in someone else's mind.

Next weekend, I will race home (the only place where I can find the necessary witness who knows me two years) and apply for a passport—still without prospects, but the time grows so short that I want to take some preliminary step. It will still take a contract and Philippine visa before anything is resolved and actual plans can be considered. In the past two months I have been busy doing researching and finally, writing the first draft of a 24,000 more words for my thesis, approved, revised; the whole thesis (300 pages?) will have to be approved in preliminary draft, revised, retyped, and be submitted to the University of Wisconsin by May 1. So you see, I have some notion of work, too, Linda. But I'm sure the writing process is no stranger to you. Unfortunately, there is no time to be both a teacher and a sociable human being, too. But something is supposed to be earned by all this sweat, and I hope that is how you feel about your own duties at school. Please remember me to Taling. Len/Ithaca. March 1, 1953.

*

Dear Linda,

So you can get choked up about other things than sunsets! I wonder which radio—Manila or Tokyo—the Japanese students complained over... Still, I don't think I would find much to disagree with in your attitude. Let me put on my false white whiskers and philosophize for the moment: there is such a thing as righteous anger and suspicion, and only the person whose feeling is involved can judge herself. You were right to ask just what friendship means to these delegated students, since *abstract* enthusiasms are insignificant…I am convinced that if I cannot answer your question, "What exactly does this new friendship amount to?" I would not ask you to apologize for asking the question…

The only question of right or wrong on *your* part is a conscientious examination of your own motives in placing the question. Were you interested in the answer? Were you deliberately trying to reduce them into tears? Were you presuming that these are enemies, not possible friends?…just to make sure that wrong is not equally divided…

Involved in the morality of such a debate is the whole direction of the discussion. I have learned…that the only fair thing is to condemn the deed, but not necessarily the doer. Not that we are not responsible for our acts, but simply that it is wise to remember that even if a particular act cannot be undone, the *doer* himself *can* change if he is willing and if *we* are willing to help…If I remember the little orientation lectures that we received in the army, Japan under the Tanaka Memorial began its invasion of the Asiatic mainland in 1931. No such invasion can begin without propagandistic preparation. This means, simply, that all these students who came to Manila had been born and raised under a regime of exploitation and imperialism. Does this absolve them as well as explain them? Of course not. We still have to believe in individual responsibility. It does mean *this*, however: probably they were not deliberate propagandists; probably they were not deceitful but only ignorant. The problem is different, therefore. You have a duty to educate them, rather than condemn them. Keep asking questions; make them ask themselves, give them an example of free discussion, free access to facts, etc…If I were *you*, I would feel saddened at the necessity of victory…Anger and the breaking off of student negotiations is not the best answer; it's a very temporary victory.

Would I make a good lawyer, do you think?

The skies are cloudless now. It is pre-Easter weather, the sun bright but chilly. Baguio weather I am told. The sky is now like plumes of cogon grass; it is like thin reflection of a burning candle in a silver mirror...soon—you will know what spring is like here. Yesterday was the beginning. Len. March 22, 1953.

*

Dear Linda,

And did you manage to go to Baguio? And was there moonlight, and if not fairies, then what? Because you are right: "there must be something to believe in." Adults like to think of themselves as adults and they believe in themselves, in other words; they have their own myths, their own conception of themselves which they must try to live up to, just as much as any child captured in childhood must believe in his own world, simply because there is no other. *This* is why, child and grownup alike, we all need humility—the realization of the walls in our own private visions, but through that we can also achieve communion and happiness, by understanding that we share these limits together and are our own best means of circumventing them. We can build windows in the walls; we can reach through gratings and shake hands, and more.

Forgive me, Linda. Sometimes I talk as if I knew what I was saying. But you must see that only by asserting a thing as if it were true, can I confirm my belief in truth-in-general. Even if what I say happens to be wrong, it is necessary to believe, and to believe strongly, because no action is possible without, first, faith. Faith without works is useless; but also, no work can ever be begun without faith, without some sense of direction, some hope in the probable effect of our actions, some informing vision. Science itself, so proud of its rationality, depends on hypothesis to guide its most careful inquiries. Law, too (or correct me), so cautious and orderly in its detailed motions, must depend upon some basic assumptions—such as the relation of two events (cause and effect), the possibility of some free will (fixing responsibility), the dignity of man (value of life) and, by extension the worth of property. These we take so much for granted that we fail to see, I think, that they too are fairies. So what? I believe in belief. I think that you, too, believe in its effectiveness and inevitability. I believe, too, for example in you, Linda and in your beliefs, as they come to me piecemeal in your letters. Do you believe in you? This is a ridiculous question, not because of its form, but because I know the answer already: Yes.

But tell me what you found again or anew, to believe in, in Baguio.

I have many things to tell you about "local color," which you say my story illustrates and to which, I must answer; yes and no. Fortunately, they are *so* many, that I will have to tell them to you in person. Len Ithaca, NY. May 3, 1953.

*

My darling Linda,

I know you will understand when I tell you this. If I didn't believe you are capable of sustained caring and devotion, how could I ever have begun to care for you? You must feel what I feel now, down here, alone against all my inclinations, taken into the house but kept apart—as I wait here for you, I don't know how long nor do I know how brief the time will be that we can spend together, when you come down as you promised. Whatever I am good for, whatever I can amount to I have dedicated to you, Linda—with finality and without reservation, almost three months ago. I wanted us to pledge to each other even then, but you thought that, though you yourself were willing, that we should wait until Christmas, the best time to talk to your father. The only thing that has kept me sane—and I wish I were not exaggerating, but I don't think that I am, has been your promise that at Christmas, surely, we would be engaged. I have not succeeded in waiting as patiently as either of us have wanted, but in those three months I have learned to love you more and more until I realize now that you are my whole life—my home, my family, my beloved. It is for you that I have worried through troubles with UP, the Bureau of Immigration, and the vast unfriendliness of a vaster city…and for you, Linda I have begun to work out plans for a writers' workshop, and annual of short stories, and other ways of helping the local writers help each other—because I believe that literature can be a mode of truth, and that the sensibility and sensitiveness of good writers is important to be preserved, for the society, the other people, among which they must live out their lives. But all these efforts need strength, Linda, and I am human and limited. My strength needs renewal; I can help only if I am helped, I can care only if I am wanted. Not just by these persons among whom I work—their affection is of a sort and quality which can hardly satisfy the full depths of my needs—but by you, Linda, *for* whom all this effort is intended. How can I help make a better world unless I am allowed to be with you, who are for me the heart of all that matters—the good, the beautiful, the true. I love you, Linda, more than I could ever have expected—more than pride, more than tears. There is nothing outside you, for me. This is the terrible love that I have wished on you; having admitted as much several times and done my best to prove it whenever I could...The goodness I have seen in you, Linda; the joy you have already returned, the peace you have renewed in me—these are my hope. Three months have been a long wait for me, Linda, because my love having engaged me to you that long ago, wants to be impatient. But I have tried to be patient, and not show the strain of being in doubt about what might happen. And the times that you have seen me reduced to anger, unhappiness or tears, none of which could be hidden, are only signs of that strain; they are not part of the permanent me which I have dedicated. Be with me when you can; I need you now as much as I ever will. This being imprisoned in a lovely room, being the guest but outsider, the still untrusted by the aunts is making me slowly into someone I do not enjoy being, someone whom you may be right not to marry. But if you will not be with me, at least sustain these hours of my loneliness…

  Christ was born to give man peace by giving meaning to their suffering; by making the goodness of grace available to them. In His name give me that same peace, Linda, on His birthday. Make these months mean something by giving us each other. Love, Len. UP/Diliman. December 12, 1953.

1954

Dearest Linda,

Probably homesickness for you won't set in until tomorrow. I've been fighting it all day, with the help of eating, sleeping and seeing two movies. I slept after you left, honey—I was so knocked out, chasing from church to BAL to the plaza: maybe that's why I couldn't find anything to say, sensibly, when you left this morning. Dick Coller keeps talking to me tonight, so this letter won't be much better; hardly worth reading, much less saying. I went to *Adventure in Honduras* (not very good though there was one good shot of some tigerfish eating a crocodile); then I circled Burnham Park, and off to *Spartacus* (which was so good that I didn't bother leaving to eat at La Patria; instead, I just went to a restaurant.) And now it's 10:30.

Tomorrow the routine will be a little different: classes, picture-taking, preparing a course for June; maybe some Tagalog. But I can see already, from today, how little fun there is in being in the nicest of places without you. A movie's no good if I can't hold your hand; and when there is kissing, I want to brush the hair from your forehead, or feel the warmth of your throat again... We didn't have everything our own way, darling, during this vacation; and sometimes when we were kept apart and I felt especially bad, I would pray that you would never be seriously lonely. Now, however, I'm just selfish enough to hope that you too are a little lonely right now.

This will be the first time we've been separate so long, Linda and so much of our lives already was spent before we met; can we ever make up for all this? We can try. You made me happier than I could have expected.

I want to hold you, Linda. Without fear, without concern, with the only care being that we are becoming one, getting ready for marriage. We must talk about these things, think of them, otherwise our lives will stand still, and the waiting, the wanting, the courtship will have meant nothing; we won't have grown up together...

And don't work too hard. I don't want you worn out to the edge of irritability by the time I arrive: let me have all the irritability in our family. Will you divorce all others, be ready to rebel, to fight for me and marry me alone?

It, Linda, may sound as if I'm asking you to live in a hermitage with me, afterwards. I'm not. I won't, But I think we both should be ready to; for our sake. I can give up anything, anyone, but you, Linda. You are my life.

Linda. Linda. Linda. Len. I love you deeply. Baguio. Sunday.

*

Darling.

I heard a *really* bad news today that means we won't be together until June 1 or 2.

Dean Panlasigui has been in Manila over a week…Originally, I thought we had a gentleman's agreement to give finals the 29th, correct them the 30th, and leave the 31st. His wife says she's certain the finals are on the 31st! I'll check with Mrs. Afable, the secretary, tomorrow, she knows as much as anybody. Pray for us, Linda, please. I want to be with you. At first I thought of giving the exams as first scheduled and leaving anyway; but there'd be a big fuss, if it's against rules; and I already had that little fuss at semester's start, you remember, and have only now redeemed myself by running two issues of a paper and handling a series of skit for our closing program at Burnham Auditorium. I'd fight for anything if I'm sure I'm right. But I wasn't sure about this issue. So, whatever's necessary I'll do this time. But I pray it isn't. I miss you so, my darling. Again, last night I felt you were close, and this time the moon was under clouds, so it wasn't that. But if it must be, promise me that we will make up for all this distance and lost time. I'm not just lonely, Linda, I could arrange an extension or get myself invited out a dozen times if I tried. But it wouldn't help. I'm lonely for you—and there is no substitute. Please write; please be with me, until we can really be each other.

This will be our first anniversary apart. Please God, it will be our last.

I took a few pictures, even though it was getting cloudy. Then I climbed up the ridge on South Drive and had just started back to school when the heaviest downpour of the season began. Heavier than anything I had seen at Manila, and ice cold. I had a raincoat but no hat, so I was drenched in five minutes. Even my pockets filled with water, but I didn't worry until lightning flashed less than half a mile away. The thunder rattled the trees; and I dropped just as you said one ought to, though by then it was too late and it was like hitting the dirt after a shell had fallen nearby. Nevertheless, I prayed; for our sake--There have been two times in my life, Linda, that I can remember not caring if I was dead or alive—I'll tell you about them some day---but now I care very much, and I prayed as I did when that fever caught me in bed and I felt as if my body was on fire and would cave in; I pray for what I don't even deserve, but what I want with all my heart—to be allowed to live, to be your husband in peace and some simple dignity, to find happiness with you.

I'm sorry if this letter is so solemn, honey.

At least I have your letter. It means everything, dear. God bless you for being you. I love you. Len. Baguio. May 21. Friday.

*

Dear da:

That's short for Linda darling--your code name for today.

Eight more days. I can see the horizon. There's a new-found land, a you, ahead; spread full sail! Take whatever wind, from whatever quarter: and God speed!

Although I agreed with your sister yesterday that I'd be at Tavera Hall by 8 this morning, for Mass, she was gone when I came. But since I was going to church I couldn't afford to be even a little angry so I retraced my steps and reached the Cathedral in time for the sermon. After Mass while I was buying the papers, who should tap on the shoulder but your father! He had just come in.

So we each watched a door, watching for Baby, but the church emptied, and still she didn't appear. So we hunted down Session Road, and I checked with Esther, who had seen her heading uphill an hour ago. Must have gone to 7 o'clock Mass. So we jeeped back to Tavera, and finally caught her by 9:30.

After reading the papers we went back down to the Plaza, your father bought us all some custard pie; and then he took the 10:30 bus for Manila. I hope he found all of you ready to make his long journey worthwhile. He didn't look tired but he must have traveled far and early.

He took along the camera, with almost 18 shots still in it, which I hope you've used on the golden showers. Even so, please make the flowers stay alive until I come, Linda; and if you return the camera, there are still a few things I can shoot here.

This afternoon I rested, then will begin to correct some papers. I'm ready to leave on an hour's notice; and more than willing. This week especially I will think of you, sweetheart. It's already a month ago that we were so close that—do you remember? And when the pains come again, think of us please. You are my need and my fulfillment, my cause and end. I love you, Linda. I hope you are thinking of us this Sunday, on our anniversary. Suppose we celebrate it the night of the 31st? You are my high sky, a fire in the fog, the unseen songbird in the morning tree. Be mine first, and others only later. Be ours. With my mouth and heart: Len. Baguio. May 23rd.

*

Sweetheart,

How sweet the touch of the sun is, this afternoon, Linda, in between clouds and before the rain; like the touch of you, Linda, or the remembrance of it. I could sit like this all day. You are the warmth that is so much deeper than skin that the cold cannot penetrate a single pore.

One week from now, God willing.

Don't be changed, Linda; don't let the inertia of that house drag you back from the beauty we were discovering. Be fierce for us, even now; need me, so that our waiting will not be stationary but a growing together. There is only one thing that can make me afraid, darling: if you choose others in any way, I hang like a dead moon, untouching and untouched. I don't want to become rock. If we can least be as together as we were here, then I will believe in life. Don't grow tired—That's one reason I want to be home. Be strong for our sake. I think you know what I mean. No more moods for either of us, except the joy and peace of existing in and for each other. I hope I'm worried for nothing—while we should have been depending more and more on each other, sometimes there have been interruptions—and sometimes they were our own fault for allowing them.

I hope you will write again—at least once. I hope you will never be too busy for me, for us—just as I will try hard not to be, ever, to be too busy for you. You are my life, you own my life: be careful with it.

I went to an anniversary last night, Linda—the business partner of one of our Baguio colleagues who teaches at the Institute. In the backyard they dug a pit as long as I am tall, and twice as broad, and roasted lechon. While we ate at that, we also took long sticks like those propping up flowers at DD, and roasted pork chops. Bangus, corn and camotes. Dick Coller and I had eaten a big meal at the Patria, for fear there would be little food at the party; and it's true dozens of uninvited guests appeared: but even so we had plenty. Coller didn't touch the lechon, because of his stomach. But I ate a full second meal.

In addition, there was wine, sour and dry, gin, and whiskey. We sampled them all... But don't worry. Trust me: because I promise you never to get drunk, never to lose control or to look more foolish in public than I do when sober. If you like, however, I could give up even this rare drinking without any real sacrifice. Actually I've had nothing since Christmas, when Fel gave me rum and your father, a beer.

Later, they showed a color film on the TVA in Tennessee, in Tagalog. By then, most of those who had come just for lechon, were gone, and we could talk a little. I met a fellow named Carantes who said how every American is like an ambassador and is regarded closely as a representative of his country. And I said, "I'm not an American, I'm Len Casper." But I didn't tell him who my county is. I am free, Linda. And freely I give myself to us. I love you. I had an anniversary in my heart better than any pig or wine or movies. It will last. Len. Baguio. May 24.

*

Darling,

It's 10:30 in the morning. In order not to tire you with the same old thoughts and letters, I try not to think of you. And instead involve myself in this Burnham day and the making of a drawing from a box of words.

A north wind barely grates the quiet pond into corrugated shadows; the boats can't be distinguished from their ripples. Triangular sails become rectilinear, flash-motivated, moving like winter sun sharp on frost. There is the unheard sound of glass chimes waiting for the wind. Slowly the boats revolve on buoys like endless days.

The trees can hardly hold their shape—this scratch of time; though everything is outlined more than ever, they have lost their reality and roundness; all things are flat, invoked on a wall, worked into oneness in the middle of change, rocklike under watery sheen.

Why does a person breathe at a time like this? The birds intrude without an answer. Gliding like an hour on the water, without question. The lake has only one shore, one shadow line at a time, now two as the little lake itself revolves. Now this horizon, now that is dark, as unseen as air slowly turns the tides of mist. The right hand has no depth, the left hand, the breath goes in and out, now green, now gray. There is a smell of underwater, of small fish, of weeds in sand. The current of sky is off the opposite headland now, the whole valley submerged. Everything is moving toward rain. Air is water, water air. The piers move in and out of darkness; midday relaxes like a sprinkled fishnet, through which all things come and go, pass and gather.

I feel like an island, feeling this is the moment *before* something: will you ever come, scrape this shore, pass through the silence? Will you happen? Even as I wait, I love you. Len. Burnham Park, Baguio. May 25, 1954.

*

My darling Linda,

Maybe it's just fatigue, maybe more. But today I feel on the verge of desperation. One more delay, one more betrayal, and the cup of disgust will run over. Not with you, but who knows what all will suffer? You know about my trouble with the immigration: how, through stupidity or lies and, then carelessness, they didn't act on my request last December for a secure status but lost the papers for appeal. Then I asked our secretary at LA, to push the matter through while I had to be in Baguio; and so far there is no word from him, although May 31 is the date the extension would have run out, even if granted! I would like not to be bitter, darling…That same old inertia which has infected so many people might kick me out of the country and away from you, the only reason I came to stay in it and in the world.

I love you, Linda. That's my only faith and hope today. Be with me; fight with me. I can't help thinking that if we were married, there would be none of this visa trouble which has poisoned my being here for over half a year now. And if I've never mentioned that fact before, it's because I didn't want to worry you and because I don't want you ever to think that I want to marry you only to stay here: it's the other way around; often you are not only the best, but also the only reason for my staying. I love you. I know I don't need to say that. But I want to, even on the edge of tears and disgust, as I am now, I am determined that my love will bring us both happiness.

Okay bless us again, my darling! Pray a special prayer for us now. If you could write, if you could say one word. But if you can't, then understand how I feel and how I must act. I need help for our sake; but if I can get none, then I will have to sacrifice our being together, for a while, when I return in order that I can try, try, try to keep us together permanently. Try with me, Linda, bear with me. If it can't be easier, at least let it be worthwhile. In your house, as you did here, be with me as often and as long as you can. Please don't suddenly disappear, when I am there, and make me wonder and wait. Whenever we can be together, let us be, to ward off the ugliness of this world. Let me mean to you, what you have meant to me for such a long time.

This was what I meant in the past, when I said that, when suddenly you seemed to desert me, I prayed to you as well as to God. Perhaps the proud thing is never to admit what I have; in this letter, but to act as if I didn't need you, or care when you were absent. But that would be a lie, and I want no part of pride that is dishonest. There are other things, too, which make today especially miserable; but because I didn't want to make you miserable, I won't tell them. I have said enough, and I feel that you are close now; and I feel better and unafraid. Even if still worried. I kiss your heart, my darling.

This morning I took my class to see the library of a Mr. Perkins, ex-Manila lawyer and consul to Thailand. Mr. Clemente, Baby's boss, is in charge; and he invited us. The estate is on Villa Azucena on South Drive, and behind the house is a handsome pine building, formerly a gambling den but now devoted to Philippiniana—e.g. publications of Japanese occupation records, Perkins own diary from Santo Tomas, the joint book published in the Philippines, a huge Spanish-Tagalog dictionary, a complete set of occupation *Tribune*. I was surprised at how much the class and I enjoyed the place. Besides the outer room was covered with brilliant prints of tropical flowers.

Which reminds me, yesterday: I saw a beautiful, deep-violet begonia in a drug store and would have bought it but the pharmacist said it wouldn't grow in the lowlands...

You restore me Linda and I love you with all my soul. Len

Nevertheless, I'm glad I got all the previous thoughts off my chest. I really do need you, constantly, darling. Don't leave me even for an hour if it can be helped. Do you think you can stand that? Your lessons will suffer a little. Does it matter much. If I didn't love you so much, if I wouldn't do the same myself, I wouldn't ask you. Len. Baguio May 26.

*

Lindissima,

If the postscript to yesterday's letter seemed a little crabby, I think I know why. This morning I had a touch of what resembled typhoid—fever in head and eyes, weak knees, nauseous stomach; and probably it had begun last night. Forgive me my trespasses. I did catch your secret reference to our anniversary, and it must have made some real impression because I dreamed a little of you again before waking. I'm coming to you. By the time you read this, I will be with you. Who will you be *my* Linda? Really mine? Ours?

I still have the letters you sent me in the States. How I used to wonder exactly what you were like! I could tell from the letters your gentleness (Baguio pines) and your violence (Japanese "envoys"); that you were capable of deep feeling and devotion; that we enjoyed many of the same thoughts. You truly are like that, Linda—I had never been disappointed in those expectations; you are truly that and more. You won't believe it, but it's true that one of the main reasons I had for wanting to come to Manila was to see the whole of you. Were you the person I had looked for? And the moments of joy you have given me since then tell me that you are more than I could have guessed.

I want to marry you. I'm ready to marry you, in every way. That doesn't mean that I know you completely—perhaps, though, I know you more than anyone else, including yourself, does. In any case, I believe that if we lived to be a thousand, we still wouldn't know everything about ourselves. Because to be alive is to grow. If we can grow together… Especially when we're married…taking pleasure in being closer to each other than anyone else has ever been to us. Just the anticipation makes me feel the world can be a wonder. Indo-Chine and the H bomb are not the essentials. Our love for each other *is*. I could die with you right now, but more wonderful will it be to live with and for and through you, darling: In our name we must claim the mutual possession of our lives. This what I mean today when I say I love you, Linda. Not that tomorrow I will mean less; but more and more and more.

This is not fever speaking. Alka-seltzer, salabat, and sleep helped break that. This is all of me. How I want you, sweetheart. Being with you as you read this, I will want you even more.

I discovered the fever after hiking to the Nursery this morning. As you'll know by now, I bought several milleflores and African daisies—but not the orange daisies I like best. SO I bought plenty of seeds, too. I hope we will have shared them, planted them together, and cared for them. That was my thought anyway as I shopped.

Then on the way back to school, it hit me. I made it back, but I had no appetite. Nevertheless, this seemed to be the best time for pasalubong, so I shopped and shopped—as you have discovered. That helped; it felt good to be thinking of you. Later, back in school, I slept, then held classes, then begun this daily letter. Even though I am not with you now as you read this, I want you to know that I had been with you every day, as I write this—just as I promised.

Two and a half more days. I love you. Len. Baguio. May 28.

*

Dearest diary of all:

The clouds are thick and heavy tonight, honey, so I'll have to delay picture-taking until some other evening. When they're not too heavy, sundown is a fine time to catch the clouds halfway across the mountains. This morning, too, was so foggy that the sun didn't come up until 9:30. Just in time. I hiked out to Camp John Hay, finished the one roll and, at the cliffside and the arena, shot half the other. Remember? The far-off hills were too hazy to look right, so I'll go once more this week. In the afternoon I scouted downtown, met an Indian who is one of eight in the city, runs a ten-cent store here, and bought a color film P11; but send three more if you can. Then I got bus tickets for Baby and me; taught my class—and here I am, waiting for supper.

The Patria food is surprisingly good. And one can always fill up on rice. This morning we had sausages and fried eggs, biscuits and coffee; this noon they fed us very fine fish soup, rice, tomatoes, cucumbers, pork and shrimp. Not bad.

Don't mind the menu, honey. Dick talks so much I can't write what I really feel. I love you, Linda. Even if the cookies and cake didn't arrive yet. I'll try to hide by myself in Burnham Park tomorrow and write *there* where I can be at peace with you.

Last night we heard a siren on the road from PMA; today we read that it must have been Recto and the doctor heading in from the airport. We still don't know if the son is alive tonight.

I buy the *Chronicle* every day and pretend we're reading it together. We have some beautiful habits, Linda, that I hope will stay with us a long time. They are our custom—just as these pictures enclosed are my sisters, their husbands, and my folks on their 45th anniversary. But you are my family, sweetheart. Be close to me now and always: I pray to you every day for us.

The movies are so bad now, that I can't even force myself to go. So, I'll try to get ahead on my work and finish the semester without trouble. How I wish we were still working on your stories. Have you begun to review yet, Linda? Don't do too much at a stretch without rest; and be careful of your eyes. Close them now for just two seconds, so that I can kiss them, darling. You are very sweet to me. Len. Monday. Baguio.

*

Sweetheart—

Naku! I must have hiked over six miles this morning. My leg muscles feel like stone. Want to feel them?

I went to Camp John Hay, perhaps for the last time, hoping to find the light in the valleys better for pictures. It rained very hard last night, so that this morning was perfectly clear. Even so, the farthest mountains were pale as gauze, and even my eyes could not distinguish any details. But the nearest hillocks were fresh green: like the pines at PMA; and the sun glint on the tin roofs of the miner huts was like the show of fire on the sea-surface at noon.

I love you, Linda.

Then I walked out through the Italian Gardens and the Country Club, over to Wright Park where I think I caught some horses in action. Then I climbed those high stone steps—you know the ones, up to that pergola or summer house or whatever you call it where the lagoon looks out toward the Mansion House. That's as far as I went, as it was already 11, and some day I want to walk to Mansion House and Mines View for more pictures. Linda. If I couldn't tell you these things or show you the pictures it wouldn't mean anything. It has become harder to please me—now that I love you, and I do, "unconditionally."

From Wright Park I went to the Navy Base, around so-called "Millionaire's Row." Although the houses are often magnificent. their wire fences and telephone poles prevent them from being photogenic. So I took only about three. I just remembered I have one picture from Wright Park that should be terrific: but I want you to guess what it must be. Then on to Tavera Hall, to check with Baby about the cookies—but she wasn't there. I walked to the Patria, stopping at the Pink Sisters where I took a shot inside the chapel. Have you been there, darling? Isn't it beautiful? That's one picture I wish would come out.

Talking about being slow: today with your letter, I will finally mail that article for Gonzalez. Our money from that will buy 3 chairs or half a table or 1/3rd of a bed. Linda! Linda! Be my wife soon. Len. Baguio. Wednesday.

*

Dearest,

The sound you hear is LC, chomping on your delectable-as-ever-cookies. The only thing sweeter than they are, is---.

Last night I had gone back to see Baby during working hours, and she said, yes a package had come, but she hadn't unwrapped it yet. Just then, Clemente, her boss cornered me, and she had to introduce me as a UP prof, so it wouldn't seem as if I was visiting over long. Then he made me read a handful of Filipino legends which had come in during a contest.

So this morning I went to her first of all, and got over, half the cake and cookies and four films; wow! I'm running out of things to take pictures of. I love you most of all for that, Linda; I hadn't really expected that, but how badly I wanted! I'm as afraid of one-way conversations as of one-way kissing. I wonder if you wish as I do, that the invitation were already true. Len, to Linda.

PS. I keep forgetting to ask: should I bring that tin hot plate home?

PPS. You have all my love, but give my greetings to your mother, Georgie, and your aunts. Thursday.

*

Dearest Linda,

In the absence of any word from you last night, I had to read your first note, for the tenth time (only). This isn't a scolding. Heaven knows I've complained enough and now it's your turn. Heaven also knows that after writing you yesterday, I felt better than I have since you left. Last night, I dreamt of you darling, for the first time in several days. That's as good as a letter, for a while. The problems I wrote of haven't been solved, but I feel that you know them now and share them, without hesitation, just as so often when we were together in Teachers' Camp you let us be together in every way, as much as possible. Because of you, other things will solve themselves— things will be solved by you and me with God's help.

After the letter I went to a faculty meeting at Panlasigui's but no business was discussed, so Dick Coller and I still aim to leave Monday. Instead we sat around and looked at walls covered with flowers—ferns, Queen Anne's lace, daisied, etc. And several Igorot fabrics hung on the walls; and ate pancit. Lumpia, mangoes, cake, strawberries, coffee and San Miguel beer. But nobody took more than one. At least we told him we would not stay any more for the conference. No reasons necessary. Sometimes he can be understanding. I felt so good that when I went to my class at 5, I shared with them the few of your cookies left.

Later, to make time pass, I went to see Tyrone Power in Marie Antoinette, an old film but long enough to bring me closer to you.

Back at the room, Coller and I had our nightly "cockroach kill," this time accounting for six, a record: under hanging clothes. Under wet towels, under bookshelves; under where? Nuisance like that, which might have made me angry, only made me laugh.

Even today seems like a holy day, because of you. God bless you for blessing me. Len. Thursday.

PS. I just picked up your note from Baby. I knew it wouldn't be able to say anything special as soon as I saw that it was open. I exist, darling; I feel, I want, I love. Please don't; make me part of the furniture, don't even treat me as casually as you might treat others. Make me someone special. I would wonder if you received my package and any of these letters. But apparently, I'll be home before you even get this. I am glad you wrote, even if only about films. All my love, Len.

*

Linda, darling:

I slipped away from Dick Coller who has to correct exams anyway, and came down here to Burnham to write to you.

When we tried to make salabat last night, we discovered that the extension cord provided by the school, (there is no wall plug only the big center socket in the ceiling) had a short in it so that it wouldn't work. So we just shook our heads and went to bed.

Honey, a strange think happened last night. I came half awake, about eleven-thirty and, felt, in the dark, that if I just stretched my hand out of the blanket I could touch you. You were standing over me. Were you really present, Linda? Time is going so slowly, and I want so much to be with you; the way we should always be. Read our poem again, dear: Baguio is 100 times more livable than Manila, but no place has any lasting meaning or attraction without you. You are my home and my heart. Be in my blood, Linda; that close. I want us to be in each other's arms. Right now in thought, but later in actuality.

The wind on Burnham Lake makes the water like cut-glass. The sky itself flows west in many layers, gray at the bottom fluffy white above. The trees are very dark this afternoon, although the morning was crystalline with sunshine. Soon the clouds like mountainous surf will roll down into the valleys and over our heads. I wish you were here: we should share our lives as much as we can. Tell me what you are doing, honey. How is everyone? Can I come to you in the afternoon? At night?

What flowers shall I bring? Early in the morning there are always butterflies on the ground, too cold or wet to move.

Dream with me. I don't know how to say it, Linda. We have trained ourselves to silence. I wish our hands and our lips could say it for us.

I love you. Nevertheless. Like the sun on the unsuspecting skin. Like the wind making the shadows of the sail turn white. Good morning. Goodnight. God be with you and bring us together soon. I have your rosary still at my side.

Sometimes, just before night or the rain falls over city hall, the hilltop is transfigured with strange cream light, like El Greco's painting. Vision of Toledo. Do you know El Greco? There are so many things I want you to feel and taste and see and like together.

This morning I shot the hills behind school, the Cathedral, Pines Hotel—then I went through the market again and found that pipe (carabao head) that I told you about, for my father. I'll show you it before I send it.

Minamahal. I will fit my cheeks to yours. I miss you even more than I expected, Linda. Len. Tuesday.

*

My dearest Linda,

Today is as bright as yesterday was dreary—and not just because of the weather. This noon the secretary assured me that I could give the finals and turn in my grades any time. So, we will be together May 31. I don't know if this means as much to you as to me, but I've been walking all day, two feet off the ground.

This morning early I hiked out to Mines View Park—but I couldn't take a picture of your favorite Igorot, the old man. I always feel as if I am reducing a human being to a piece of furniture. So, I just gave him fifteen centavos and walked back. Later I took a few shots at the Mansion House and then I crawled down Wright Park and visited Baby, taking a few pictures of her and Misses Cordero and Cruz. By then I must have walked nearly six miles. So, I crept back to school and there I got the good news about us.

This afternoon, the students gave the skits which you saw, in program in one of my letters. They were surprisingly good, despite the fact that after I had a final rehearsal with all 15 acts Thursday, people were still revising, recasting, and expurgating. Classes were at a standstill Friday while everyone rehearsed. What school! But the costumes and visual gags were handsome to look at. I wanted to take color pictures but some of the girls were too shy to come outside in their grandly crazy dresses; and then later, it rained. So—I don't know. Maybe it wasn't really so good; maybe I just feel good. But anyway.

Dean Panlasigui announced that maybe next year, a UP Extension, year-round, might be instituted at Teachers' Camp, the teachers residing right there in the cottages. A person would really have to work hard to make the cottages livable especially the plumbing. Probably it's just a dream. Nevertheless, add it to your hope chest, honey. Some day we may really reside in Baguio—and later on, on our own property. Pray. Pray that Linda will give in and keep that promise about marriage in '55. For our sake.

I don't want to be separate from you anymore, in any way. All my love. Len.

*

Last night the rain stopped just before sunset. Then I saw the biggest rainbow I've ever seen, in the east. A whole half a horizon. I tried to put it on film, but probably it won't work. Some things have to stay in our eyes and heads and hearts; no machine can record them. Saturday.

Also, Jimmy hinted, without committing himself, that I would easily become permanently appointed but not before May 31 when my present appointment runs out. He has already spoken about it to Dean Fonacier. I love you inside and out. Len.

Linda Ty-Casper's Note

I found some letters from Len, a packet of notes, undated but presumably between 1953 when Len arrived and 1956 when we left for the States. I will add them at random here. Now that Len has passed away, it is heartbreaking to read them, but somehow comforting. We happened, as he said, past the silence, out of dream. I hope if heaven exists, we'll live there in our glorified selves, not interchangeable wisps of matter; but in the soul and heart and mind we co-created while on earth. Was this also Len's wish?

*

Linda, I will be the songbird, if you the rain/I will flower into feathers, Darling. I awake to you and the night. Last night, we were together, and you were a soft wall of rain, making us alone, and you were the quietness and the dark. And you were peace and you were love. You are my love, my beloved, my lake, my island when it rains, the heart of my growth, my goal. Len.

*

Linda, does my love give me the right to feel this? To say this? Why wouldn't you let us say good night? Why wouldn't you wait? But I say good night to you. I want to marry you once and for good and for always. That is the way I have to love, too. Not off and on but always. God help me make it possible. It is ten o'clock.

*

May God take away my sins and my faults—there are plenty—but never my love for you. I see you smile in the picture. I can feel again the hard softness of your hair. There is the touch on my fingers of the soft flesh between your fingers. Well, we are not so far apart. Are we?

*

Still apart. I feel better to be able to write this. This is a prayer, not an ultimatum. It's a question, not for you to answer, but for us, by being one.

*

I write this last of all when your absence hurts badly. Though I have tried not to let it, because I remembered the afternoon. Why couldn't you come out? Don't you suppose I don't care? Don't you really care? Thank God for God. At least I can pray, even if he doesn't seem to answer the prayers. This is the third night in a row now, and tomorrow we will be apart. Linda!

*

No more than rivers can ever fill one single sea
    Can my loving, day by day, flood the outer shores of my beloved
        Because she renews me:
        Because she restores more than she is ever brought
        Because we are two parts of one. Len.

For Linda
        Who splits
            long-shadowed day
            with her sunlight
        Who is
            air for breathing
            because she makes light
        Who is
            wingspread for birds
            and green trees
            all year;
        Who is
            the shore-to-shore
            of ocean's laughter;
        Who is
            the unheard
            song of nighttime insect;
        Who is
            the running joy of spring.
            the inner blossom,
            flood time's delta,
            mountain pass,
            heron's flight,
        the color of a cat asleep…
        For her whose touch trembles
            with the thought of touching,
                creation's week is always

                    this one
                       now:
              Now:
       beginning to be new: We,
               Because she
        makes light of the world,
               with her light.
               Makes eye-light.
                         *

Good night, Linda. It has been another happy anniversary. I wish we could kiss goodnight, but if we can touch hands until tomorrow.

*

I love with my whole heart and new happiness. Good Morning, darling. As often as it is plucked out, love's heart will beat still, like stars behind daylight's glimpse. (Written on The Sanitary Steam Laundry, Calle Arlegui card).

*

Darling, Tuesday I can be with you only less than two hours of our wholly being together without interruptions. My darling I miss you too much to enjoy being with you "in company." I need you, that's all there is to it. The others have you the rest of the week. But I dare anyone here to say he or she loves you more than I. And I feel very passionate towards you tonight. Your books have occupied you, but you have been on my mind constantly. I do not like the circumstances. For the present I am happier with you this way than when I am alone but I would be happier if we were alone.

*

We can be alone though there are people around. It is a state of the heart. Then you are satisfied? You need a saint! I need you. Will you say you will be you? Or be a saint? I surrender.

*

You sometimes say I get angry when I do not get what I want. For two years and more you have been all I wanted. Next to you nothing else seems important. Good or bad I know that is true. Don't you need me or want me even now, more than this? I want you very much alone. And I love you even in this traffic, even though you are tired. I need that tiredness and I need your strength. That is love. Do you forgive me all the quarreling, petty holding back of ourselves that we did this weekend? Were the good moments enough?

*

The stranded years. I was equally, if not guiltier. Can we forgive ourselves? I love you so much. I forgive me. Will you forgive you? Can we have any happy seconds yet tonight? I wish this anniversary were happier. Shall we visit? For us. Tomorrow before you leave. And Tuesday and Thursday? As long as it will be before we are finally us. Yes we have to wait. I love you Linda, darling. Perhaps those were to be their own rewards. I have prayed for us. I will sleep now. God bless you even if we are this apart. Because I missed you all day. I looked for you. I waited. I miss you now, sweetheart. The day started well. Thank you for that. I have your picture to kiss.

*

What I need is for you to need me so much—perhaps as often as I need you, that I can feel it. We come first. You come first, for our sake. Nothing is more important than that. You know I feel this way. I won't force you by speaking for you.

*

Sweetheart, I am with you always, all days. Remember that even in the dead center of other things. You are my dearest truth. I will never wear out my belief in you. Len.

*

We/Two/are a multitude./ In the days of my errors remember the happiness we sometimes made, and be kind. I will love you better than I love you—at least show it better. You are my life. Len.

*

Friday. Linda, please give me the right to care for you when you are sick. At least to talk with you and to serve you at your bedside, despite all others. Otherwise it will continue to be as it was today. I am tired of being chased away from you, when I think I should be near. It's like being kicked out of home because I have no other home but you. I want only to show my love and not to have to hide it as if with shame. Len.

*

There is no fear greater than my love for you. I will try to go to UP this morning so that we can be together this afternoon, darling. Be home by noon. I love you darling for this morning.

*

I tried. I called; I cared. My back is really hurting, honey. I feel as shaky as this pen tonight. If I thought you would come, it wouldn't matter. When you type tomorrow, be sure to rest in between. Remember you have to reach 180! (years not pounds) Your company while I worked meant more than you know. God bless you for that and help you tomorrow. If I can't say good morning, this will have to do for me; but I wish I could be with you when you need someone, darling.

*

Linda, There are dozens of ways and times that you have helped make me feel alone and therefore, unloved…When you cut me out of conversations, or rather don't let me in; when you promise and then welch or say "Later" and seem to mean "Never": what am I to think?

I think nothing. It is very seldom, if ever, that I even come close to being angry at you. But the fact is that I am left alone at times I need you very badly. I've exaggerated the ways I can feel deserted. These are the only ways; not many. But the times, sometimes seem many. The week we had of perfection, not long ago is the exception. I don't expect it to happen often. But you mean more to me than anyone or anything when I feel that I mean something of the same to you. But when you are distant—for instance when you choose to talk to me one minute out of twenty and meanwhile keep up a happy chatter with others—I'm lost; I'm almost forced to be locked in my own mind with unpleasant thought, because you've helped close the doors. The so-called "adjustment" is merely open recognition by each one that the other one exists and are important. I want to be loved hard and surely and constantly, I think that should mean being put above -- That's how

I feel about you. For the sake of us, I could stand public or private humiliation; the only torture is to reach out and not to touch the only one who matters. You are the dearest and the only. I've only been describing my love, which, yes, make me appear more unmannered than I am. Help me if you love us. Len.

PS. Probably you don't notice it, but many times yesterday, in just one instance—I have only a slight idea of what's going on. Maybe what I've written will hurt; but since the weekend has been unpleasant, let it be a little more unpleasant, if need be, and honest, and maybe with our feelings bare, we can make something pleasant out of these pains.

*

Linda/Len. This is not a valentine. This is the mural of the drowning lotus, exhaling itself like a tangerine flame even in the dark and lifting itself with every breath to the rolling wheel of night stars. It is my flower for the flowering of your body and heart-seed. It is my quiet watching, like a calming hand or the moonlit river over you. It is not a valentine, it is love.

*

Darling, I love you so very much for what you did and said last night, that I can't be more than a little sorry that maybe I was one of the provoking causes. But I hope you slept well (for the cold's sake); I felt bad to see tears in your eyes when I last came down. God bless you, Linda, I am with you, as you are with me. No one can separate us. My love, Len.

PS. I love you, Linda. And I do love you so much more than anyone. But even love grows; it has continuity but it is not a rigid, brittle thing. I love you more and more, in newer ways without losing the old. And I respect you for what you are and for what you make. If I fight for you, even with your family, it is because I want you to be free—so that when you love me, I know it is a love freely given; it is because I love you for yourself, not for some concept into which anyone would mold you. And when you fight for us, I know it is for us, not for fun of rebelling, not for some abstract concept. If I were more docile, I would make a good son-in-law—and a bad husband.

*

Sweetheart, Is it one of the penalties of being in love, Linda? Listen. You know how hard it is for us to be together, alone, in the way we should be sometimes, ever since Saturday night, I guess. How many interruptions there have been, both malignant and accidental...Because you were so good to us for the moment or two that were possible, I had to be good, and I'm tired, and I looked forward to our ninth anniversary and hoped, at least then, we would be lucky. But it is only a Thursday, only a morning—so little time to celebrate. Besides there will be the usual breaks in our privacy. So, I prayed especially at 6 o'clock and 9 when we are apart. That we would be together somehow. I don't know how. God help us to know how.

Sometimes you have seen me desperately looking into your face, begging you to help find a way that I can't find alone. So I thought of our tickets to plays which we never have used. And when you promised to go Saturday, I was very happy for us. Then I discovered there was no Saturday performance. And the dream about us sharing public life together even if secretly, collapsed.

Then I saw that you would have a conference Friday and I thought I might go along, that we could have that...I am so tired of us living separately. And I was going to suggest that tonight. Then I thought that maybe we could even see the play. Thursday, if necessary I would come home with you. And this could be a good thing because it was our anniversary, and might be better perhaps for part of our celebration that I thought you have come to want as much as I.

Darling, and all those were hopes, and prayers and not even finding a chance for expression but encountering these facts, to decide then: Baby needs the car Saturday, you don't like plays, you had no intention of being alone with me in public anyway, apparently. Friday night, I guess, is for the girls. What I wanted never sounded like demands, even in my own mind. They were only hopes, suggestions.

The "penalty" of love is that one can't even outguess one's beloved. So that one makes dreams but can never expect those dreams to be satisfied. I don't know why I am telling you this, Linda; except that maybe there's some important truth here…and maybe because I had dreamt of saying most of this to you, then suddenly there was no chance and no reason and the wrong ears around anyway. I don't love you less for not having any part of that dream, Linda. Nor will I stop planning and dreaming and hating everyone, not you, but who disturbs those plans; not you because you are the dream. So help me God. Thursday.

*

I want to write this now, after finishing your notes because what I say probably won't be nice and if I say it tomorrow to you, it might spoil the few hours we might finally have together.

Linda, I love you too much to give you up like this. Even before we had only 6 hours a week out of 168 when we could be sure of being on an island alone. This week it has only been two hours. Am I selfish?

Was I selfish in Baguio when I resented a friend stealing precious time from our being together when she could have had you other times? Am I selfish when I hate the jeeps for stinking so that we are robbed again; or when your friends make you break a promise so that 1pm becomes 5? Do you think it makes no difference to me? That's why I resent these past three years of chaperonage, feeling frustrated, and now our wedding date delayed time after time, as if it was nothing. I'm scared, honey, if we always let others do the deciding, the more they will think it is their right, the more they will keep us dependent after July; and our marriage can be destroyed just as easily as anyone else's if we put it in other people's hands. I want that island with you, Linda; we planned that so long ago. What happen to our plans?

*

I need you, Linda. I tried to tell you Thursday; I came in the strike, and I came when I thought any minute my appendix would break, as I have always come because I need you. If you give me yourself only ten minutes a week, I will come. But my need will eat that happiness soon, and be hungry again.

*

Darling, I can't sleep right; the lights are on, and I worry and get up too early, and I can't sleep during the day. I come back from classes many times with work to be done. And I could do it if you were there, just to hold me for a while, to talk to me. Am I selfish? I get groggy, I get cranky, the communion must be a sacrilege but I won't give them up. I am lonely, lonely, lonely. It's been so long since we're really together. Almost two weeks. Georgie will be there tomorrow; if I prefer sitting alone with you to eating merienda, you will hate me and deprive me. While I need you and the less I have of you, the uglier, the tireder, the sicker, the more hateful I become.

*

Next Tuesday we cannot be happy. Next Thursday? And again? Everyone first, we come last. Are we selfish? And what happens to our love practiced at a distance? It becomes words like this, a "lecture"; and you are there and I am here, and I am lonely to death for you, Linda. Won't you believe me? Won't you see that even the six hours wasn't enough? How much less so now? My chest hurts sometimes so that I wake up and find myself sleeping on my back. It's not food I lack. Linda.; not sleep. It's you.

Where is our island? Where is our peace and loveness together? I might as well die fighting for that island and you, because I will die without them anyway. Believe me, sweetheart, before it's too late. I don't know what miracle I expect from you, but I have always expected miracles from you, and you have worked them. I miss you, Linda. I want so badly for us to be us, everyday; and I want to come home to you, I want you to come home to me. If you need me as I need you, will you understand my bitterness; it is not aimed at you but at other people, other things. Only you, or you and I can set them right.

I don't feel better for having said these things, but they had to be said. I am dying, Linda; that's not melodrama. As you love me, give me life; give me us. I cannot work anymore. I cannot think any more. I am no good. I am bad without you. I will read your notes again because there was much of love in them. It's that love I appeal to. We are not immortal, Linda. God must despise us for wanting our chances to love in the name of some false Christianity, a distorted commandment or custom. Your notes will help a while longer. But Tuesday! And all the other times. I need your voice and touch. I am not happy, darling, only less unhappy because you have written. I love you and I love you and I love you. Len.

*

You say I have moods. So do you, Linda. And I don't deny my own faults. Last night was one such --time. You didn't get angry when Baby or George refused what you offered, only when I did...And I offered you the part which you preferred and only ate to keep you company. When you refused half of what I gave, I didn't get angry. But when I rejected, you did...

The point is sometimes do you punish me for faults of which some other people unjustly accuse you? But when the love and something-like-disgust come too close together or alternate too quickly, I'm mixed up. Help me help you help us. Please. I love you too much to let these quarrels rattle off my back without taking them seriously.

*

My Darling, Linda, I must really be evil, insane or tired beyond help to be unable to respond to your love this morning. Please forgive me. None of my mood was your fault. Even the incident of the night before was too slight to deserve the fuss I made. I know that I was unreasonable...But the strain cannot be shaken off that easily. Even now I have no time to rest because there is an important lecture to give tomorrow, from 2:30 to 4:00 which I'm not fully prepared for, this is an added worry, though temporary. Please understand and forgive me. I love you. Len.

PS. What I spoke to you this morning or rather what wouldn't, was not myself, Linda. It was something like a sickness, only that. The way you acted in return--your patience, your gentleness, has almost healed me, as I write this. The ironic thing is that I may not be able to prove it to you too unless you can overlook this physical sickness. It has nothing to do with my feelings, Linda. Don't listen to it.

*

Darling, the Registrar gave us news which mean that things won't be easy, but nevertheless will probably turn out okay. I'm 21st on the list of people waiting; but about 9 or more already have houses and are just trying to change location or have a better house. So I'm really about 10th. However, many of the houses are being kept for Fulbrights and FOAs; if either of their programs are curtailed, my chances go up. So I will ask Jimmy to request that I be on permanent status, starting in June; and the same if I am married or openly engaged—the presumption what I will stay here being confirmed. So as soon as we tell your father, I will tell the Registrar: Okay? Besides the Registrar used to be in my department, and the actual assigning is abetted by the committee's "discretion": so we'll have to keep praying, but I think everything will be okay by October, when we're actually married. Maybe I can even have the house as planned, to get it cleaned and painted. Stay with me, and all will be well. I love you, Linda.

11

1961

BREADLOAF: MIDDLEBURY COLLEGE/VERMONT

Darling,
The place is lovely but how time drags while one waits to hear something really fresh and useful! Agents &/or publisher representatives won't be around until the second week of the workshop.

I'm glad Gretchen is happy but forget the ants awhile. All my love, Len. Postcard of the Barn.

*

The leaves haven't turned this much but a few are taking color for fall. I hope I can find some way to bring home some tiny pine seedlings. Between yesterday's horrendous rains I saw three deer on the fields' edges.

I'll probably stay until noon, August 30, to take Bert Florentino to his bus. But whenever I come, would you like to celebrate your liberation by going to Boston & the stores some morning soon, on a spree? I imagine both of you would like to get out of that house-trap as badly as I would like to see you, dear. All my love, Len. Postcard.

*

Today it snowed for the first time, but lectures have improved. Points are beginning to fall in place, where before they seemed aimless. Also I was sometimes depressed to see all the nuts who have published books (these are not people on the faculty), but more recently I have met more fully developed persons and writers. One might be able to guide your works to his publisher, and in any case to his agent. More in a day or so.

Are you both well? Each day I have to talk myself into staying. I love you dearly. Len. Postcard.

*

Dearest Linda,

I hope that my not having heard from you since that first time (I didn't realize how much a letter would mean) does not mean that you or Pipit are in trouble. When I worry about that, I tell myself that you will call, if any real emergency develops. Please write, honey—even if the days don't seem to pass as slowly for you as for me, here.

Our days are filled--with lectures: workshops start tomorrow: "clinic" they're called; but in the midst of a lecture, I find my thoughts drifting home to you. Not just remarks that I wished you'd heard, and that I try to remember, to tell you; but thoughts of us together. I wonder if this is really worth our being apart.

On a typical day, lectures begin at 9am; last till 4:15, with an evening talk at 8pm. Meals are fixed: we must eat at 8. At 1, at 6:15 or not at all. The doors are literally closed, so that waiters can clean up and attend lectures, too. At night we have a cup of coffee together, and a little discussion in The Barn, and get to bed by midnight—and up again by 6:30 am so we can all get washed in time.

Let me tell you who "we" are, because we're all that keep one another sane, almost literally (and only one week has passed!)

The summer campus is 1500 ft above sea level and as soon as the clouds leave us, I'll take pictures. The mountains are quite lovely with a layout vaguely like this. Theater for lectures, The Barn with chairs and coffee bar, Inn, dining hall, Annex, Brandy Brook College, Ciardi, Fellows. Most of the older people (Len was 38 then) are housed in the inn-hotel or nearby annexes, a few of the more able-bodied like me, are in the skirts of the campus, though within walking distance.

Our cottage, stucco or rustic, with a mouse we have been trying to trap or poison all week is Brandy Brook on a brook; a two-story affair, with luckily some very decent fellows on it. I say "luckily" because otherwise the self-imposed restrictions in this secluded campus are as bad as any army camp.

The others on my floor, second, are as lucky as I am. We enjoy each other's company, but largely as a substitute for something we miss badly. There's a Canadian jet pilot and aviation management editor, Chuck, to whom I feel more attached, and I guess, because we can talk World War II, so we can take our minds off shoptalk, and our families (he has two little children). Then there's Bert Florentino on a leader grant, observing theater in this country. I knew him at UP as a playwright. He'll be in this country 6 months altogether—from here he flies to Chicago, then San Francisco, Dallas, England and India. He's quite close. Then there's Joe, a very bad poet but a fine person from NJ, who teaches high school there, and is unhappy, and we're trying to talk him into teaching college courses so he'll feel less frustrated and exhausted.

When I first came there was a fifth fellow on our floor, a young poet who also said he lamented leaving his wife behind—then within twelve hours had moved to the Fellows house on the other end of the campus which is practically a "whorehouse" for the "famous" like himself. Rarely do I see him or the Fellows at lectures and I know he is not busy writing. I thank God I didn't become a Fellow, not because I couldn't resist the flow of women to that cottage. I could: you may not believe it, but I love you; and I was as virgin as you are in our marriage, despite the army and innumerable opportunities and a longer history of celibacy than yours; but precisely because I could resist women and would have to move out or fight the other fellows. Anyway, we are keeping one another company, and after all the lectures are there for whoever wants to keep busy. I *do*.

I have learned more than I expected. That is, although some of the early lectures seemed elementary, they have deepened cumulatively; and even the lecturers who sometimes were bad have also had their extremely valuable performances. Above all, though, I have learned from discussions with published writers who are non-Fellows, somehow—though one Fellow was disgusted with the sex activity that kept him awake and is now in our cottage with us. One gave me the address of his agent, for your novel; and having read portions of you book, even thought that his publisher might be interested. I have not seen the agents that Randall spoke of and may not ever: but perhaps I will see publishers' representatives themselves, coming up to see their people, and get ten minutes with them about your book. This, I already know, darling: it's better in conception or even in execution, in this early draft than any novel ms here I have seen—and we show things around among ourselves constantly while awaiting private conferences with our critic.

Mine will be Richard Yates, younger than I, who has a first novel just out. I doubt that there's much future of my collection, so I'm not disappointed in having to see Yates.

I'll write about some of the people here, perhaps each day I'll try to stay awake and *apart* long enough. But please write, also, sweetheart. I miss you dreadfully, and I want to hear how Gretchen is taking it. Love, to my only, Len. Tuesday.

*

Dearest life, and darling pie:

How lovely it is here. How I miss you both and hope you are well and we need never be separated like this again—already I am ready to come home—in spite of the fact that from 6:30am to midnight the day is filled with talk, and the fact that Bert Florentino is my roommate and about ten of us have a little cottage. On the edge of this very lovely mountain campus, and the upstairs five of us are rather close or friendly—all clinging to each other out of loneliness. We ate and attended lectures together the first day. Lectures are not yet impressive, although it is the incidental talk afterwards that helps.

Starting today, however, we'll be assigned places at talks to mix us up socially—perhaps not as bad as it sounds. I hope since almost everyone here seems to be an active writer (and or teacher) so we have something to talk about between gulps of food, which has been mediocre but at least not repulsive. I need exercise, which I sometimes get with the help of a Canadian pilot-editor, running around.

Nights are the loneliest—from 9pm until we finally get to bed. We seem to talk from habit, having already worn out our interest in each other. The sky has been so absolutely clear these last two nights, it seems like Texas: no clouds or lights to dim all the magnificence of stars which I haven't seen so clearly in years.

I wish we were camping together. My hands miss you...you are girl and woman, wife and lover altogether--and I don't know how I will be able to stand so long from you. All my love, Len.

...I think I will get tired of the shop talks fast, although every fifth person seems already to have published a novel or collection of poems. The real workshop—discussion of ms—won't occur until the second week. So far, it's possible to avoid the staff who have no special care for us—or vice versa. Kiss Pipit for me.

*

Dear darling,

Happy anniversary! I think we should get back to celebrating the day you promised to marry me. Especially this month, thinking of that night two days before Christmas, it helps bring us together.

Today it did not rain but still was cloudy and bone-damp. Tonight, after a poetry reading by Howard Nemerov, everyone is over in the Barn community singing. I'm back at our cottage, listening to Brandy Brook outside, and writing.

Yes, I received your August 17th letter, and not your August 22rd. I'll write Fr. De la Costa when I get home I guess. When I read about your stamps and food, I feel more guilty that I am here, and almost got in the car to come.

But the second week has officially started today—with more exceedingly important publication figures and library figures from a publisher last night, and the first critiques of short stories and novels today. If the panel of critics was sincere about the sample writings which they said they liked, there is very great hope for your book. The Canadian who lives with me read chapter VII and insisted on seeing more. He couldn't believe that a woman could write such action scenes.

For example, one Bread Loafer is about 22 years old and author of a book about an American girl—real tripe. Doubleday published it; Columbia Pictures is making a movie of it; Book of the Month may take it. But you can't talk writing to her. She took a course with Caroline Gordon, and its' funny to hear her repeat Gordon's rules...as if they were her own. She doesn't know I know Gordon. But in any case, what's funnier is that she has not applied any of those rules of density, suspense, etc. to her own work. It's a potboiler. Anyway, Chick's only criticisms were that the sentences and paragraphs were too long—perhaps good advice, but small criticism for a first draft.

It's wonderful to hear that your novel is going forward. I still have no date for any personal conference but I'm not nervous about it at all, as some people are, facing criticism.

I hope the weather improves so that I can take you both to Rhode Island before school.

Apparently, Sears has not delivered our cabinet yet. If you want to call them about it, I think the receipt is in an envelope in the refrigerator.

This week has seemed like a month. Do you miss me as much as I do you?

Last night just as we were going to sleep, the mountains roared with fire siren—we have no news—so when we didn't see any flame in the dark, we thought it might be news of war, and that above all made me want to get in that car and go to you and Gretchen.

Chick and I ran down the road, just to be sure: but it was a false alarm. Somehow a sprinkler in one woman's room which should have spurted only at a certain temperature let loose, and her things were drenched, no worse. Ciardi, the poet director, is a good hard worker; and his wife, also kindly, brought a change of clothes, etc. But for a moment, in the still stark black with light radiating from many curtains, I thought of El Greco and your novel.

God bless you both, but especially you my only love, if I could only kiss you goodnight. Len August 23, 1961.

12

1980

Dear Linda,

    I have finally done enough research so that I feel confident to write the big section on the Philippine economy. If I can only get a lead, I know I can get through it. Even though school starts on Monday.

    Yale accepted my reluctant offer to write about the image of Filipinos in Western fiction, so I guess I have to make *that* effort when the encyclopedia article is done.

    I intend to send your Windsor poems to *Berkeley Poetry Review*.

    It has stayed in the 70s mostly and rained enough that nothing has burned yet. I hope it stays nice so that I can do all these things and still be a good father. This weekend I want to take the girls to the wild Animal Farm in Hudson, NH. Remember?

    And I think we all appreciate better how well you prepared the freezer for us before your departure, in the midst of so many things; and trying to keep up with the potted plants gives me additional clues to how much you loved this house and cared for us all.

    I pray night and day that you will really feel good—restored—during these months. I almost forgot to say that I am signing this for all of us. Len. June 19, 1980.

*

Dear Linda,

    I hate to ask you for help when I know how difficult transportation (and cooperation) can be there. But you are my last resort. I have tried both the NY Consulate and Washington embassy. They can't provide information.

When I last did the *Americana* article, I had access to data from the 1962 *Statistical Handbook on the Philippines* on the number of Filipinos speaking various languages and the number of population represented. Now they want as good an update as possible; but it frightens me that my 1962 data is better than anything available here.

The embassy person at least gave me two Manila addresses, and maybe you can reach them by phone? The Ministry of Education on Arroceros and the Bureau of Census, R. Magsaysay Blvd in Santa Mesa. The latter surely should have a more recent *Statistical Handbook* since they put them out.

I need new numbers and % of population for the following languages spoken by Filipinos: Pilipino, English, Spanish, Chinese, Cebuano, Tagalog, Iloco, Hiligaynon, Bicol, Samar-Leyte, Pampango and Pangasinan: 12 languages in all; none of the minor ones. There was an actual table in 1962 with these figures and I hope something like another table was made. I must send my large and small changes to them by July 15 and I know these dates is almost absurd for you. But in hopes you can mail me the information on languages by early August?

I'll write later when the work is done.

I took off today to bring Tina to a parade (July 4th) at Quincy Market, where we snacked.

Stay well. It's strange to send an urgent request and still tell you to relax; but please do relax. Len. July 5, 1980

*

Dear Linda,

The Northeast has had a heat wave (high 80s, low 90s) for nearly a week. It finally broke last night, so we're writing while it's halfway decent.

Last week I finished the Encyclopedia article on the Philippines and gave my judgement on a monograph written for Donn Hart: a series of sketches by a humorist, about an American bureaucrat telling Filipinos about "benevolent assimilation" at the turn of the century. Not very sharp or even funny' and the introduction was only 11 pages, so I suggested Hart reject it. Speaking of rejections—a sad subject but one all writers have to get used to—let me ask you about a few things. If Australia rejects your mss, may I send them to you in Malabon, for New Day? At least *Hazards of Distance* really requires Filipino (or Asian) audience, and Heinemann's will take only what they have? Please say yes, and don't quibble about revisions. You should be getting on to new things.

If Atlantic Monthly Press sends back your tobacco novel, and Helen's agent does not reply, may I ask John McAleer's agent to consider it? He's had luck with John's novel about Korea. Guggenheim sent a list of awardees. All south Americans and none in fiction. Don't take those things harder than they deserve. Have sent the poems from *Windsor Review* on to *Berkeley Review*. *Georgia Review* wants to see more of your fiction; but not this summer.

We haven't had a letter from you in over a week but hope you are all well. We also hope our own letters are getting through. I've meant several times to write about the plants here. The sun scorched the ajugas but they seem to be recovering. The yuccas (five of them) came and went. The gaillardias have done well and many survive. The evergreens seem to prosper, for once, but gypsy moths are flying thickly at times, and I have my fingers crossed. The small apple trees and peach tree seem to be bearing all right.

Soon I should prune the shrubs for the winter. Should I just let flowers go to seed? The zoyzia is OK so far and the rhododendrons have absolutely recovered. I don't dare to tell you how hard it is to accomplish anything when it's this humid. I have no real plans to paint the fence before Fall.

I'm reading for the Yale Filipino image in the western literature article slowly, without enthusiasm since there is no compensation and there is no way I can account for British and Australian uses. A lot of work for nothing. Jock Netzorg is doing something of the same sort with children's lit, for a different book. Maybe Yale should have asked him. Anyway. I'm trying not to get angry or upset about anything. Life is too short. There's too much goodness in the world to waste time on things going wrong.

I hope you received my request for distribution (numbers and %) of languages in the Philippines. I see OD is now secretary of Education and Culture. Either he or the Bureau of Census should have data.

Stay well. Relax, Be happy that you're at least in a new set of problems. Don't brood. Consider your writing. Galdon's book on the Philippine Novels in English mentions *The Peninsular* with respect several times. Your writing is great: I wish I had done it and would trade all I have written for your novels, published or otherwise. Len. July 23, 1980.

*

Dear Linda,

(Lined paper has spoiled me so that I find it hard to write on anything else.) Gretchen and Tina wanted to send you a birthday card together, before Gretchen leaves for Michigan; so you may get this a little early. I take great (objective) pride in your writing. I've always held writers in high regard, and you are one of the best, and it has been an experience beyond description to have been so close to such a hard-working writer, filled with imaginative powers for extending reality. Every word of this is true.

My gift--a basic gift than this truth about my esteem for you as a person—is $500, half of what I earned from the *Amerasia* article (which was a pleasure in itself to write). The other half has gone to motel rooms to Michigan and back, a new starter for the old car ($80), and a pair of black shoes for me from Filene's—plus little gifts for Gretchen and Tina. I can't very well send you the dollars, as far as I know; so I'll hold it in escrow, to add to the Money Market Certificate which is your mother's inheritance to you, when that comes due this November, or whatever; unless you direct me differently.

I'll mail your two novellas before the end of this month and have delayed only in the hope that you would tell me the safest address to use: Marikina or Malabon. We sent the package of jellies, etc, to Colonel Ramiro in Marikina, in the absence of better instructions. I hope the box arrives. I just received galleys for my article on Warren, which will appear in the fall issue of *Southwest Review*.

But first, Gretchen and I will try to see if we can take the back seat out of the yellow car, to allow room for her things.

Because things have just gotten too hectic to manage everything, I have written the fellow at Yale I am resigning from the project on the image of Filipinos in western literature. I had warned him months ago of my limited access. He said then, okay but don't forget to look at Australia, etc. literature! Each time I warn him this is all I can do, he says fine, do some more. The fact is that I've spent half my life reading Filipinos, not Westerners using Filipino characters. This would have been a fine job for a 2-year doctorate or a 1-year full time NEH, so I had to drop out completely, only suggesting that Jack Netzorg might have done the kind of reading he has in mind.

I feel suddenly relieved, having time to do a little pruning; take Tina to Hopkinton (and of course to ballet and piano in a few weeks.) and Gretchen to Michigan without having a breakdown. Incidentally, does Tina have to be enrolled in CCD? If I try to teach her myself where/how do I get the texts?

I hope you concur with decisions I have had to make about agents, publishers, etc. I think too highly of what you create, to let it all just sit. Happy Birthday. Len. August 21, 1980.

*

Dear Linda,

Only because I might forget it later, I have to ask first—we know you're arriving Nov. 2; but on what airline…?

Congratulations again on being asked to join workshop/staff at Ateneo and UP. You have so much to give. I was looking for that Focus acrostic which you said might be in your desk. I tried not mess up what you so elaborately put in order, but I was astonished/delighted to see all the volumes-to-be, the piles of handwritten and xeroxed notes. If the authorities in Manila could only appreciate the stretch of your reviews of the Filipinos struggle to rise, stand erect, and be recognized (and assuming both intelligence and objectivity on their part) you would surely be among Malacanang's honorees.

Fall is in the air here; though it was near 90 a few days ago, last night was near 40. I must begin to bring in your plants, most of which seem to have done well.

Tina has been to piano twice and seems to enjoy tinkering—even composing. This week she will have her first ballet. I've signed her up for several symphony concerts; Girl Scouts; Iskwelahang Pilipino (due in two weekends—but the second meeting falls on the Sunday I'm taking her to the circus). She is diligent in her homework: she has a house key; I arrive about 15minutes after she does, and she's usually working already. She's lovable, if I do say so. And putting on a little weight and becoming beautiful, really.

My Evening College is both Monday night and Saturday morning; sometimes she stays in my office; sometimes comes to class.

The cars are all set with inspection stickers. Mine needed a rear brake job and one new tire; and in November I'll start having them both tuned up. But this is normal maintenance. It's good to know people like Charlie who (like Mario) can be trusted absolutely.

One night we had a cloud burst and some water still came into the basement; so I guess our bags should be used when advance notice of a real storm comes. Otherwise, the drainage is much improved.

As I write this I have the feeling that some of this is old news to you already—the problem of communication at a distance.

Gretchen has managed to move in with Erica. She's closer to class, libraries. She is also closer to a few fellow grad students. And she can cook her own meals. Things seem much improved, though she is mature and never complained. She knows how to take care of herself.

A man from Groliers called: three volumes on Philippines ethnohistory, politics and the arts, commissioned, were completed, and they need someone knowledgeable to spot check it now, for authenticity, completeness, and discretion. Morehouse (Groliers does *Encyclopedia Americana*) suggested me. I received the first volume today, and we'll see if I am asked to do the rest. It's a more fascinating assignment than my teaching, at present; maybe because I am on my own. It has to be a fast job however, because their deadline is overdue. I'll save the last page for Tina. Stay well, be happy. Len. September, 1980.

*

Dear Linda,

I am sending you "Standing Sun" as you asked; but also "Swarm of Sun" which I consider a different and far superior story. Can you enter both in the PEN contest? I realize the subject is "freedom" but...Later this week I'll airmail the novella.

Your letters arrive in clusters and they are not always wholly clear, but I'll answer as I can. I'm confused about your remark about Capiz "lamps." I hope your father can clarify this for you... Sorry to go on and on about light fixtures.

I know you want to hear about our trip. It went rather well. 500 miles the first day, 300 the second. We arrived in Ann Arbor shortly after noon, as I recall; took several hours to unload and help Gretchen unpack and settle. Then it was supper time: we found a good German restaurant; later took her around (a dark) campus, then--with tears all around—Tina and I went to our motel.

I had divided the return trip into three days, (though this added to expenses) and went via Pennsylvania whereas we had gone west via New York. Tina was almost magnificent—never complained, read portions of *The Empire Strikes Back* to us aloud, coming and going; acting as navigator coming back. I really enjoyed her company and she enjoyed the scenery, ate well, got up first for breakfast so we were on the road by 7:30 each morning, so we could quit by mid-afternoon when it was hot. She liked the motel foods. Now, of course we're both back at school, and things are somewhat more hectic until we can get better organized. Miss Gill suddenly announced that Tina's proper class is Friday' and Mrs. Robinson will be vacationing another week, so we can't see if an alternate piano time is possible: but something will work out. I will also sign Tina up for skating, beginning in November.

We have not asked about the CCD book yet, because we've been attending 11:30 at St. George—good music and excellent sermons.

I hope the anniversary cards arrived and that all went well at your parent's ceremony. You are luckier than Mona, who called last night to deliver your message and the sad news, and word of her father's death. We talked at least 15 minutes and she told me all she could.

Your reference, Aug 13 (after attending the WILOCI) was cryptic. Is that law organization? Do you still feel you have to compare yourself? I feel sorry if you do. You are unique—if underestimated and under rewarded. Your writing will probably affect the country in the long run more than law practice might have. I know—better than anyone else—how well you write. What kind of knowledge and insight and craft go into your "fictions." Of course you cannot expect recognition if you don't cooperate, at least minimally, with someone as sincere as Frankie when he offers an autograph party or something like that. There's nothing dishonest about such an effort, especially, so modest a one, as Helen can tell you.

Helen is back, asked about you, and misses your company on Thursdays. Gretchen is missing you, too and will probably try to come home in a few days around Thanksgiving.

I know you are a writer, whatever else you may; and that you write well—if too meticulously perhaps.

Simpson Drive is quiet and now, greatly cooling. Absorb all you can there; come back replenished. We will see you and welcome you in less than two months. We are keeping the house and even the grounds in reasonable shape. Gretchen will undoubtedly write to you directly. Stay well. Len. September 7, 1980.

*

Dear Linda,

Surprise. Surprise. One letter of yours, airmail, took 12 days to arrive; yesterday, after 5 days, your essay came. Safe and sound. I have only scanned it.

It looks powerful. I think I should query the NY Times (&

Globe?) first. Since that's the safer procedure. That will also allow you time to change your mind.

And nothing happens in print that fast here, as you know: Antioch has sat on Gretchen's article for nearly two months. So it goes. However, we expect galleys from *South Atlantic Quarterly* any time. I figure you plan to arrive 6-7am, Boston, TWA, on Tuesday, the 4th. We'll be there—unless, after reading our earlier letter and talking to Luz, you decide to stay on a while longer. There really is no need to rush home now; but I'm sure you must have mixed feelings. We'll go with whatever decision you make. As long as you don't arrive unexpectedly on a Monday night or Saturday morning, my Evening College class times, there'd be no impossibility of reaching me at home or at school. Tina even has a house key which she used regularly, since she sometimes arrives before I can make it.

So relax. Enjoy these last days. As far as the fare goes, I'll pick up the entire tab, since we're paying for it at this end. I told you about my editing—after the first 3 volumes for Grolier's. Well, I've done 1 ½ so far. Then I'll have enough to cover the missing fare amount, with some left over for Christmas presents.

I'm sending this from BC, to get to you as soon as possible. Len. October 17.

*

Dear Linda,

We're doing this in haste, in hopes it reaches you in time. Your airletter took 12 days to get here, I did mail *Hazards of Distance* and I hope it is only suffering from those same hazards; and was not lost or whatever. I mailed it two weeks ago with two $5 stamps on it.

Anyway, Tina and I agree that as long as you arrive before Thanksgiving (Gretchen is definitely coming and is anxious to see you), stay as long as there's a chance you can join the reunion. Tina and I have settled into a routine—she may even watch Heineman's Nazi films Monday when I teach. And everything is reasonably well. I just got rid of a third stye on my eyelid; occasionally a quick storm puts a little water in the basement if I haven't put out the bags; two ferns are drying up etc. A trivia really. We miss you and your cooking; and we know you miss having a quiet place to write. Still, enjoy this chance.

It's in the 30s sometimes; we've had two frosts. But most days are briskly clear. If you do stay on, maybe I'll have more time to vacuum, clean the bathrooms, etc. everything else is fine. And even CCD may work out. Jeanne Prifti called a few nights ago. She works in Weston and seems satisfied.

I'll close here. Have the vacation you deserve. Len. October 17, 1980.

*

I'm awful glad and proud about *Dread Empire*. You are the author I never could be, but far from envying you, I honestly take pleasure on all your works, and especially your public successes, since I know how hard you research and how deeply, you contemplate.

13

1982

Dear Linda,

I'm halfway through your ms—or did I tell you that before?

It's bitter cold; and some of the drifts are 3-4 ft high. I'll shovel a little at a time, (I've been out many times already since last night), after I mail this. We first want you to know that we think of you regularly.

U Washington Press has asked me to look at a ms of reminiscences about Bulosan by P.C.Morante. The name is familiar, yet I can't find him in any anthology. Also, I bought you for Easter (and received already) the book edited by Rosenberg on *Marcos and Martial Law in the Philippines*. (Cornell)—from Cellar: expensive but worth owning.

Did I tell you that I got rid of the old trousers you said had a hole in them? And bought a replacement.

Take care of yourself. Jean, Helen, Luisa all promise to write. The storm has kept me out of touch with Sister. All our love, Len. March 3, 1982.

*

Dearest Linda

I want you to receive this as soon as possible so I won't wait for Tina to come home. We'll both write again in a few days.

I want you to know how much I love you, and how very much I felt your love the last days before you had to leave. I can still feel your arm around me and your breath on my cheek, from bed and the touch of your lips on my beard at the airport. Although I know you were under terrible stress, you kept reassuring Tina and me every way that you know that we are not out of your mind just because Lola has to be very much in it. We love you that same degree, she is in our minds, too; but you are still at the center and always will be.

I can only hope that the transfer in NY went alright: and that the flight, too, was only tiresome; that you arrived as planned, were met, are now with your parents. We pray for you regularly; as we always do, and of course, for Lola. I hope she is resting easily, in mind and in spirit: I'm sure she is in the best possible hands.

I also know that you will tell us what you can when you can. It's more important that you care for your parents, and for yourself, than that you concern yourself about us.

Tina aside from having a messy room has been excellent-- getting herself up, doing at once what I asked her to do, working at her homework. Her math grades suddenly are her best.

You certainly left us enough cooked meals until almost the end of the month! I called Gretchen, and her advice was to wrap and freeze some of the meals. We'll finish the sinigang tonight. Tonight, Tina will sleep over so I'll make a small fish just for myself.

Saturday will be a busy day: Girl Scouts until about 2:30 (gymnasts), then Luisa I presume will pick us up. Sunday, we'll probably take it easy. If I get a little ahead, I will start sprucing up the lawn for Easter. This morning I did a wash load, so we're ahead on that. Tonight, Tina has agreed (she can be very agreeable) to go see that Columban priest with me.

When I finish this letter, I'll write Ben Santos, congratulating him and giving him a little news. Then I'll write Netzorg who saw the Glossary on DREAD EMPIRE…he's going to read the novel.

The weather has remained as it was the day you left; frosty at night, 90s during the day. I hope the change to tropical heat doesn't wear you down. Gretchen said she's sending a few simple recipes, like lasagna; but since I saw you baking pork and chicken and already know how to broil fish and steak, it will just be a matter of scheduling cooking time and doing several things together. I only hope you will be as well as we will be. Eat, sleep, drink: don't overdo.

We love you and miss your goodness. Tina keeps saying you may be home in two weeks; and I know what those simple words imply. Take care. I really love you, Len. March 25, 1982.

*

Dearest Linda

I thought you might like to see and keep this card from Bonnie Crown. I talked to her in New York this morning; and she is genuinely excited about *Awaiting Trespass*. I will send her the basic Knopf correspondence. Although she is querying Knopf, Harper and Farrar Strauss Giroux simultaneously. She is quite willing to accept "a letter agreement/understanding" from me, in your name. She suggests that you try to retain rights to Plaza outside SEA, provided Heinemann takes the novel; but she is more interested in future works (understanding that New Day will take *Stranded Whale*). I'm working on the preliminaries this week.

However, after some discussion, we also agreed that the ms should be retyped (better margins, darker pages, no write-ins, etc.) to make the best possible impression. Since that would run over $200 if someone else did it, I offered to do it myself, if she can wait for the new copy until after Easter vacation. She concurred. I have already paper and typewriter ribbons and hope to start by next weekend. It will be backbreaking & eye boggling and time-consuming. But I'm convinced it's worth it; and I offer it as my Easter gift to you.

I reread the novel this past weekend: and it is fantastic. I wanted to take extensive notes to satisfy the promo materials she wants.

Yesterday, Sunday, I took Tina to the Castros so she could practice the tinikling with them; and finished reading the ms there. Mabini was fertilizing the ground although it felt like winter awhile.

Next Sunday, I'll take her to IP (or maybe type if I'm ready and let Luisa take her.) The meal at Goulets was good; the other company were the Allens (Maritess and Richard) and the Bakkens. Pleasant—largely talk of mystic experiences. The solar apparatus, according to Roger, is not working so great; paid a lot of electric bills regardless. And it was freezing while we were there.

I'll save space for Tina. She is well and more cooperative than usual. Our love to you. Lola and Lolo. Len March 29.

*

Dear Linda,

It isn't really that I have so much news, but I write to you this often (We sent some cards yesterday) because I miss you—being close to you, exchanging thoughts, making decisions together, holding hands, clinging, raising a child together—and this seems one way to close the distances a little.

On the other side is a copy of the "jacket style" material that I sent to Bonnie, which she'll forward to several publishers. The idea is to solicit interest, then send the book itself. Meanwhile I am typing, typing. Yesterday, I finished the first 25pp (33pp in the new format) and I want to be able to xerox right after Easter Monday, that also happened to be Tina's spring vacation; and we'll want to do something together.

I can see why typing tired you so. I had three consecutive eyestrain headaches (easy to handle) and a muscle pain in my right shoulder side (I lay down about 10 minutes each hour or did something else. But the book is beautiful, beautiful.

So I said to Helen, who like Sister called to know how things are, with you and your mother. Helen herself has until September to revise her Twayne book.

Tina actually cleaned her room yesterday—though I think she needs to sort out her clothes. Her drawers are so full. Gretchen sent her two more shirts: a nice batik-type and denim. Gretchen's professors have virtually guaranteed a pass, in prelims; but needs a vacation break. She may also need more money, because the minority funds for May and June don't seem to be ample, anymore. Probably she has written you directly.

Helene also passed on word about a drama on Louisa May in Concord, all during April. So, I'll get late-month tickets for all of us in the hope that you'll be back by then.

Don't worry about anything, anybody here—though we both like to think that you are thinking of us sometimes, and perhaps sending mail via PAL and the West Coast. But I know you must have many other things on your mind. Tomorrow, Tina has Girl Scout gymnastics (which she likes a lot), Sunday, IP. Cris Castro has already invited us (including you if you can make it) for Easter evening meal. That afternoon there will be more tinikling practice. I tire easily now and sleep at 10-10:30; but typing makes me feel where I want to be, close to you. All my love (and Tina's), Len. April 2. 1982. **PS**. My essay on Bishop Labayan will appear after Easter.

*

Linda dearest,

It was marvelous to get your letter from a week ago, even if the news itself was hardly good. I type in our bedroom (60 of the original pages (of AT) done so far—71 in the new format) with the picture of Lola and Lolo there. Sometimes the pain seems to leave your mother's eyes and she tries to smile.

I'm taking a break (1:30) so I can write this, but so I can last, too. My eyes were fine until it clouded up (we expect terrific rains tonight), and my right shoulder blade (why just the right?) aches. But I want to keep doing this as a sign of, and to offer up the pain to relieve your mother's, even if only a little, my real love for you. God seemed dissatisfied that Cain didn't offer his best for sacrifice. But reading your novel, I begin to wonder if one's best is sometimes one's worst: that is our weaknesses—our infirmities of flesh—if we could offer those up, give them up, how much more meaningful than "offering" something we publicly pride ourselves in?

Typing is tedious, but it allows a prolonged meditation on your novel—AT—which can stand that.

. . . . .

Leon Comber wrote, but rather than xerox the letter, I'll first save it and relay the basic news. March 29, he received *Fortress* just before leaving the country. He is arranging to have it read meanwhile. He will send on *Dread Empire* here, and I will return *Perspectives*. He enclosed a xerox of a March 6 (?) 1982 issue of WHO, describing a speech he made in Manila, in which he mentioned you and a few others. I'll just put that aside for you.

It looks as if you won't be here Easter. Tina and I will be at the Castros; and we hope that you have some respite, some pleasure this Easter; and your mother, too. I am confused by the medical report—but as of a week ago, perhaps you were also.

I went to Mass (9am) Tuesday and Thursday; and Tina will sing several times Easter week. After that, she has vacation. I have Easter Monday and, of course, Tuesday off though I may be xeroxing the new "version" of the novel by then. But Tina and I will find something to do when the time allows. She occupies herself well, helps cook. We're going to try chicken in wine sauce tomorrow, actually cleaned her room once without being asked, and of course, misses you, as I do, but we're not complaining. Love to all, but to you especially, Len. April 3, 1982.

*

Dear Linda,

I waited for the mail in case we were lucky enough to hear from you again. (Everything is okay here except that we both miss you.) At least there was this letter from Gloria Rodriguez which I'll return to you now. We can pay for the books from here, so what little money you have can go farther.

Also, I'm enclosing a sample of the pad that Tina made for her Lolo and Lola. She couldn't enclose it in yesterday's airletter of course. She wanted to bring the pad next summer. And you received an Easter card from Bill.

The remains of yesterday's history-making blizzard (never so much snow in April, nor so cold: 17) are with us. Yesterday because of high winds and drifting, schools were closed: that's when Tina made

Easter eggs. But today's a full day for her. The sun is sort of out, we got mail after three days, so I don't have to shovel until Friday night when a little more is coming.

Instead, I am (at noon time) on p. 160 of Trespass (200 in new format; I figure a total of 260, when I finish Saturday). As the end approaches, I keep worrying the machine will break down, twice during the storm the electricity went off briefly, and I thought it was the typewriter.

Tina and I will attend services tonight at 7:30, and probably the same time, Good Friday. (April 9)

I think I have written so often (it seems you've been gone more than two weeks) that there isn't much news left. Tina vacuumed, and dusted the house last Sunday, cleaned her room several times. I feel like painting some ceilings, but nothing will interfere with getting this mss to Bonnie Crown. Typing I can see where a sentence here or there could be cut, and a little more information given about Telly's mother and Severino's wife: but boyoboy, what a richly wise and moving novel this is!

I hate to leave all this blank space. What more can I tell you?

The snow is not quite the depth of the 78 blizzard but imagine so much snow not in February but in April! Driving is still treacherous because the wind keeps drifting the snow, and the streets not taken down to bare ground is very icy. We're not planning to drive much at all until Easter, when we go to the Castros. Maybe Spring will return by then.

Linda, I love and miss you and I wish I could hold and comfort you right this minute, and care for you as you are caring for your mother. I hope these new trials take away all old doubts and bitterness and mistakes in judgements and confusions.

I'm going back to typing. That's where I can be closest to you now. Love, Len. We both send our prayers to Lola. I hope this mail gets through to you. We've been writing at least every other day, and sometimes every day. Holy Thursday. April 8, 1982.

*

Dearest Linda,

    I grieve with you. So do our daughters; each in her own way has lost a good friend. The afternoon after your call, we (Tina and I) attended Mass, then asked Father John Morris to say his next Mass for your mother. So, Friday, yesterday, that was the afternoon Mass; and he mentioned your mother, and without special elaboration, took every ordinary occasion to point up the resurrection, the faith/hope we all have of joining Christ, and so on. Then he came down and shook Tina's hand and mine. Tina's head was on her arm part of the time, and I was trying desperately to wipe away tears from my right eye—funny how one eye cries more than the other.

    This morning I was finally able to reach England; although Luz was out, Ely answered and we had a long talk. Ely wanted to call you at Marikina, but I said it might be next to impossible, and anyway the connection leaves one shouting—hardy right for what one wants to say.

    Father Jim knows, so do Sister and Helen, and the Fitzgeralds. I'll tell Luisa tomorrow, Sunday when she takes Tina to IP. We'll ask her to eat out with us that evening.

    Today, I'll take Tina to Louisa May Alcott; the play got decent reviews, I hear, even though it is an amateur group.

    Meanwhile I am doing a wash load.

    Monday, Patriots' Day, I've convinced Tina to see a colonial parade in Lexington in the afternoon. Spring seems to be here for good now (all the blizzard snow has melted) and I want her not to feel too sad.

    Tuesday, I'll take her and Jenny sticker hunting, and also go to Sudbury for sneakers for her. This will be her week off. Friday, I take her on campus for a good lunch in the faculty dining room where I've eaten only with committees.

    My essay on Marcos et al, finally came out yesterday at BC; and Tina and I will see the last Filipino in the BC series, Thursday: Father Saguinsin of the National Federation of Sugar Worker; but I won't send you any copies now. We're hoping you arrive by Mothers' Day, if you can. Even the Easter cards are waiting, and Tina's eggs.

Gretchen was so choked up when I told her about Lola—she really couldn't talk. She was offering (if you received her letter) to come to care of Lola in May, after her prelims.

We are all anxious, too, about Lolo's operation: Ely said he had had a hernia operation previously. Please take care. Love, Len and Tina. April 19, 1982.

*

Dearest Linda,

I am sitting here, this Thursday, in the library, trying to help Tina have a pleasant day. Yesterday I brought her on campus, but since she really couldn't come to any of my classes (two were so small she'd be noticeable and the other too adult a work), she probably become bored, hanging around for nine hours. Tomorrow she'll come again, we'll picnic on the Charles (first decent day since you left!), then she'll practice for the folk festival in the afternoon. Saturday will be the festival; Sunday will be a book fair at the library. (Oh yes, I did take her to the Mobile Book yesterday afternoon, but she didn't find anything she liked; I found three books that I'll have to teach.) Monday night we drove to Maynard to see a Turkish film, Yol, which you would have liked: prisoners on furlough find that the police state is no better, and the status of Moslem women worst of all. An underground film but handled with delicacy. We didn't go to Aquino Tuesday night—storms verging on snow—but the Heights report made it sound pretty good.

Tina has almost not at all been sullen, and that's a relief—for we both miss you. It seems so long since you've been gone. I try to go to bed dead tired, but then I drag the next day. We'll make spaghetti tonight; but generally we've been eating food you prepared, which Tina prefers. And we both realize how much love went into those preparations.

Father Donelan was here briefly last weekend. We took him Sunday night to Bergson's which he liked very much.

Unfortunately, they were out of lobster, so he had scallops

instead; seems to like seafood; and never had Coors beer (instead we had a fine, heavy California beer: Steamboat something) We had a good time together, from 4-10.

Word just arrived that *Solidarity* will come out 4x in 1983, so I expect when you see Frankie, he'll remind you of your story. I wonder if Gretchen has reviews with him.

As soon as I reach home, I'll type our reviews for *Filipinas*; and arrange to have the lawnmower sharpened, although cold weather like last year has stopped growth short—except for your tulips. We'll try to take pictures. I knew that school is almost over but forgot how much student work comes in at the last minute. At least, however, I have read far enough ahead now to account for the first meetings of summer school: 1 ½ weeks' worth. I also have orals and department meetings while Gretchen is here, but we'll do the best we can...we'll feast on the stuffed chicken you left, as well as on fresh lobsters. It's hard for Tina and me to imagine what you're doing, now that the memorial service is over, but I hope you are managing to see old friends—or making arrangements to do so and getting the flavor of the times; and still resting. I know you haven't forgotten us; but I don't expect you to have us constantly on your mind either.

We'll probably try to call you the first Saturday of Gretchen's arrival—which should be Sunday morning there—at Lolo's. But of course, you'll probably receive this after we've made our try.

My mind is in a daze from trying to keep everything here in order and for reaching out for you and remembering that you're gone for a while. But at least the days pass. God bless you and Lolo. Love, Len/ April 21, 1982.

*

Dear Linda,

This is turning out to be such a busy week-off for Tina, that I'd better write now (we're at the main library briefly), even though the week's not over.

Last Saturday we saw Louisa May Alcott, not too bad an old theater (though the wooden floor was noisy from kids' shuffling around) and the production was quite professional, fast paced, well-staged. Tina liked it.

Sunday (our time), you called; Tina has IP; then we invited Luisa to Yenching for supper. Monday, I took Tina and her friend Laura (Patriots' Day) to Lexington, for a two- hour costumed parade and she shot her first film there, which we'll pick up this afternoon. Wednesday—my long day—Ging picked her up for tinikling practice. I forgot to mention that Tuesday I took Tina to Sudbury for sneakers and stickers.

Tomorrow (Friday) I'll take her to Boston College, and we'll eat at the faculty dining room.

Saturday, all day, we'll be at the folk festival in Natick, where she'll dance twice. Sunday evening, she sings at the 6th grade liturgy, and at night we babysit Sandi's daughter.

I forgot again that tonight we go hear Fr. Saguinsin at Haley House. It's been busy-busy, with that and cooking and trying to do wash loads and dusting. Tina made hamburgers for us this noon, and leftover pilaf. I have the Morante with me, to check out, so I thought I'd let Tina come to the library while I work. She has been amazingly undemanding.

We both love and miss you very much though, we're doing our best in your absence. Your mother's death was noted in last Sunday's bulletin, and since then some (unopened but I guess) condolence cards have arrived, and a few phone calls, including Mrs. Bradley.

Other mail includes forms for renewing your car registration, so since I can't find/haven't received your current one, I've xeroxed this one and maybe it will suffice for Charley's purpose.

I raked the lawns and most of the flower beds Tuesday, but it's been too windy to spray. Nor do I know whether fertilizer or Malathion comes first. I'm glad Fr. Donelan reached you, and maybe you'll be able to see Luz, et al, in case we don't go next summer.

Gretchen will have had her prelims by the time this arrives; and have done well, I believe. She so far has no grant for this summer, though she'll stay there to prepare for Fall prelims. The good news is that she did get a full grant for next year.

Please take care of your health—cry hard if you can, Helen says—but come soon. Not only we, but all your friends here miss you. Love Len. April 22, 1982.

*

Dear, dear Linda,

I'll try sending this to Malabon, since you said a few days ago that you had only now received the pre-Easter Letter which we sent a month ago! to Marikina. No wonder you think everything is fine here. You had been gone only two weeks, you were at your mother's side, we didn't want to add to your concerns…But you must realize that by now, you are sorely missed; and we are disconsolate, trying not to be depressed each time you delay and delay your return. A person can hold his arm aloft for five minutes, but half an hour, half a day…?

There's a cumulative strain. We are not fine and dandy; it is not the same as if you were here. And we are bound to wonder if we are missed; and if all this delay is necessary, or are people using you so they can return to easy lives. I have tried to be considerate and generous, out of love for you; but that same love wants you here…

You write that I should start my novel. That's so unrealistic, honey. I cook, I wash, I help Tina with her classwork (math is up, but Spanish down) I take her to school sometimes and to piano and Girl Scout, and to various Filipino affairs and she has been exceedingly uncomplaining: but that doesn't mean that she doesn't miss you. I teach, I shop, I clean, tend the cars. I've painted both our bedrooms and the kitchen, so you won't come home exhausted to find a deteriorating house; and now I have to cut grass, fertilize, use insecticide and weed killer, and in a week, fight gypsy moths…and still this is largely maintenance, not progress.

So we do live minimally, but not effortlessly; and days are so filled with busyness that I get confused about which is which and fall asleep dead tired at night. That's how things are. And we do this for you. I just wanted that clear, since you are still reading mail a month old…

Last Saturday we were invited to Joanna Bunuan's First Communion; and Tina enjoyed playing with the girls. And food so much better than I can prepare. The Briones will go into private practice in California. Mothers' Day we especially missed you. Luckily Luisa's mother flew in from Texas and we took them to a Chinese restaurant in Marlboro—excellent food. That day was also the last IP for the year. May 29 will be the Santacruzan at the Endrigas, we have a map. Gretchen will be here and will accompany us to the lechonada.

But it is not the same without you. We were becoming so close just before your mother's death—closer than we've been in years, I feel; and I have to believe that she will touch your heart now, to close the distances again; how close she and Gretchen came to be when they confessed their loneliness—I miss your mother, the wisdom, her understanding and caring. There are so many personal things I want to tell you, Linda; my heart is filled with love for you and a need to be loved by you, to feel you close—but many of these feelings can't be put in a letter, or even into words.

I hope you get this before June. I am so disappointed with Philippine mail which only aggravates this sense of remoteness. Come, Len. May 11, 1982.

*

Dear Linda,

I want to give you a kind of accounting; but I really don't want to start with money. First: the dogwoods are magnificent, so are the cut-leaf maples, the apple trees have almost no flowers because of last year's gypsy moths (I probably have to start spraying next week: inch-long caterpillars have appeared occasionally); the lilacs are pretty good. I've fertilized twice, sprayed all plants and trees twice with Isotox; and I'm hoping that though you won't see the flowers on the trees this year, everything will survive until next year.

I haven't had time to paint any more recently (two rooms done) because I've a June 1 deadline for a 3000 word article on Villa to do before Gretchen arrives next Saturday. Wish you could be here.

Yesterday I watched Tina and the Girl Scouts do their final

gymnastics at Dana Hall for two hours. Tina is quite limber. She talks of doing ballet next Fall, and I'm investigating (not strenuously yet) possibilities in Sudbury. Today is Romy's son JR's first birthday, (remember the christening last summer?) everyone was there. Cris, Luisa and her mother, Vince and Lourdes; and on and on: all at Chit and Bert's. A nice several hours and good food—pinakbet, dinuguan and curried fruit, etc.

Saturday night at MIT's Kresge Auditorium, we'll see UP youngsters sing. I tell you this so you will know we are making efforts for Tina to have a decent life in your absence. But you know, I sure hope you realize—that we both miss you terribly. It's not a family without all of us together; and we hope you will not stay away from home one minute longer than necessary; in fact we are a little puzzled by the delays, though we have to live in hope that we, too are loved and missed.

Now, you already know (if the mail ever arrives there) that I hold the interest in March for your two certificates...to reduce the $1168 which was due on our income tax (for over $4670 in interests in 1981) ...As for the $10,000 certificate that I have held in trust, I want to stay below $7000 for your car. I'll wait until you return, of course, though my red car is not in very good shape. I have tried to save $3000 for Gretchen...

But once again, though, I want you to have some knowledge of what's happening here—or not happening—the main thing is that life is not the same without you. Linda. We survive though I worry sometimes what Tina would do if something happened to me: we do not prosper, we do not enjoy.

Come back. Bring us peace and comfort, let us bring the same to you. Love, Len. May 16, 1982. With note from Tina.

14

1983

Dear Linda,

It seems that you've already been gone for weeks, but at least it's not as desperate as last year when we didn't know what was going on, and when we did hear from you, you sounded confused and exhausted.

Gretchen called about an hour ago, just to stay in touch. I had to tell her that Father Donelan just arrived and will leave on Monday, so they'll miss each other. He moved his schedule up by two weeks, to spend more time with his mother, who's really ailing. This is Saturday (and I've just finished my review of Yabes' book: with high praise; will type it and yours next week); tomorrow 2-4 Tina will practice her dance; then we'll pick up Jim and take him to Bergson's while it's still daylight and he can see some countryside.

I've been so busy I hope I can remember what we've done. We've had several meals of chicken so last night I took Tina out for Chinese food; and we'll have lasagna tonight. You left so *much* food frozen! Tina will catalogue it Monday. I'll take her to campus with me Wednesday, and again on Friday, then straight to her practice again. I guess Saturday she'll perform and Gretchen will be back from Chicago to finish her last and most important paper. In between Tina and I will hear Aquino at BC.

I bought white paint already for the living room, although I'll wait for Gretchen to leave before doing it. Exactly when will depend on how far ahead I can prepare books for the summer course beginning May 17th. I still have 4-5 books to read for summer. I also looked in vain for Rapid Gro along Route 9. Luckily, I found we have a whole big can of it, enough for 3-4 sprays, so I did one on Thursday.

You received another thank-you letter from Our Lady of Fatima Church in Bukidnon; and a letter (I hope you don't mind my opening them) from Father Galdon, saying he's back in the P.I.; in remission and reasonable spirits. I'll drop him a line, explaining where you are, in case you are not mobile. He says he misses teaching.

Tina and I went to 5:15 Mass on Friday, and Father Jim Hession was glad to offer the Mass for Lola. He was in an excellent mood, though so rattled by doing IRS for his legally blind mother that he actually came and started Mass 5 minutes early!

We expect to call you while Gretchen's here, unless some especial news comes up first.

That reminds me: I did *not* get the SSRC grant for this summer. My only disappointment is that I wanted to be able to turn it down—as a little sacrifice, remembering how you once turned down a Smith-Mundt to the U.S. because you couldn't marry or stay in the U.S. otherwise.

The Fitzgeralds sent a card from Greece. Having a good time.

I'm not: but I'm keeping busy and somewhat productive, I hope. I feel good about our reviews. Tina has been *very* cooperative, like last year. I guess she realizes this is an emergency, however strung out; and she actually enjoys taking on a few new responsibilities.

Our regards to all, but especially our love to you. Len. I hope you got your luggage from conveyor belt to examination spot; without a hernia. I'm serious. April 12, 1983.

*

Dear Linda,

It seems more like two months than two weeks since you left. But it seems both us and Sister Helen have heard from you by now.

(perhaps others have had, too, and have not told us) By the time you receive this letter, we will have tried to call you—in Malabon when Gretchen's here; and I hope we're lucky, since Sister's letter as she interpreted it made it seem as if where you are is unpredictable. But we will have tried.

Tina and I are so pleased to hear early from you, but especially that all went well...last Saturday at the folk festival, Tina danced the binasuan very well. The Philippine group was easily the most interesting, although one Irish group (much older) did some splendid choreographing, imitating various Irish treasures at the Museum of Fine Arts!

Sunday, it rained so hard, we were both so tired (and I had 35 term papers to correct) that we forgot to go to the Saxonville Book Fair until too late.

Incidentally we have tickets to the Congregational Pancake Jamboree May 1 when Gretchen is here.

I hope by now you've adjusted to the jet lag and can sleep. We had to put our clocks forward one hour for Daylight Saving.

The food would not have been severely diminished before Gretchen arrives and, of course, she will cook several of the things in the freezer. The only "hardship" is the difficulty of finding time to do all that should be done, and still rest reasonably. I should read about five books, yet, since I have to start teaching May 17. "Luckily" it has been raining so often, that I haven't been able to do any outside spraying; so I sent out the lawnmower to be sharpened.

Cutting grass though is the smallest problem; the flowerbeds probably need a lot of work, and dandelions are beginning...

The *Americana* commissioned me to write 3 brief articles—Aguinaldo, Osmeña and Palawan—by July. Maybe I'll ask Gretchen if she wants to do the first two. Exactly, at least what year did Aguinaldo die, do you know? And is there easily available population/economic statistics on Palawan?

Your birthday present is en route here; so will Tina's come early. Gretchen will get an American Express card as part of hers.

Just when I thought I'd be with Gretchen and rest a little for summer school, the department set up two meetings! And the students wonder why I expect them to do their best, too.

I dreamed of you and your mother two nights ago, I can't remember what, but it was domestic and pleasant. I'll save Tina some space now. She's been nearly perfect. Love, Len. April 27, 1983.

*

Dearest Linda,

I'm still going to wait until next week to answer your April 30th letter. So will Tina, I think, she's so excited about her musical...But I wanted you to know about some letters that have arrived for you, some of which I've opened. The "unopened" ones include a renewal form from the Harvard Coop, and a BayBank statement, and two airletters from that priest in Bukidnon. Scott and Lita Haskins had a 6 lb boy in mid-March (and a new address). I sent money and a card. Rose Kodad wrote a beautiful thank you note for all your kindnesses (that reminds me, Father Hession asked about you at Mass, and Sister called twice to say she got your letter). Were you still here when Father Galdon wrote, from Hawaii, enroute to Ateneo? He's teaching there this summer. Please give him my regards if you see him and tell him that I always list his books in bibliographies and essays I've done for Magill and other encyclopedia of literature.

Jack Larkin acknowledged our reviews and was happy with them. P.E.N. sent a newsletter and a request for annual dues. Shall I send $20 to Nancy Eddy?

Do track down your book ms. If necessary, I can airmail you a duplicate. Same with 10.000 Seeds. All my love, Len. May 6. 1983.

With note from Gretchen re staying in Marikina, being asked to teach this summer at U Mich, political science course on the Philippines and Mexico for $2000.

*

Dear Linda,

Gretchen is writing her airletter next to me on the porch (where we have placed the sofa: spring fresh air, cardinals are all here) and perhaps on Monday, I'll write you a personal letter, of love and longing.

But this one, I thought should be straight "business," the state of the budget, especially since we made that account transfer, from money market to money market account...Credit: a love gift to help you defray travel/ease your enjoyment there...

I know that figures like these are cold. In fact, though they represent hours of labor devoted to a simple principle (trying to live within one's means, and still leave something for dreams), in turn devoted to helping you and our children safe and sound, with opportunities for reasonable happiness, and saving enough to continue that care should anything happen to me. IRS averages 25% annually, but the whole % withheld is over 40%.

I am trying to tell you what the very carefulness of figures may *not* succeed in telling you: I love you deeply; I care *for you*. Len. May 6. 1983.

*

Dear Linda,

I'm sitting here on the porch, 9am, in cool sunshine (we had a near frost last night. Tina covered her seedlings), listening to a variety of bird calls and wishing you were sharing this peace and pleasure. The flowering trees are deflowered (except for dogwoods), but other ground flowers are starting and some tulips remain. Little by little I'll try to pull grass and *identifiable* weeds from beds, but when in doubt, I'll have to let the plants grow until you come. So far I see no insects, though my eyes may be missing scale. Just before almost a week of rain, I sprayed with Malathion, so we'll see.

Tina's recital was *not* last Sunday, but this coming one! Which means that it's the same afternoon as the santacruzan, but Tina absolutely prefers being Reyna Elena. Tina practiced her piano piece well, and we're all disappointed, but a decision had to be made. Sayang.

I've been kind of nervous, as usual before a new class; but I met them last night, almost 2 dozen! And apparently willing to sit and let me lecture for 3 hours and again on Thursday. Next week discussions begin. So I felt relieved, except that the tedium of taking notes on new novels (three of which I have yet to read) keeps from really tending the house inside and out. (I do. keep up with laundry, cooking and cleaning; but it would be so nice to garden at least an hour a day: maybe that will come about.)

I called Gretchen last night, and she had to make a drastic revision in her thesis proposal, but whatever it is, she'll find it wise, she says. She wants to clarify it in a brief, to be sent to Father Carroll at Ateneo (IPC), then with his consent apply for especial visitor's visa at the Chicago consulate. She still has enough time unless Chicago needs Manila's consent and there's some hang up again. On the other hand, she doesn't really have to leave in September, if she can't.

The last letter we received from you was 5/5: so mail seems to be much better than last year. We're all glad to hear that Lolo checked out reasonably well; and enjoyed the Center. He deserves that kind of comfort—and yes, too bad your mother didn't have the same opportunity.

I made adobo, and we'll try it for the first time tonight. I was pleased with the sinigang and will try it again. Tina is literally counting the days until you return. I can tell by the way she hugs me when she comes home and kisses me goodnight that she misses you--as I do, terribly sometimes, if I let myself.

Once again, I hope you find your novel and fix its place. Your novels are truly relevant. Please let them be published. Love, Len. May 18.1983.

*

Dearest Linda,

It's the day of Tina's recital and, though fine weather was promised until this evening, it's raining out. Perhaps it will clear by midday. Why do so many things have to be done the hard way? At least this fine rain, however, may help the seeds that Gretchen helped Tina plant in small containers.

It's 9am. I expected to write this out in the porch. We put out the sofa, for Gretchen's coming; and I'm grateful that most of her week was pleasant. (she did a lot of gardening), Tina and I took Gretchen to Bergson's (partly celebrating Tina's grades, which have improved. Gretchen bought her a pair of earrings) then we went to Colonial Inn in Concord, also Dim Sum on Saturday, and lobster at home.

We tried to call you that Saturday, which would have been Mothers' Day there: no answer. We tried again on Sunday (I'm confused: that's when it would have been night there). No answer. So, Gretchen had to fly out around noon; but she wanted you to know that she had tried. Finally, Sunday night here (Monday morning there) Tina and I reached you...

The main thing is to remember that you are, warmly, in our minds, Sometimes I think of you so passionately/desperately, missing your presence, that I have to turn to other activities, of which, God knows, there are plenty here. My last exam was last Wednesday; this Tuesday night will be my first summer teaching. I don't dare think how few will show up; I can only try to stay ahead of whatever students show. I have only two more books to read; but that means five to take tedious notes on. But I'll make it. I've cut the grass twice; Gretchen cleared Tina's flowerbed; Tina hand trimmed some of the grass edges in front. I'd like to spend at least an hour a day on the out-of-doors; right now the weather having been dampish, I am recovering from a muscle spasm.

Whenever possible, I have read on the porch. Weather aside, this is one of the most beautiful times of the year...The forsythia came and went; the apple blossoms are already falling; the lilacs are about midway; some tulips are through, some just starting; the strawberries are blossoming; two yellow flowers are erect in the strawberry patch; the red bud tree is in full bloom; and all the dogwoods are lovely, including the young wild ones. Of course, the cut leaf maples (yes, the "little" ones too) are great. I've put some Malathion everywhere but had time to fertilize only once. It helps that the gypsy moths aren't around. (But I need to weed!) Once you sit on the porch sofa and realize that unless you glassed in the entire porch, you'd lose much of the visual pleasure (not to mention the air) you might want to reconsider and perhaps put the money planned into the kitchen, and/or upstairs bath. In any case it has been a consolation to me, so that there has been a little rest between school schedules, I mean rest for the mind.

The yellow car didn't pass the emission test, first time. Charlie's back from N. Mexico, but up in New Hampshire; but Richard said the car didn't need a tune up, only a carburetor adjustment: and it passed the second time. So I have no stresses left for the time being.

Tina has done most of her studying at my desk, while I read; so I know she's trying. Her musical went fine. I'm taking her to Ken's, after the recital; she says she went there only once. Mama gave us kidney beans and a vegetable dish in return. She liked your gift. Next Sunday is May procession: Tina's back is too broad for your wedding gown! so Luisa will bring some dresses from Cris. We still have two lasagna meals from Gretchen, and morcon and half stuffed chicken, otherwise we're now on our own. I made sinigang pork chops (for three meals) and it was quite good. I'll try adobo this week; and we have plenty of steaks. Tina never complains; but really the food has so far been superior to last year's. I'm writing this in the kitchen, making pork sausages for lunch.

Hope you can track down your book! All my love, Len. May 15, 1983.

*

Dear dearer, dearest Linda,

We received your mid-May letter a few days ago, so you can see how delivery is much improved over last year.

Of course, we'll continue to pray for you. Part of me wishes that, since you have to be there, you should be doing interesting things, absorbing a lot, enjoying your friends. Another part misses you badly, so that I wish you were here. We've had several near-frost this month and lots of rain; but when the days are beautiful...! I wish I had time to be outside doing more. Saw a cardinal and an oriole the other day. The dogwoods are about ready to drop their flowers, but still looks good. And there's peace and quiet. The neighbors are putting in a brick walk and continue to keep the grass cut.

At least you can feel that you have moved Lolo a little bit in the right direction towards health…and also Tia Pinang.

Be sure that you have our prayers. And be sure to take your blood pressure pills.

I'm in my second week of summer school; the class averages about two dozen; and our first discussion meeting went well. So even though I am busy trying to stay ahead of them, I have less to really worry about them.

I took some pictures of the santacruzan (luckily the sun shone). Tina looked lovely. You'll see. And I'll let her write about it… This Saturday we'll attend Paul's Confirmation. Then Sunday or Memorial Day Monday, whichever is sunny, we'll go to Faneuil Hall. Tina's morale is good (though one night she dreamed that you arrived and then left again.) And my cooking has improved. I made my second good sinigang today; and we've had some excellent spaghetti; lots of steaks and hamburgers…My first adobo was overcooked because I kept it covered. But I'm cooking a second batch tonight.

I have a book to review on Warren this weekend. The second book on him didn't appear. I love you *and* Tina *and* Gretchen, I want to live with and for you a long time. Thank God. Len. May 26, 1983.

*

Dearest Linda

Mail coming here seems faster than mail to you. Your May 26 letter came today, while you only now received the May 15th from us. We write at least once a week, although I stopped numbering our letters. I hope, at least that the pictures and card that we mailed to Lolo two days ago arrive safely.

We've had rain, at least showers almost daily, wish we could send the Philippines some, to offset the drought. But still we haven't had the wicked weather of Texas and Utah; and I think it will still be a pleasant relief for you after 100.

I'm glad at least that you will see Luz and Hermy. But what of Alex? Can't you call him at the Cultural Center library? Or write him there? It must be frustrating to be so close and yet be immobilized. If you can at least find out where the ms is. If it's lost, we'll just run off a copy and send it directly to New Day.

Gretchen wrote Father Carroll who, I'm sure will let her work through Ateneo. I worry more about red tape getting the visa; but she'll apply through Chicago, and with his and the IPC's prestige, perhaps there'll be no trouble.

Tina and I attended Paul Castro's confirmation last Saturday; the day was pleasant, the ritual intelligent. Afterwards we ate at the Castros with Mama and Luisa.

You received books, I think, from Raffel; and the Radcliffe issue with your review. I went to Horizons Unlimited, and Tina and I think we have a (one and only) escorted tour through much of Spain and Portugal (although it avoids Barcelona; some other time.) Two weeks at a competitive price. We won't decide until you arrive, but then have to act fast…to enjoy plane discount—that will be in August.

I've given up on adobo: it doesn't seem to taste right. But sinigang is always a success

Father Donelan's mother is hospitalized but he had to return before July 1st and must be there now. All my love, Len. June 2, 1983.

15

1984

Dear Linda and Gretchen,

    (8am) Tina and I, two nights ago, went through the booklet of courses at North; and prepared a 4-year plan (tentative) that looks good on paper but, of course, depends on the teachers. She'll get basic requirements in English, Math and Science out of the way early, then take history, psychology, sociology, and such. We were to present this outline to a Walsh advisor this morning; but we had a semi-blizzard (white out, followed by just enough snow to make walking hazardous) that's only now tapering off, so classes were cancelled. Just as well since Tina seems to have a little of Leslie's flu. And having shoveled three inches, I may go to bed myself.

    I had hopes to take Tina to *Cats* during Lent, but all the ticket are gone. She never complains. She's basically like Gretchen: mature for her age.

    We got our Ashes Wednesday, with Father Joe Flynn officiating. There were paper footprints down the aisle and sand instead of water in the fonts. Father Jim helped distribute but seemed out of focus.

    Tina will try to reach Luisa soon about Filipino school this Sunday. Meanwhile she promises to keep her calls under 10 minutes in case someone wants to reach *us*.

I have tried to perfect my notes and organize them, so that I can see who my main characters have to be. I have lots on MIFF 1983; my concern is how to organize scenes, especially of *action* so it's not all talk and editorializing. I am getting closer to a plot, in the sense of relationships between people; but the events so far seem *background* only. I can appreciate how you bring characters and national and personal events together. This is all new to me, that's why I don't want anyone to know I am working on a novel until (and if) it succeeds. Next, I think I will go back to reading Graham Greene, to recover a sense of scene and pace. I have 8x11 sheets of cramped notes to absorb!

Sionil Jose sent a copy of a Russian magazine, w/ a review of *Hazards!* It's all in Russian. Tina says she'll ask her teacher to translate.

All of your other mail seems routine (statements, etc) so I've left it closed. Just finished washing Tina's sheets and mine, yesterday: it was sunny.

(10:15) Now, just received fine analysis of *A Season of Grace* from VA Quarterly Rev.

(Noon) Tina feels better. We'll go see *Never Cry Wolf* and get food on the way back.

(7pm) It was a great movie—only a few actors: virtually 1 man and wolves. And mountains. Made its point (respect for nature) w/o saying so. I'm trying to make adobo, but I think it's not cooked through, so I'll put it on the grill afterwards. Tina babysits tomorrow (Sat,) morning, so I'm telling her to sleep. I am tired, too: up at 6, to shovel. I'll save Tina some space. Below 0 tonight. Love to all, Len. 3/10/84. Good to hear your voices and know all things are moving. March 12, 1984.

*

Dear Linda and Gretchen,

It's snowing again and slippery, the temperature belongs to January. I think I have a touch of Tina's flu. Mondale may take a beating today (primary in several states, including MA) so why don't I feel depressed? The news you passed on by telephone Sunday was elaborated in your two letters which we received on Monday. (So it takes airmail about a week) I like the *Philippine Studies Review* very much, because it seemed to understand the novel, and avoided fancy phrases. I'll make a better xerox here (BC takes PS). All the more reason I encourage you to give New Day your *Fortress*. I've been begging you for years, literally; you were afraid it might make waves, (but what of *Dread Empire*? And now is time for waves, (you said you didn't want to have so many books at New Day. *Fortress* must be 10 years old. Now is the *time*, don't change your mind for the tenth time. It would please me so much as publication of my own Firewalkers: and I like your idea of making a "reading" for Gretchen, even if I may not be able to match it.

I'm amazed at how expensive a barong can be (equivalent of Harris Tweed suitcoat here) but I appreciate it and will wear it at the wedding. Tina likes her gown design, too.

As for your long letter, Gretchen, I'll take care of Frank and our Detroit-Boston tickets this week as soon as the storm abates. Also, right after this airletter, I'll write him that Ginny should have to prepare dinner *only* for the actual rehearsal group. I see no reason to make things complicated. Among the reasons, I suspect most of us will not be in Ann Arbor long; the real problem will be how to "entertain" everyone in that short time. I'm quite willing to substitute paying for a meal somewhere just for the Casper family. But it may have to be a lunch, because I assume the rehearsal will be Friday, and Saturday is already the reception buffet. We ourselves will be leaving early Sunday; and I think all the other Caspers, too; if not sooner.

To get back to the pleasant news—the things that have reinforced my euphoria, caused by feeling close to you both through these letters: last night was Promotion Committee celebration at the Pillar House. Great company and of course, excellent meal. I can't believe that IBM will buy the place, level and put up a building there; that's the rumor...And Saturday I'll go to the Fitzgeralds for St. Pats. But the bigger news is Tina: the school variety show this Thursday night, her playing at the Callahan Center Friday (I'll attend both, of course) But especially what her teachers seem think of her: we talked over her first semester at North with the guidance counselor today, and all of her teachers think she should take/is capable of taking the college prep courses in English, Spanish, Science & math (tho she won't take accelerated algebra, she will take advanced.) You should have seen her quiet smile of pride/confidence because some of the teachers surprised even her. Hope their grades confirm it.

Take your medicine, give New Day *Fortress,* rest but enjoy yourselves... Love, Len. March 14, 1984.

*

Dear Linda and Gretchen,

(11am) The sun is out again, brilliantly; and there's some hope that—like yesterday afternoon—it will rid us of these mountains of snow. Classes were cancelled yesterday (second time in 5 days), but this storm was much worse because it not only dropped 6+ inches of snow but turned to freezing rain which coated everything. I think a pine branch is down, in back; but I won't trudge out there for a few days. The birches bent to the ground but are erect again. The sky is cloudless.

I continue to read Greene, now that I think I have my characters and need places and action, if possible. I can see the need for patience with a novel. And have to laugh at word of women who sometimes do Harlequins in 3 weeks!

I'm listening to WCRB on a GE transistor radio (probably worth around $12) which Shopper's Panel finally sent. I'll be finishing your manicotti for lunch. Last night (third try in 3 years) I made a *very* good lasagna, which will last us for a while.

Yesterday, Marilyn dropped by with an application for BU. She said the snow was too sticky for cross-country skiing.

Instead of Centrum, I will take Tina to Framingham State where a "rocker" is supposed to appear in April. But we have to let students have first choice, so that's up in the air, too...I'm so tired of shoveling wet snow.

(12am) Without you it really is Lent.

(3pm) There will be a program tonight at Walsh, rehearsals notwithstanding.

(3:16-8:30) Tina and Michelle went through their performance perfectly. The sad thing was there was so much audience inattention (90% kids) that I don't think they were audible throughout the auditorium (though the rock bands were allowed ultra-volume!) But to show Tina's maturity—she said later, that other performers almost cried because they worked so hard for so negative an appreciation: and she cheered them up, saying the performance was what mattered. Granted, some of the singers and dancers were mediocre, but even the best were barely acknowledged and not during the performance, unless they were loud. So it goes. Tina had to sit on stage; it was a kind of variety show.

I passed by the library and got two more Greenes. Funny I can't remember details from those I've read since Xmas, but of course I'm not teaching him; and I just want what might rub off, not clone him at all. Love to you both. Len. March 16, 1984.

*

Dear Linda and Gretchen,

(3pm) Taking a break from *The Quiet American* while the lasagna defrosts, waiting for Tina to come home from rehearsal...I took her to the Book Fair yesterday, but while I was choosing Le Carre's *Tinker, Taylor*...she preferred reading magazines upstairs, and brought home two *Architectural Digests*.

The Fitzgerald's St. Patrick Day was, as you'd expect, all fun/food/games/song. The McCues, the McCaffertys and Longos and McBrides (remember the ex-banker whose nun-sister played the accordion once?) were all there. When Dan sat down at the piano after dinner, we sang for two hours though only John and Kathy seemed to know most of the words. It cheered up a dismal day.

Today is a repeat of cloudiness, and the snow has certainly not melted. *Carmen* is at Maynard, and I'll try to convince Tina to come see it with me later in the week: we stayed up talking last night until after midnight and will probably doze early tonight. She is well over her flu if that was what it was. The interim comments (no grades) from her teachers are all encouraging, so I'll let her see a movie with Audrey next week.

Today's *Globe* announced a luncheon celebration for Duhamel downtown, which he surely deserves. (In fact BC owes him about 3 years sabbatical). Longo says the second person hired in English is Italian and seemingly decent, if she can only be uncorrupted by the female caucus that has formed.

(3/19-8:30) Freezing rain, hard to get Tina to school; glad I don't have to go to BC. Tomorrow is the first day of Spring! Today is a good day for reading. (3/20-8:30) Still drizzling. Colleen and her two brothers have colds, I have an Enrollment Dean's Search Comm meeting, 1-2 (Monan will announce his choice), will race back to pick up Tina. She has a science quiz today. I must read/review Oates' *Mysteries of Winterthrum* for *Herald*; it arrived yesterday: 500 pp. Must get a haircut this morning.

3/21-8:30: Now, the great news is from Djerassi: you have a residency, though not for this month. The Djerassi letter reads in part: "I am happy to say that they (the Board of Trustees) were quite interested in you, and so I am able to offer you a residency." I wanted to be able to give your decision to Djerassi. I tried to get their number this morning, and they have none; so I already mailed Susan Learned-Driscoll your thanks and appreciation, and in order of preference: a stay in November, 1984, as we keep either July or August: 1985 for taking Tina to Venice/Munich/Vienna.

In any case, congratulations. Tina and I will somehow manage, whenever it is; and I know that success is (tends to) breed success: ten years ago you were a Radcliffe Fellow, and some good (if not all you deserve) came from that. So *do* leave *Plaza* with New Day; and, when you return, do keep after *Whale*. Don't waste your time on things someone else can do. I am trying to take my own advice. I could have written two articles this winter; but (aside from some book reviews which I've promised, I'm really reading Green for pace and point of view, and trying to get into my characters, so that whenever I do write I'll feel inside.

It's really disappointing to hear letters I wrote late in Feb, or early March (and 3-4 since then) haven't arrived yet, where *your* letters took only 10-11 days. With love, Len. March 21. 1984.

*

Dear Linda and Gretchen,

This is probably airletter #9 since I have averaged 2/week. (Tina wrote on about 3.) Yet Gretchen's letter of the 21st took only 6 days to reach here and says none of our letters have arrived. Perhaps this one won't either; but I'll send it to Malabon, just to see if something is wrong with Marikina. I can't tell you how disappointing this is—really. Not that I remember telling you anything greatly important (I would telephone for that). But I have kept a virtual diary, so that you could know what we're doing and how we think of you and want to be close to your heart…Well, let me practice what I preach about thinking positively. I'll assume this will reach you.

At least Gretchen's letter was full of good news--that you will give New Day *Fortress* and are considering publication of *10,000 Seeds* there. As for Djerassi, take it (like anything else) while you can. I am just as grateful as you are for this recognition even if the Italian grant shouldn't come through.

We'll celebrate my birthday whenever Gretchen returns, it'll be dual that way. Northeastern U is having a poetry book-publication contest, 50-70pp, by Sept 1. I will duplicate your ms and send it long before then.

We attended Father Jim's concelebration. I'll see Father Messer this Friday about where he might publish his dissertation on T. Wilder.

We are managing. I have been reading Greene widely (w/ part of a week off, to review Oates' later novel: it will help pay for the barong, which I never thought would be so expensive.

I am writing only in my head, trying to get used to the characters in depth, and to find some *action*. I can appreciate more what Linda goes through, writing a novel—its complications, and not just its length, compared w/ short stories; and I can understand the need for "distraction" (reading, shopping, cooking) because that's when problems seem to get solved "fortuitously".

What I can't reconstruct here is all the love that Tina and I have felt for you both, our good will, our dreams (no more Mexico, but Italy/Austria/Switzerland for her in 1985). Etc. All our love, Len. March 27, 1984.

*

Dear Linda,

How good it was to hear your voice, we could tell that not only had connections and flight and pick up gone well, but that also you were pleased with the Peninsular scenery and with Djerassi and its own view, and your rustic accommodations. You finally seemed pleased that you had decided to go. So, your happiness completes ours.

We thought you might not call until after dinner there (about 10pm here) and were trying to stay awake by napping a little beforehand. So we were surprised when your call came early. I imagine you were just as sleepy and hope you did make it to the joint meal.

We had just finished our pochero (what I couldn't remember last night) and were about ready to start on the grapes. We had gone shopping late in the afternoon, for fish for today (Tina will cook it in an adapted N. Orleans style!) and more snacks-drinks for her. But you left us so many meals (for at least two weeks. I think, though we'll also make spaghetti a few times): that's tender loving care and while we'll think of you often—especially hoping that you'll enjoy your entire stay—we'll think of you warmly at mealtimes.

Tonight I'll go to the Sons of Mary (with cheese and your story); tomorrow Tina will be at the BC library while I teach, then we'll rush to get your book at Harvard Square (and look for her ring, if we can park), then hurry home because we'll have to pick up Luisa for caroling. Sunday I'll finally try to review Mojares' book, so I can get on to the MLA panel piece before Thanksgiving—after which there will be Galdon.

In case *Time* magazine isn't in the Recreation (?) Room at Djerassi, I'm sending the xeroxes of the five articles on Ver and Agrava, which you may want to mail overseas later.

A cold front passed through this morning (good you left yesterday), and tonight may be in the twenties. That will test out our solarium for the first time.

I received first-choice reservations, Dec 27-30, in Washington, so all that is readied. You'll have almost four months' rest in between. Tina has half-cleaned her room already and seems eager to take charge of shopping and whatever she can do. I guess it makes her feel more adult, and that's fine.

I'll go pick her up now; and mail Gretchen's book to her on the way. All our love, Len. Enjoy! November 2, 1984.

*

Dear Linda,

We just received your November 2 letter and I'll answer it while waiting to pick up Tina. (She can write her own letter, so they'll be staggered better.)

If you pack your novel with as many details, it should be a great sequel to *Three Cornered Sun*.

Sounds as if winter is starting in the north borderline states (NY state is supposed to get snow today; we have warm mist, alternating with heavy rain: no ice slick. I'm so glad that the trip down from Frisco was picture-perfect. Especially the animals and trees on the Santa Cruz (?) mountains sound lovely; restful. As Brother says, treat this as a retreat for meditating. By now you will have found out who's available to talk to--& worthwhile. That is, when you get tired of talking to your characters. Some of whom (including several in *Tobacco*) I really can see in three-dimension and can imagine as interesting partners in conversations.

So you might get to see Palo Alto—and maybe the Stanford campus where I met your mother 33 years ago (!).

Saturday, we lunch-snacked on your (cold) cordon bleu at BC so we could save time for shopping. We got Sr. Teresa's book (I've already mailed it) and an extra copy for your pleasure later. We didn't think we could park, but on the way out we found a place almost across from Orson Welles (traffic was so thick because of a football game that we went towards MIT instead, on Mass Ave) so we stopped. Tina likes her cotton rug, though it's only 4x6 (she didn't like the 6x9s), so I let her decide.

We barely had time to rest before we had to pick up Luisa and go to the Castro's, arriving at 5—but no one else came before 5:30, and they straggled. Tina ate lasagna, I banana fritters, dinuguan, & some wet vegetable mix. Then Lyna made us begin to learn a very difficult, syncopated version of the *Drummer Boy*. Maybe we'll catch on eventually. There will be two more new ones (including "Do you Hear What I Hear?"); and plenty of golden oldies, which we sang well.

The days plunge on.

Sunday, Tina made brunch (waffles, eggs, Sizzlelean), then I copied out 10 index cards, on literature, so I'm ready for Tuesday. Then because we had discount coupons we ate at Chi Chi's which is really interesting in its décor (but a little crowded at 5pm). Tina had Chimichanga and I had Cancun, which is crabmeat in a crisp cheese covered roll, and a Mexican beer. I think you should try it sometime minus the spicy dip.

We rushed to get Tina to Confirmation. Sister misplaced her workbook, but no matter since she's already confirmed. But when Harding's group talked about St. Thomas More, Tina said something one should be ready to die for, and all the dumb kids laughed although John Harding said she was right. She felt bad enough, telling me so at 8:30, that she cried a little. Your calls and now your letter help cheer her up, though she's really remarkably resilient.

Dave Casper sent pictures of the wedding, along with the negatives (I'll have 2 sets made, for us and for GG), so you can do with these photos what you like.

I *had* planned to do the Mojares review this week, but since it's not due till Dec 11 and I'm getting nervous about my panel piece (for after Christmas, but I promised to share a draft with that other panelist in Newton before Thanksgiving), so I'll start reading Nick Joaquin's latest today: he's half my presentation (Nolledo's the other).

I'm writing this on my lap in the solarium, which even on a darkish day is the lightest place in the house (and which kept steady at 60 even on those freezing days and otherwise rises to 68 just from the sun's rays). I know you'll work hard, but at the same time collect memories to share with all of us once you're back here. Love, Len. November 5, 1984.

*

Dearest Linda,

While Tina is still sleeping this morning and I have a wash load going (the skies are clear, it is 60* at 8 am) 1 thought I'd write to you even though all the important things seem to get said now on the phone.

Yesterday I dropped off Tina, Audrey and Jenny near Bowditch Field. I myself watched BC beat Army on TV (I don't fully understand the new count rulings but apparently it allows freer negotiations for TV coverage, and while Flutie is a candidate for the Heisman, we seem to get a lot of coverage). It was *very* close, though the score (45-31) wouldn't indicate that. Flutie was passing beautifully—a touchdown each time we had the ball. But we did win.

Framingham North didn't. Tina came home a little disconsolate. I told her that Natick has won 32 games in a row, so don't feel bad. I think we were both very tired yet from not getting home until midnight after a wearying choral practice. But she soon perked up and made us a steak supper (medium rare) far better than my typical dry steaks.

I know you're concerned about our eating, but we still have 1 hamburger meal and two adobo meals that you left, plus a spaghetti meal that I made. We haven't touched the relleno yet. And this is a good month as far as days off: Veterans Day and WThFSat around Thanksgiving. The only pressure on me is my Xmas paper which I said I'd show what's his name in Newton, from Tufts, before Thanksgiving. But yesterday I finished Joaquin's book; today I'll take notes. Monday

I'll try to write the piece (less than 10 typed pages). However I can't yet foresee doing the solarium ceiling until maybe after Thanksgiving.

I haven't had to rake since you left, thank goodness, because occasional stiff winds have sorted out the leaves. Almost all the mums are gone, of course. Should we cut the heads, or let everything drop? Actually, we've had a very decent fall so far, considering the storms elsewhere.

BC's *Biweekly* has agreed to use my piece on youth and the May election in the Philippines, so I'll update the material telling how Cardinal Sin stood by the Mendiola young demos, confronting Marcos. I haven't kept track of all the mail we've sent you, but I hope you got the xeroxes of Time of Marcos and the Agrava Commission.

Tina is really a great person, not at all resentful when some others do things she misses. I'll save her space now, and she'll call about 8am (your time) next Saturday. Love love, Len. 11/11/84. (Forgot to say in previous letter, that I had your checks to pay Harvard and Filene's)

*

Dear Linda,

According to this noon's weather map, it may be snowing where you are. Here we had heavy downpours yesterday, and off and on sunshine today, w/ cold blasts and possible light flurries by midweek when your storms get here.

Because of the rains, only a few families showed up at Iskwelahan, I'm told; but I'm glad we did go to Drabik's concert because at least we filled 2/3 of the church. 4 of the 5 Sons of Mary were there; and many Filipinos sent their regards to you: Joey Briones, the Bunuans, Feli (his birthday!), the Morenos, Minichiello, Dr. Lily and others. The concert was magnificent, like a partial rehearsal for the Dec 14/15 production—which I think we should all see. All 4 voices were great, but of course, knowing Drabik I was amazed at his power and virtuosity. The Filipino songs, w/ their constant shift in modulation—not to mention the words—were *extremely* complicated;

but so far as I could tell, he did them beautifully. (They strike me as being more Spanish than pre-Spanish, but still a mix.)

We didn't eat out for lunch yesterday, after all, because every place had lines by the time Mass was over; so we did try it today instead—at Bickford's next to the Post Office. Still crowded, but lines: 10am! And last night, after the concert--7pm—we found no parking near Ming Garden and China Sails so we ended up at the Chinese Restaurant in Newton Centre where you and I once ate, and you and Tina. It's refinished and the food was so good, we had egg drop soup, chicken lo mein, shrimp and beef: and no leftovers! I had a Chinese beer.

Today I'm taking notes on Joaquin's book, a curious piece with a strange ending which perhaps I'll have understood by the time I write of it; and Frankie's *Mass* for Galdon; just now I need only about 4 pages for half my panel time in DC; and I feel confident that I can do that this week. Gretchen has helped a lot. Remember she sent me a long critical resume from Manila when I was trying to decide if I dared include it in my panel. Well, after reading the novel, I found the resume even *more* meaningful than before, because it caught some emphases that I missed. Indeed, I could do the panel piece now first on the basis of her notes, but I'll take my own for the sake of the longer Galdon article which I'd like to be "definitive."

My being impressed with Gretchen's mind, in the past, is only confirmed now; and somehow, I think, whatever job(s) she may get, she will enjoy living in that mind for a long time.

Tina too makes me very proud with her adaptability and maturity. So I'll save this space between her piano practices. (Notice the plural.) Love, Len. 11/12/84. We just got your phone call. Hope, whether you can do many chapters or not, you at least reacquaint yourself w/ your characters so that the writing will be easier on your return.

*

Dear Linda,

I was contemplating this letter (writing it in my mind) when you called. Duhamel had told me the news about "a serious kidney operation on Marcos in Manila," though I too had heard earlier that he was expected to come to the US for health reasons.

Anyway, while things are at least half clear in my mind let me tell you about the despedida. There were more people Saturday than even on UN day: Castros, Javiers, Bunuans, Morenos, Feli (+Drabik), Minichiello and his wife, and many I recognize. Chit was also there with Linda Ott. The religious service was splendid, w/songs and prayers in three languages and very sincere. We ate plenty. You'll be here for the next one, Dec. 1.

Brother Francisco has been too busy to see our house. But we'll see him Tuesday when Phil reports; and maybe again. His departure is not wholly clear to me.

Then Sunday we gathered at the Bolandrinas for a heavy brunch. He had made arrangements for the entertainment at Cushing, w/ the help of some teenagers planning on being confirmed. At Cushing we set up Christi Anne's synthesizer so that, after 3 dances (Tina did the binasuan beautifully. There were 3 sets of tinikling-ers). Raul Manglapuz on the guitar led us all in old-time favorites. Finally, Tatang did *Bayan Ko*.

There must have been 100+ in the audience, half in wheelchairs, some asleep (since it was right after lunch; but some sang heartily. And there was a persistent fellow in front who knew a few words and didn't seem to be able to read anymore (there were sheets passed out) but who kept the melody and beat perfectly. Tina and I went back to the Bolandrinas for coffee and cake, and let him explain how he was looking for opportunities like this one to let people know that Filipinos exist.

It does seem a shame to sing only two weekends, after all the practice necessary for the complicated new songs that we've had to learn. I can't pretend to have learned them perfectly.

Between school and Filipino doings this has been a busy month, but I regret only those late Friday practices (we arrive at 7, start at 8, get home at midnight) Tina comes with me Saturday morning, so she doesn't get much rest either. I've hardly had a chance to sit and enjoy our solarium.

Today is Tuesday (continued from last night after your phone call). Tina will have to walk home while I see Dana about my blood pressure. Tonight, Phil will talk on the economy. But at least I have no obligations for a while, until rehearsal Sunday afternoon. I'll try to do my book review. That would leave only the Galdon article—and the new end for my novel. This happened to be the time that some term papers come in but they can slip through the cracks between times.

Thanksgiving we'll eat at a Greek restaurant on Mass Avenue, beyond where we used to go on Easter. Tina wanted Thai food, but they all close on Thanksgiving. I tried to call Romagnoli's and several other famous Italian places—all closed. But the Areof sounds interesting. Anyway, we'll celebrate when you return.

Gretchen probably told you: she'll go to Philadelphia in March and then to Chicago in April, on panels, professionally she seems to be doing well.

Sorry I was groggy when you called yesterday. I was snoozing before eating supper and going off to teach again.

I'll call about 3:15 your time next Monday (I don't teach this Saturday). I'm glad you do both some writing and see something of where you're at. Give my regards to your characters. Only a fraction of you in Vitoria, Linda: the rest is lovable and loved. By the time this arrives, you will have less than a week left. Enjoy it. Love, Len. 11/19/84.

*

Dear Linda,

(8am) It's freezing out. But the sun is shining. I had 7 hours sleep last night. I felt relieved.

Phil was supposed to talk last night, but a reason was never given, Sister Ignazia did instead—on what one might expect to meet in the Philippines, especially in relationships... She stressed the community, as a "first family." but really these men are not novices. We had hopia and since it was Francisco's last night w/us (he leaves the day after Thanksgiving), we sang "for he's a jolly old fellow." I've grown to like him very much and will miss him. That's almost s true for the other four: the Sons of Mary will not be quite the same for the next several years.

Meanwhile Luisa called and asked for more cushions, having finished one already. So, we'll bring a few over tonight. I paused to hang out a wash, although at the moment it is only 40. But this is Tina's half-day; I'll fetch her at 11, we'll have hamburgers, then I'll take her to *Garbo Talks*, her (comic) choice of movies. I give her credit for not choosing something dumb or teen-age-ish. Tomorrow: Mass (we'll pray for our family, then for the world's poor. Tina still isn't earning, but she gave some of her money to Ethiopian relief).

I hope your own Thanksgiving is not negligible. However, as I've said several times, we'll celebrate several times in December, in Boston and in Washington: to make up for it. By the time you receive this you will have only one week left there. When I call Monday night (3-3:15 your time) I'll have confirmed your flight. Only a non-writer would expect you to have written 40,000 words; but I hope your old friends from *3-Cornered Sun* visit you more often now, with suggestions and counterplots, and the like. I'm enclosing one of the remaining fuschia. The paper narcissus are showing about 6 blooms today, and the hibiscus dropped its second flower since you left, a few days ago. Love love love. Len

I just called Brother Francisco, who wanted your number and perhaps by now, would have called you; and I told him I have mixed feelings about his leaving because a good person always influences one's life. I really will miss him, them. (The Sons of Mary missionaries are going to Manila to open a shelter for street children. Also, the radio says Marcos denies being ill, again; that he has been at the U.S. The embassy in fact, denies this. So it goes.) 11/21/84.

16

1985

Dear Linda,

Thank you! I know that sounds strange; but today (Saturday) I read as much of Wings of Stone as you have written, and it's good. I think, sometimes, that I have access to your best self—your most mature insights and feelings—as you write (Perhaps that gives you most access to yourself as well.) And I am glad/proud to be your husband.

The faults I've found (or marked) in the mss are minor: too much repetition of time overlap in the first several chapters, considering that this is a major motif and will be picked up later in variations, maybe too constant a double-name reference to Rose

Quarter—Sylvia Mendez; not enough recollection of Johnny's experience as a professional.

But your greatest strengths are there, as usual: the deeply felt characters; and the suspenseful pace, which allows surprising information to be introduced just at the right time—especially a knowledgeable way of ending chapters: a short story writer's trick.

Johnny (once his professional dimension is added) is convincing, including his seeming sentimental/emotional attachment to Sylvia until she too turns out to be complicated and worth considering. The father, in his silences, seems more profound than merely shadowy: how they miss each other regularly (and will this have anything to do w/the mystery of Johnny's birth?) is moving. So are Rio and his ghetto people. So even is Martin wholly conceived. You have exposed the rich-and-irresponsible before but Sylvia and even Martin are fresh portraits. One can conceive of them as existing in the same society with *Trespass* and *Garden*; and still they are distinguishable, personalized.

The texture is less descriptively rich than Telly's, but I think that is closer to Johnny's sensibility. Yet at key moments (often with Sylvia) the right metaphors rise. I'd say that this novel, like Empire, depends more on understatement. Yet it is unique in some ways by having several plot lines going on simultaneously--drawing in internal crises (characters) as well as on external events. (the May '84 election). How will it end, I don't know. But there is already so much substantiality, it doesn't matter.

Do you wonder why it means so much to me, needing to be loved by you—held in high regard and special regard—when I realize how very special you are, in these novels? Love, Len. June 2, 1985.

17

1986

Dearest Linda,

    Tina and I were excited to get your 4/7 letter yesterday. That means it takes about a week. Also that your back may be okay, and the jet lag less than usual.

    I wanted to get this to you at once, to include a xerox of a xerox of a *Hudson Review* review of *Awaiting Trespass*, that NVM sent. It's lengthy and accurate even if it misses some of the religious overtones. I'll send another xerox, in time, to Sherman, to whom I sent your "egg photo" last week.

    Tina measured me, and 21 ½ (across the shoulders) 25 ½ arms, & 29 ½ (shoulder to past hip) turns out to be perfect! So I get a barong after all: hope you have the same luck with rings.

    Because of the continuing turmoil, even if it's not violent, I hope you will be prudent where and when you travel. For that matter, we are watching carefully the results of Reagan's attack on Libya (apparently, they did not hit only military targets but were off enough to injure civilians: will Spain, Europe in general be safe?

    But I wanted this to hold only good news. Yes, we're well and very busy—productively, I hope. Tina has temporarily gone out for tracks (running) until babysitting starts again; so we eat a little late, but that's good; keeps me from over-snacking at 10pm. The weather is still cool at night but on alternate days close to 70. So things should bloom (including your houseplants: only the geranium is losing petals, maybe naturally). I don't look forwards to bug season and spraying; but spring otherwise is always nice. Did I tell you that I have until June and August for encyclopedia entries? And someone at Aquino Foundation promised to get birthdays of the Aquinos; so once I sort out my clippings, I should be set—before summer session which is one week before your return.

We had your chicken last night, will have sotanghon tonight. You left a *lot* of prepared; food so I've only made spaghetti once, will do lasagna tonight for freezing. We won't eat out this week so I can give the money to Tina for her trip to GG.

The Moro brass pieces sound good.

Use your time well, rest, take medicine. My eye feels better, after soaking.

Remember: seriously consider hanging on to *Garden*, at least until Bonnie hears from Sherman. I'll try my own novel *here* again, in fall: North Pt, Grove, New Directions. But you have a steady audience. Love, Len (for Tina who just left for school.) 4/15/86.

*

Dear Linda,

I'll start this tonight—Saturday—and finish it in the morning. I'll go to 8 o'clock Mass, because I don't feel like singing, with everyone gone.

Tina had lovely weather, as you did, to fly to Detroit. We picked up 3 lobsters (Capt. Bob opened early for us) and whisked off to the airport for Tina's 10:30 flight. Now I miss you both and really will have to work this loneliness off. I gave Tina an airletter, so she can write you from Ann Arbor: so I'll let her explain her new adventures in track; and how she likes the Impressionist gallery at the MFA last night. I can tell you my impressions: this was better than Renoir because there was a greater variety of canvasses (Cezanne. Toulouse-Lautrec, Monet, Gauguin, Sisley...), the food was better (great roast beef, e.g. on special breads), and there was the BC chorale (part of it) singing in the Rotunda. Oh yes, there were St. Gaudens sculptures, with frames and pedestals by Stanford White, Sister Elizabeth's relative. She was there; so were the Longos, McAleers, Chens, McCaffertys, Appleyard and others from elsewhere: but it wasn't crowded, so it went well. Kay Hastings, the AVP's assistant whom you met was nice to Tina: so maybe in the future we can rotate?

I made some great pork sinigang tonight: great, really! At first, I couldn't find the powder but I kept poking. It will make 3 meals. Tomorrow I'll keep working up the Aquino data for Gretchen (did I tell you that the Aquino Foundation gave me their birthdays?), so that Monday I can work outdoors for a while (rain expected in pm).

From the solarium I can see distant tulips coming up, plus squills and other blues; and the ajugas are getting ready, and whatever under the apple tree. And the indoor plants are showing new leaves.

Writing you, I feel better now; will sleep, and write tomorrow.

Sunday: I forgot to say we received a card from the Moores, the Fitzgeralds. And a letter from Louie, who split his head from a fall down the cellar steps and Mary is losing a little vision in her left eye. But they're both as chipper as usual. Latest word is that Cardinal Sin will be our Commencement speaker! – morning of the night you return. A far cry for when Bush presided.

It's still about 40 at dawn, but by now (9am) it's very pleasant—because sunny. I should open the flower beds, tomorrow, rake leaves off.

At 8 o'clock Mass were the Bottis, Cavatorta, the Hungarians, and others whom you know but whose names I don't. I may give blood this Thursday, at St. J's. I saved the only bad news for last. Sr. Mary Helen apparently died last Thursday, though we heard of it (in the bulletin) only today. The funeral Mass tomorrow is at St. Agnes' in Arlington—which unfortunately I wouldn't be able to find. But next Sunday's Mass will be for her, at St. J's. Her "peculiarities" were always pleasant ones, and she was a real personage: a hard, efficient worker; a real carrier of the faith. All her flaws were minor, her virtues great. She was never aloof—and I can't believe that she will be, even now. All my love, Len. April 19, 1986.

*

Dearest Linda,

    I postponed writing this letter, from usual Sunday morning until Monday, so I could report on the Tagalog movie. The crowd was very good, for a rainy day (not heavy enough to relieve drought): some 200, I'd estimate: good for Sons and for Mindanao. Fr. Coss looked pleased, though he had to leave early (they delayed start from 1 to 2:30), sold food—some trinkets. It was not a comedy, though we never got its title (movie started with direction credits: Lino Brocka). Fairly easy to follow, except some relationships were a little vague.

    Tonight, Tina's track running permitting, we will see BC—Boston Symphonic Orchestra practice Beethoven's 7th, then I have to settle down to giving exams and *really* getting ready for summer session in two weeks—just before your return.

    Tina's a little disappointed that we've had only one letter from you: but I say you're probably in Baguio. Coss says you've seen the Brothers *several* times.

    No major mail for you this week. I have article on Santos in *America* this fall; and I quickly did galleys for *Firewalkers* last week. If you see Gloria, please tell her I airmailed them 3 days ago (but not registered: no such thing to the Philippines). Mail coming this way takes about a week: hope it's the same going there—and that she has a respectable cover illustration. None sent.

    I followed your directions—watering everything when geranium dry—but found some were overwatered. The foul weather will soon end the small tulips, but the big ones are appearing & look strong. I've cut the lawn once already. Trees getting leaves.

    We're off Daylight Savings now: but I guess that won't affect your flight. Tina seemed to have great time with Gretchen: brought home G's Mothers' Day present. Sr. Mary Helen's Mass yesterday was well-attended. Love, Len. Sent two more boxes of books to Lolo. April 28, 1986.

*

Dear Linda,

It's frustrating—and makes you seem farther away than at other times I have felt you were—to receive your April 24th letter which sounds as if our airletters are slow in arriving there (your two letters have taken only one week each) or are lost.

It may be useless (perhaps the 4-5 letters which we've already sent will arrive by now, or this one will be lost, also): but here is the substance of some of those earlier letters (we've written every week, plus our regular letter w/ a copy of the *Hudson Review* on your novel).

The largest measurement for a barong (21 ½ shoulder, 24 ½ arm, 29 ½ torso) are fine. One letter mentioned Bonnie Crown's advice to hang on to *Garden* in case Sherman Carroll wants it next year (she will try to verify his policy of expansion, which seems in effect for *Wings of Stone*, without committing himself to an actual text in advance).

Perhaps you could manage with Pacheco this way: she can have my novel if she cares (this is no longer important to me) but buy only the Philippine rights to *Garden*, so that RI might have access.

I'm sorry these communications, which are important, come at a time when it is next to impossible to reach you. I feel *awful*.

But I do want to end on a more pleasant, less depressed note: Tina's grades are as follows—Geometry: 93; Acc English: 90; US 20th C: 98; Spanish: 96. Bio 87. Her best scores yet. I won't wait for her to come home but will try to "speed" this on its way. Love, Len. April 30, 1986.

.

18

1987

Dearest Linda,

Is it old age, stress or both? Today I locked my keys in the car, at Pinefield—first time in years (remember Newport?) The AAA have a simple tool for opening the door though. I can see why locked cars don't mean a thing to a thief.

I had bought some envelopes, gone to the car to fit into one the original pamphlet of Salonga on extradition, got out to mail it, slammed the door and realized the keys were inside!

Saturday Salonga spoke at Third World Conference at the Kennedy School of Government. He remembered meeting you two summers ago. Heherson was also there, and I gave him Cellar Book Shop's address for a friend who is interested. Aquino was also there & Phil Suva. Also a US correspondent for AP, persona non grata in Manila; and a Locsin —plus others I couldn't identify, except for two nuns, a Maryknoll and a Columban from BC. Anyway, Salonga was great, synthesizing basics from a 28-page pamphlet a Filipino group in Hawaii (where he now lives) printed. Boone Schirmer was given the pamphlet. I borrowed it, xeroxed a copy for us and for Phil, and returned the original.

I hope these visiting Filipinos keep coming in the fall. They save their own lives, by becoming visible; and they've already convinced several US Congressmen to rethink extradition w/ a country that doesn't have habeas corpus, etc.

Tomorrow, I hope to paint the walls in our bedroom (ceilings done already; so is the kitchen ceiling which took two coats). I try to balance cooking, washing, schoolwork, attending these lectures, & doing minor writing. By June I have to do a long article on Villa; by July1, on NVM: for a Virginia encyclopedia: &75 each, so I can at least buy a suit in the fall. When I get my $50 for reading Morante's ms (UWash Press), I'll look for a summer suit or jacket.

That reminds me, Comber said that they suddenly got orders to suspend all publications except textbooks—I mean new commitments. From Heinemann's in Britain. So, he has to return Plaza. But I think, with very minor, insignificant deletions it can be sent to New Day. Really. Just don't mention the Marcoses, any more than Dread Empire did. The political situation will still be valid—and as I reread it, it seems an indictment of many frivolous people, of all classes.

We received your letter (dated April 27) already. But since you used Philippine stamps, I have to assume the US stamps were pirated. That's why I advise everyone to write you, using airletters –though one week ago I sent more stamps.

When you hinted you might not be home for weeks, I opened a gift from the Castros, from a week or so ago: our mother has been enrolled in perpetuity with the Franciscans. The "record" is lovely.

Saturday, we'll go to Joana Bunuan's First Communion celebration; Sunday is Mothers' Day (which, like Easter we'll celebrate on your return) and IP. Luisa's mother will be arriving.

I hope your knee is now healed. Please, please take care!

The two MM certificates fall due this month; I'll just let them roll over, for you. My own I will cash briefly, but not buy the car until you return, since it will be yours—anniversary gift.

I know you want to stay to clear things up for your father (what happened to the hernia operation?) and for Baby. But we need you, too, remember.

Do you miss us sometimes too? Gretchen will have written you *her* news, here's Tina/ I love you, only & much: Len. May 4, 1987

Father Flynn and I agreed to have Masses for your mother 9am on all Sundays in June. Chinese key wasn't where you said; can't find it.

…..

Mom, I just got my report card today. I made the honor roll again. Come home soon. I love you. Take care. Tina.
PS. Toby says hi.

*

Dear Linda,

I know this will reach you only in time to let you know that I received Joe's letter. He obviously didn't know that you were going ahead, but by now I'm sure you have reached each other, and you have begun to think what historical fiction means and doesn't mean to you.

I'm grateful that I now know what my topics are so I can bring the right notes. I'm sorry that Tina and I will be missing *your* talk—we arrive two days later (I think: this time change has me nuts if I try to think it through).

Not much has happened since our last letter, so I might just as well quit here.

The Celtics (nothing wounded) somehow managed to win game #3; but I can't imagine their getting 3 more since games 6 &7 are played in LA—if it goes that far.

Tina's giving me a burgundy shirt for Fathers' Day (I'll bring it along) & Gretchen is giving me the book on the Marcoses. Pedrosa just released her update on Imelda.

It has been raining fairly constantly (the seasons are still in transition, & Canadian cold keeps meeting southern heat), so I've watered outside only 2-3 times since you left. The white daisies are everywhere.

The lawnmower came back, so I did the front today fast; & will do the back on Wednesday. Then once more just before we come.

Tina thinks she has low blood pressure but isn't worried: the health book says that's good for the young and the elderly. My pressure is fine, but I think a sty is trying to form in my right eye: so, I'll bathe it.

We'll probably write only once more &, if an emergency arises, try to reach you by phone. Father John was in a great mood, Pentecost. Love, Len. June, 1987. Monday.

*

Dear Linda,

I hadn't really expected to write you again before Tina takes her SAT tomorrow. Because it has been a routine week: drizzling everyday so that no outside work can be done (the sun will come out today) teaching to grad students who straggle in; the Celtics exhausted and crippled, getting trounced twice by the Lakers to no one's surprise...The one bright spot was Tina's A- on her osteoporosis paper.

But then this letter came from Joe Galdon, and I thought I'd try to get it to you, so you could prepare your mind—in case you haven't seen him yet. His letter to me was not at BC yesterday when I taught, nor here, but I'm not panicky yet. My semi-refund request can be made late, even (if it's honored, the check probably wouldn't be available until July...we could use it for expenses if we go to Wisconsin). But I do need to know what notes to bring along if I'm to lecture on things not on my fingertips. You can just tell him how you view history, what your research methods are, where your characters come from, etc.

It's 8am and I want to get this in the mail. The dogwoods have lost their flowers, and the rhododendrons will go soon. The red trees and the purple mounds will have to provide color, the next few months.

I worry more about the SATs than Tina does, but I'm trying not to let her feel my anxiety. May God keep you all well. Love—to Lolo, too, Len. June 5, 1987.

*

Dear Linda,

Probably this will reach you after our arrival. But I wanted to mention a few things, lest being exhausted as well as busy with adapting I forget them when I see you. The most important thing is that we received your June 5 letter and will try not to be pickpocketed at MIA; thanks for the advice on how things work, we will likely not be able to bring queso de bola, simply because we are already bringing so much for others that our clothes are minimal. We will try to add the candy and dried fruit, as much as possible.

Secondly, FILIPINAS has accepted your MIT talk on women writers. I had to add a hasty biblio, and make a few corrections, retype pages their reader has scrawled on but I'm mailing it back tomorrow. They wanted it in Kansas ASAP. Congrats.

Also, the BOSTON REVIEW finally answered: she wants me to do an overview (I suggested telling of writers in exile, those who compromised with Marcos. Current prospects: so far she sent no details; only wanted samples of my writing—which I readily sent her, asking her for a deadline and word-limit).

NVM, thinking you were still around, called and we had a nice talk. He seemed unsure of what Galdon wants him to do; but I told him that my own letter from him, though it suggested two topics (which I've accepted and am collecting notes for), gave me free rein. NVM doesn't even know if he's being paid transportation. He had asked the Ateneo Association of SF for support: no answer. Like me with the Embassy cultural attache, but I did xerox Joe's letter and petitioned BC for $750 (their limit) though I won't know until my return.

I hope we have as much rain (about every 3rd day) in our absence as we have now. The bougainvillea is gorgeous, a much deeper color. The peonies have come and gone; the day lilies are about ready, so are many of the smaller flowers around the trees; and the purple mounds in front thrives.

You decide where we should stay and when. We do want to see Lolo, Sr. Teresa, Brother and Galdon, of course. I will have to carry several routine medicines, to stay well. Maybe Tina will have less allergies there. (She's now at work and I think mail pickup is 1pm, so I'll rush now.)

Romel sent the jack to bring. It's packed.

Tina called Gretchen but also wrote down word for word your sketchy details about IPC so that she will have a rough idea and at least the name of the director and know how much to ask for support when she does.

We're doing okay, except that emotionally we miss your presence; but we keep slugging along (the Celtics on their 6th game today: their last? --- they are underdogs—help!) and time passes fast. Tina's exams are coming up, and we hope you prayed hard. We'll be back before she knows about the SATs.

Another book about the revolution of 1986 (THE FOUR DAYS OF COURAGE by Bryan Johnson) has come out; from the review I can't tell if any new details are there. You're learning more things useful for your novel in situ, I'm sure.

THEN Gore Vidal has added a new novel, EMPIRE, to his list of novels on major moments in US history. This time it's about the Fil-AM War, though the reviewer thinks he spends too much time with the big names, and seems not aware of labor movements, here etc., and I guess is less interested in the Filipino side. So, I hope you get onto STRANDED WHALE by January, next year.

Now I better mail this and give it a head start. You are very much missed by us. Love, Len. 6/14/87 Sunday.

19

1989

Dear Linda,

    After about a week of springlike weather when I didn't even have to wear a jacket, it is so bitter cold (though no wind) that my hand is shivering as I write this.

    Still, this cold is better than the freezing rain of last Friday when we were tempted not to go to school except that Tina had her history section meeting plus a paper to turn in. So we went and made it, partially because relatively few cars were trying it.

    Tina has mailed both her income taxes (two refunds) and I mailed our Federal yesterday but will withhold the state for a while since there we owe $300 (the state unlike the federal taxes all income, including pension savings which the Federal lets go.)

    Tina is out this morning, giving Cheryl more driving practice. Last time the Marlboro registry officials said one of our stop lights didn't work and wouldn't let her take the exam (a poor excuse but the weather was bad and maybe he was afraid). Actually Richie found the lights okay—but it's just as well that I went to him because we found a flat tire. (I think I wrote this once before.)

    She will do an anthro paper this afternoon while I consider redoing my paper for Louisville.

Did she tell you that last Sunday we were asked by Jackie Reichert to bring up the gifts? Today they announced the Kodad's thanks to all (unspecified) who helped them get to St. Patrick; and Fr. Quinn's brother Joe died. It is St Blas, today.

Wednesday is Ash Wednesday. We've actually been overeating so we certainly can fast one day. The portions you left are large. But I did buy a few small steaks to vary the menu.

The NEA acknowledged receiving your manuscript; and according to Tina, Gloria someone called for you, saying she is now in Washington, as a resident. Is this Bella's sister? You also received two reviews of *Awaiting Trespass* from R. Kwan Laurel, a self-described fan of yours, from the *Sunday Globe Mag* and *New Horizon's*, today, 5-600 pp long (identical pieces). NVM gave him the address...it's wonderful to know that somewhere in Manila—*Trespass* is available.

As usual we hope that you are seeing your friends and especially checking on the availability to Readers International of *Small Party*, as well as the publishability of your stories.

We meanwhile are more or less on hold now that winter's here. Tina is excited about France, and a little less so about Louisville. She received back her final paper of last semester from Mrs. Zeltzer who continued to write all over it, but this time gave it (and deserved) high praise.

Frankie was kind enough to write, despite the fire, that he has accepted my article on Rosca's novel (glitzy, wf a depth, especially moral depth) and urges me to put together another book. Perhaps by *1990* I will have enough. Perhaps by then *his* novel on Ermita will be out. If you see him--& NVM—please give them my highest regards. And if you can find Yuson's novel...After Louisville I will try to do a piece on Cirilo Bautista's epic poetry for Wally Bacon. I suppose being too busy is better than being bored. Until next week, Love, Len. 2/5/89. Sunday.

*

Dear Linda,

All the good news first. That's terrific that Gloria will release

A SMALL PARTY IN A GARDEN to Readers International, as long as it does not compete in the Philippines (or in any case would be a hardback for those who might want to afford it). I wrote Sherman at once, telling him the news just so he could start thinking of SPG in this year's lineup, although he probably would want to wait for an actual release form from you/Gloria. I feel good about this.

Secondly, I called Mr. Capalbo at BC Housing and finally got through to him, and he assured me that a space (no specifics at this point) would be saved for Tina. Friday, we went to housing and got the brief application form and made the $200 deposit. The assistant director knows all about Tina's situation, so we will be sure it ends up in her hands.

Third, but Tina can tell you more about this), PHIL-AMERICAN NEW in LA called and wanted you to write something for them (again, no specifics) and then the editor heard that you wouldn't be back until mid-March, he said he'd call again then.

Fourth, I was able to review Seagrave's THE MARCOS DYNASTY and send it off to Frankie, with a note of thanks for his accepting my Rosca essay especially while he is busy repairing his place. I said I was intending to do an essay yet on Bautista's poems (two volumes that I know of, unless something came out since TRELEX MOON, Yuson's novel, and Frankie's own if it appears this year; so that when you go in 1990, I may ask you to take along a book ms.

Fifth, I attended the Jesuit Institute luncheon and Fr. Daly made a wonderful presentation of their intention and yearly focus; when two faculty seemed concerned that awards (research) be open to all projects, I made a quick speech that creative tension being good, but destructive tension (extremists of either right *or* left) not. We did not have time to explore my implications; but I knew that some people will try to subvert the Institute itself by asking for money for projects that in effect challenge basic church doctrine and common sense: I've seen tunnel vision at both ends; and of course I'm aware of the anti-clericalism/anti-Catholicism in our department. In the name of openness, things will be closed down.

Sixth, Tina is packed; and I will pack after this letter (our last). For a while we were worried, because there were floods in Kentucky—but not in Louisville, as I found when I called. We may finally have a snowstorm here before we leave Wednesday; but we only have to reach the bus line and the rest is in God's hands. Will call Ruth today.

Seventh, we saw Joe Kodad yesterday—in the hospital with heart condition brought on by lung congestion; but he was more lucid than ever; Tina can tell about that. We had a long, good-humored talk.

I don't understand your references to Scott (Wm H.?) and ILOCANO HERITAGE/ILOCANO RESPONSES; nor to Cora Bolong at IPC, but we'll find out when you get home. We can hardly wait. Take care of your cold! All my love, Len 2/19/89. I also paid a real estate semi-final bill of $970—auto insurance may come down, to compensate for water going up. Tina wrote in back.

*

Dear Linda,

This looked important or I wouldn't have opened it. I've already replied to Bonnie, though I said *you* would give your own reply early in August. What I remember saying in essence was *10,000 Seeds* is excellent, but since it is about the late 19th century, Readers International probably wouldn't be interested. I also mentioned that Beacon Press is *looking* at it (only), and that it should be of interest to an American audience as the centennial of the Philippine-American War draws near. As for *A Small Party*...that's closer to RI policy but *perhaps* too recently released for New Day to allow for reprint. Therefore, I think I concluded, to me *Dread Empire* seems the best bet. (It occurred to me *later* that *Dread* and *Party* might make a good double release.)

Meanwhile I said a *little* about *DreamEden*, predicting that it too is close to RI policy; but adding that it's not yet finished and available; and why not try it on one of the US publishers now? God knows your achievement ought to be sufficient if Bonnie could catch someone's eye. So I said a little about Montreal. I think that was it.

Tina has now registered for the fall, assuming the courses are available when she wants them. But she probably has written about all that.

She helped me with the ladder so that I could—finally—cut off the two dead limbs on the mountain ash. We had occasional rain while the Midwest sweltered; but now face Philippine heat and humidity.

Gretchen will arrive one week from today—I assume she'll leave before this arrives.

Except for aphids on the fuschia (despite soap treatment), your plants seem okay. Outside, the lilies are coming and going in a lovely rhythm

I'll take Tina to a half-comic/half real-life movie today, and tomorrow on my birthday, try a Thai restaurant in Waltham.

I remember being so event-clogged when last I wrote that I said the Sunday before Louie and Mary left we simply lolled around. No, we had plans but Mary managed to reach Angie in Quincy and I arranged for Louie and her to meet at Shopper's World. They ate at Houlihans on Rte 9, across from Shoppers World, and Mary said she felt so good about Angie.

It was a good visit, if sometimes strenuous (and I thank you for all you did to make them overwhelmed and the week memorable). Tina had an especially good time with the girls; and, as I wrote, she too was tremendous, driving to Plymouth and to the airport. I hope (and expect that your own stay with relatives and friends is equally satisfying.

If you go/get to a bookstore, there are a few things I wish you'd have them send: Vol. II of *The Writer and His Milieu*, and any issues of *Solidarity* since 'mid-1987 which might have reviews or articles by me. Frankie used to send me contributor's copies but probably is too detached from the magazine now.

Time to make the "doughnuts" (luncheon sandwiches). Love, Len. July 5, 1989. If you happen to see Rodriguez you might ask her if she'd allow the reprint of *Party*, w/ or w/o *Dread Empire*.

20

1990

Dear Linda,

    I'll start this letter now, although in less than an hour I'll be going to anticipatory Mass alone. Tina stayed at BC to give Elsa a weekend there, but she just called and said that the father needs to go to the garage, etc. A snowstorm (6-10" like the last one, also on a weekend) is promised, starting tonight. Nothing will move tomorrow, except shovels and backs. At least I finished drafting our IRS forms, we owed about $300, but only because they didn't withhold enough. So I won't file until April.

    Before they slip my mind, newsprint copies of *Awaiting Trespass* arrived today from New Day. Mailed in September! If you haven't already told Rodriguez, remind her to put Tina's name into future printings. It could be done without using an extra page if it's entered just before the copyright information (When you do talk to her, please make sure that my ms has reached her hands, too many little slipups over there.) And did I tell you that a check for $30 awaits, from Greenfield Review for "Hills..." Also, in checking my notes for the IRS, I found that in fact we *must* have received a royalty check: June 21, P224.09 (my share was $94, according to notations on my checkbook). So let Mrs. Rodriguez rest in conscience: I don't know why she thought otherwise.

Heritage arrived, but they gave you only a page—largely a summary of what I (vaguely) remember you gave *them*. Still *some* kind of recognition.

We have finished deciding at BC, whom to offer slots (2) to, so I'll be able to use my "off" time now more propitiously. I *must* start on Warren now. (A fellow from Duke, in NC, wants me to be a charter member of a Robert Penn Warren Circle.)

Tina's schedule is working out fine; we get to Brandeis and I get back to my grad class, w/o a hitch. She likes *all* her teachers. Though I tell her she'd better approach her new math professor, admit that high school didn't prepare her well, and ask where she can get some help. Otherwise, anthropology, archeology, etc. seem to be pollenating one another now and she has interesting texts.

Keep praying for her in math—as well as in her social life. I worry only on occasion, like this weekend, when the plan w/ Elsa fell through. *Two* weekends this month she'll be in Southborough; and we'll be getting her ticket to Wisconsin next Wednesday.

It's lonely here with only the bunny to talk to, though the IRS today and snow tomorrow will make *these* days pass. I can't imagine that you know how much I miss you, that's such a cliché. Especially when I saw a fine, somewhat hopeful—only program on Alzheimer, a few nights ago. So did Al, whose mother also probably died of/with it, though no diagnoses were publicized back then. But I think sometimes how much I have never been able to communicate to you the extent of my love, my need, for you; then someday, I'll be silenced beyond even the groping for the words or the right gesture. I wish I were *really* a writer and could at least get some of these said to you. Particularly. I think Tina knows how much I care about her. Maybe Gretchen occasionally guesses…So it goes.

I've gotten Tina a great anthropology book for Valentine. Too much for her to absorb just now; but if she's serious, *some* day.

Neither Tina nor I understand what operation Lolo had, but it is heartening to know it was successful.

Stay well yourself and fill yourself with the Philippines.

I'll try mailing this to Araneta, the address you.ve been using. Love, Len. Finished before Mass after all. 2/3/1990. Saturday.

The Jordan M sofa is still $1300. Teak has one at $800--the one I think we saw before—it looks better by daylight. But we won't make any purchase before you return. Teak will have a sale again in July. No typewriter key yet.

*

Dearest Linda,

Your letter of Jan 26 (postmarked Jan 30) arrived here February 9. Not too bad. I only hope our own letters take only 1 ½ weeks to reach *you*.

Of course, we look forward to every word from you—this was your fourth letter to us. (Tina, before falling asleep last night, mentioned that you would *soon* be home: unfortunately, not true, but it showed her eagerness to see you again.) At the same time we realize from those very same letters how restricted you are, I hope for your sake but also for *yours*, that Lolo is back in Malabon. As usual there is no vacation for you; first Rolf and a camcorder, then virtually a patient yourself, and the bills eating away at money you expected for your property but apparently may not get! These circumstances could make me continually angry if I dared brood over them. You deserve better and the possibility of your seeing Hermy and others, finally make me sleep better.

You want good news from us, and I'll try to give some. But first I have to tell you that Bob Monahan died; his funeral was yesterday, but I had to teach. Dora collected for flowers, but if Tina and I can find a Mass card, well send that, too.

Tina had an exam yesterday (math) and may not have done well. Tina will see if she can get a tutor of some sort, since no one on her floor is helpful. But otherwise she seems happy—happier by the week. She'll write about her flight plans. You arrive in NY March 4.

Tina leaves for Wisconsin early March 5: so you may miss each other! You never said exactly when you might return to Boston. *I* sure hope *soon*. Roma said Rita fell on ice, New Year's Day and hurt her head and neck somewhat though Rita didn't mention this when we called to get Jan's phone.

Tina went to the Primate Center today & will again tomorrow. She not only has been assured a job there, but two different departments are after her. *That* keeps her spirits up also.

Tomorrow I will go to St. Mary's chapel (BC) for an anniversary Mass for Evelio Javier. Invitation by Phil Martin, just back from the Philippines after years.

I did receive two copies of *Solidarity* (July-September issue) w/ my piece on Salonga, Yuson, but not yet the issue with my piece on Rosca, which I mailed him one year ago, and possibly would have been used w/ shorter reviews, before July. If you can reach him by phone…He once said that if these issues don't arrive, he'll airmail one: well, Rosca is overdue. On the other hand, my article on Cirilo Bautista appeared in Jan in Wally Bacon's magazine so I feel better – more productive. If only now Rodriguez has my ms in hand & will use it.

Tina remains enamored of Dumas—even asked to be brought home Sunday despite a snowstorm which made me hesitate at first. But Dumas is frisky and needs to be walked soon; for which they have leashes, believe it or not.

I made a respectable sinigang, so I'll try again, and an adobo, much darker than yours but according to the cookbook by Reynaldo Alejandro. We'll try it tonight.

We're both glad to hear you feel healthy, though we worry about your lack of sleep. Life (people) just isn't fair.

I have applied for a summer grant, to organize a new course (I'll call it tentatively "Third World American Literature) to "supplement" the AHANA course which is exclusively Black Studies. But knowing campus politics & also possible competition, I have no illusion. Just thought I would do it and forget it.

Despite storms the weather has been normally in the 40s and 50s.

Stay well, try to have some *fun*, try to see Tina before she leaves. Love, Len. Feb 10, 1990.

*

Dear Linda,

Two of your letters (Feb 1 and 13) arrived together (!) today; but that's not why I'm writing. I have been waiting to have enough clear time, so that I could read your novel. The department took forever to hire two persons (neither one my choice), then of course I have been taking Tina back and forth to Brandeis, caring for the house, bunny and plants; & teaching. Finally, I turned in my applications for a summer grant, then spent all of yesterday and today, reading. I've finished despite all that, only Book I: 232pp. But I want this in the mail, as my last letter to you. I hope you are in Marikina: what a run around you're caught in.

Although I read making punctuation corrections, etc., I think Bk I moves well. Benhur is somewhat too sad to stay inside him too long; but the mailman is there, Sally Vergel, Osong, Mig and Joel, to help break the first 100 pp away from pure melancholy. Then Sr. Madeleine! Brilliant. And after that, an introduction to Cayetano (who, I presume, will end the novel), and Patro (her 30pp too long w/o a break? I'm not sure). Anya and Patro's mother-in-law (fine scene): the vaciador (*always great*), and the Osong party wf/ word of the coup. Proportion and pace I haven't been able to assess perfectly yet; but they seemed ok to me. As long as *something/someone* of interest has the readers' attention...

Only occasionally were there stumbles, and always from the same source. This is a novel about "the people," I know; fine; but sometimes too *many* people are mentioned in the same breath; without adequate identification. I had to figure out who Lola Sula is because *everyone's* lola and because you don't give her name at all when she's first mentioned, chapters before the third from the end. So, she just needs to be given a name sooner and the reader be reminded who she is, later. Almost the same with Anya: the reader (I, for one) will think she's Loreto's sister unless reminded. And in the first part of Patro's section, it took too long to figure out that Cleophas was the husband, Demetrio the son, and the children, the latter's. Easy to remedy. Just be kind to your reader, who first of all doesn't know Philippine culture where everyone's related and second, the exact *pattern* of identity you have in mind.

But the impression I get is that these 232 pp are *polished* with those few little glitches; &; and I'm anxious to read the rest--& I will this weekend, when Tina works two days w/ her monkeys.

Today she made a good impression on Uritam (in War & Aggression) because she answered back a boy who said if it weren't for the US, the Philippines would collapse, etc. Uritam even invited her (half-jokingly, I think) to lecture on the US-P relationship. *And* she has also impressed her Brandeis teacher on her knowledge of primates. Only math—And she's supposed to get a tutor. Those courses where she can speak up are her best--& give her confidence.

I'm sorry your father hasn't recovered easily and that Baby has to tend now to a sick Rolf just makes me angrier, w/ people's unreasonableness. As usual you will need rest when you arrive here. I've been writing, I guess, how much I miss your body, but reading this novel—a *major* work—reminds me of your heart, & of your soul: & I (Tina, too) miss that also. By the time you receive this, you probably will be packing. I hope no one gets some new idea of making you a beast of burden. Enough! Already!

The *Hawaii Pacific Review* will run "In Place of Trees" in April & wanted biodata. So I just sent your resume, w/ a hasty note. I don't know if your Ateneo collection includes acknowledgment of source.

Don't worry about the gold chain, if you can't get down into Manila. I understand. It means more to me, actually that Rodriguez received, I hope, my ms, because some of those essays are too timely to be reprinted in 1991—if possible, it should come out this year.

The good news here includes a sale at Jordan Marsh of the bed-sofa you liked, at $300 less than the Xmas price. But we'll wait for your arrival, so you can decide if it should be red, green or blue. I remember you especially liked the springs: Posturepedic.

I can't think of anything else.

*

Dear Linda

It was good to hear your voice…

I'll write a separate letter soon, knowing it takes almost two weeks to get to you.

But I wanted you to know that Tina's test scores are no fair indication of her preparations. What can one do, if a teacher tries to test memory-work on 300 pp, for example. But her math is improving, and her classroom presence persists. If only these teachers do what I do: use classroom participation as the *principal* source of grading (because most extensive)…Your call really lightened some of her remaining burden of inadequate self-confidence. We help each other a lot, that way. *We miss you, because we prize your opinion of us.*

You have received Mass cards from Rita Alberini, the DMG, Polleys, McGiverns, SOM (ourselves: a novena), the Puliaficos, Scotts, Louie/Mary, Rita/Joe, Rose Kodad, notes of condolences from Darlene Arden and her mother; Nancy Eddy, the Wellesley P.E.N. Your father was so good and suffered so long, surely God does not need these affirmations of worth. He must be happier where he is now, and maybe some of the grace of prayers can be "spent" by him on others like us still in need. You also have a cryptic, friendly letter from a Father Kwiothokowski, now in Rome. God and your parents bless you. Len. March1990! Letter from Tina in back.

21

1992

Dear Linda,

 It's 7:30 am, one week after you left. I've had no breakfast because my belly is about to burst, from overeating, "psychological compensation"? While I wait to get a haircut let me get down some of my thoughts.

 I hope the typhoon that hit Guam has missed you. The Mid South US states had a series of tornadoes, but all we've had here is torrential rains: everyone, but Dumas, has a cold; we're not complaining. Did I tell you that taking her to the vet went without a hitch (except that she wouldn't speak to me the rest of the day). They gently put a dye in her eye; and examined it under a special light (which Tina understands, we've exchanged about three calls so far). Result: no scratch in eye but a slight infection. I could barely get Dumas to behave so I could put medicine in her eye. But it's cured now, and I am probably overfeeding her as I have myself.

 I've gone to Yen's Wok once, made spaghetti for two meals, pork sinigang for two (with cabbage). Otherwise, I am eating what you left—and will on Thanksgiving as well: the Rock hen, etc. Josie is taking medicine...diverticulitis (avoiding food with seeds), and Luisa doesn't really feel well and may drop out of caroling; so they were both gracious about inviting me, I just as graciously just wished them a

Happy Thanksgiving. (There will be a 9am Mass that day. Dumas won't go)

Friday, of course I ate at Edna's and passed out Tina's questionnaire (with my annotation and self-addressed envelopes) about 10. The kids generously agreed; but I warned Tina later that, despite their real affection for her, and their good will, they are very much involved with caroling and rondalla and may forget. I'm depending on Cynthia, Krishna, Christi Anne to remember and remind. Anyway, we practice again the day after Thanksgiving and Sunday as well, so I'll carry spare questionnaire for anyone who lost theirs. We finally have one old song, "Do You Hear What I Hear." The men's song is clever but too rapid for Bob Ott and myself, so we'll be straggling. Christi Anne's ear is so sharp, though she sort of avoids eye contact with me when she's complaining (to her father) about the bases. We start performing the first weekend in December|.

I find I need vacuum only 3 rooms: porch, kitchen and study. I'm taping Poirot and Secret Agent. Hope everyone there enjoyed the tapes sent.

Now for the heart of this week's experience. I miss your presence, I miss little conversations with you. I miss your body. I really think I'd go wacko without Dumas (classes of course are virtually non-existent this week). What helps is your manuscript. I have often said that you write beautifully about lovely people, the 100 pages which you left, of *Stranded Whale* are as good as anything you've ever done (though different of course from your contemporary pieces) I think the 9 chapters are so readable because you had large characters to draw on and because each chapter is virtually self-sustaining: not quite as complete as short stories, but filled w/ detail, movement and suspense. And you have orchestrated the narrators in masterly fashion, and together they move the historic background forward. Aside from miniscule changes in punctuation, the only negative "complaint" I can make is that I think each chapter needs, at the top, a reminder of where the location is (I'm still hoping for an American audience), as well as minutiae of time. But if each book can be kept to 100 pages, this should be the best in your trilogy of the late 19th century. I couldn't be prouder as the dedicatee, if I had written these pages myself.

I have also sent "Happy" to *Story*.

Give my respects to Tia Mameng, my regards to Doding and Frieda (the way she should really spell her name) and to NVM if you see him; and Frankie, of course You have my love always (it can never be adequate to what you deserve). BC beat Army and will go to Hall of Fame Bowl in Tampa; Flutie may win a Canadian award; Tina's Saints keep winning. Love, really: Len. 11/24/92.

*

Dear Linda,

10am and I just came back from Mass—for Tina's report but it also turned out to be Henry Bradley's death anniversary. I sat with Dora.

Today will be a busy one. Besides preparing my grad class, I'll make spaghetti for the week, and if there's time later, put lights outside. Irene who asked about you doesn't plan to decorate her tall evergreen this year, because both boys are in the Carolinas. But others have begun to put lights outside, and it is so nice coming home in the dark. Besides the weather will be clear. In the 40s today.

I tried bathing Dumas the other day, and I didn't know how to get under her except with the spray; but at least she doesn't smell any more, yet. She was angry for a day, but now follows me around as if anxious. I probably over-feed her…but her eye seems fine.

TIAA at least is on their toes and asked exactly *when* I would retire. Benefits to begin in August, after they send me another form and information. It's only the health coverage now. (We should be under Pilgrim until August, when Medicare should kick in, supplemented by Cobra (for 15 months), then Medex. These are matters I'll go to BC about in February. I will teach only in the fall of 93, and exactly the two courses I suggested: Cross Cultural American Lit and Recent Fiction by American Women. That frees me the winter of '94, if you can get a Bellagio grant anytime in that period.

This Friday we carol in Medway (Luisa dropped out, I'll be with the Abriams; Saturday noon at Liloy's house, so I can get to the caroling. In the afternoon we do Forgacs.

The men's song is "Ikaw ang Mahal Ko"—and I dedicate it now to you, if the translation is as Mabini said: Ikaw ang mahal ko/Ikaw ang mahal kong tunay na tunay/Ang lagging panaginip ko'y tanging ikaw/Nguni't ang totoo/Madalas mong mapag-alinglanganan/Ang puso kong tapat sa pagsintang di mo alam/ Ang pag-ibig kung lubusan/Kay hirap maunawaan/Sa puso ko ang pagsintang Dalisay/Laging wagas kahit mapagbintangan.

I try to keep busy enough to fall asleep easily at night, so that missing you won't be as bad...

Tina tries to keep in touch and seems calm, less anxious than Dumas. I'll be sending Gretchen and Frank the batik and cookies soon.

Since Doding won't come to LA until January, all the more reason you should mail the books and carry one bag only. I did receive your airletter yesterday. That helps.

Good to hear that Tia Mameng is still with us.

I am sending a belated anniversary card separately.

I hope you actually get to see Hermy and the others and that your remaining weeks won't be all bedside tending. I will write weekly for a while, and perhaps call on weekends for whatever I will remember I did not include here just as soon as I seal this.

I also want to reread as much of Stranded Whale as I can (probably Thursday). I have often said that your works are filled with wisdom and penetrating perceptions. Some day you will find time to read more of your works and find your best self, there.

Now I should make my sandwiches for today's lunch (and tomorrow at school). It teaches me to appreciate how you have had to interrupt one thing to get to another. Love, Len. Dec 1, 1992.

22

1998

Linda dearest,

    At 7:30 pm there is lightning around us and a promise of heavy rains. So far we have received little, but anything is better than seeing the grass brown so soon, before summer and we hope to have real rain during the next few days.

    I overate as usual (at Rileys, getting a haddock plate that made two heavy meals), rested while watching (in the dusk) wren-sized birds flirting on the apple tree, then I thought of writing you, even before it will be another week before you get this.

    The best news is that, of course, your voice does not delete on the new phone; and even if you don't quite sound like yourself (transmission, jet lag?) there you are, and I can hear your voice every day.

Tina and I have spoken ever since you left (daily), but soon she'll be in Orlando.

It will take me a week at least just to eat everything you prepared in the fridge. By then I'll inventory what's in the freezer. It teaches me, on a small scale, how you always thought out our meals and prepared them twice a day. Although I miss your bodily presence, these tokens and your telephone voice give substance to your saying you love me

Sunday, I went to church to have Olan Miller do my photo. Apparently, our paired photo will be kept towards the "album's" rear, in black & white, and only my photo taken, today, in your gift of that blue Turkish shirt, will appear in the normal lineup.

It was 90 today and humid – but I can't complain knowing that it's the same in Metro Manila; and at least I can drive to church and to stores; and it will go back to the 70s soon. In fact I have to be careful not to let my sinuses fill up again. Your cold sounded ok, on the phone; but you should take it easy, too.

I painted the back steps that's why I didn't hear the phone at 2pm, until I came in I saw that you had left a message. I hope there is some way that when you call the charge will come here. But I know that, usually you'll be too busy with parties and preparations and seeing old friends (my love to Luz and Hermy), so that I really don't expect calls or letters. Enjoy your stay. I hope that all goes well—and that some small part of what I sent you become a birthday present for Kate.

I think the rain is going north and south of us, even the thunder seems far away. But I put up our three window fans today, and that will help evenings, for sleeping.

I am so glad that God is with you. Love, Len. May 29, 1998.

*

Dear Linda,

The last day of May. But not the end of May.

It's 7:30 am, Sunday morning, but my dry cough bothers me so I may simply attend Mass on TV. I hope your own cold is faring better than mine. But I still have 2 ½ weeks to get well.

I am sending separately (so you'll get more mail) a nice note from Bonnie Crown (But I'll save your check from her here). She's still bouncy and one of your real fans. Did you ever send her a copy of *DreamEden*? How nice to have someone who reads and reads well. (Like Tina's response) Makes the work of writing worthwhile.

That reminds me. I reread *Circular Firing Squad* straight through yesterday. I know it can't compare with your own novellas; but it moves fast and has some things to say about 1983; so I'll retype it and send it either to Anvil or Giraffe. It has some evil characters, prone to violence: but that's true of the Marcos years. I wrote it probably, about 1985; before his fall, one summer while you were away. I wrote it for an uninterested US audience (paperback?), knowing it was unsafe to try for a Manila publication. Now, let's see.

It has been in the high 80s and getting humid (I go out only early or late), but rain is predicted off and on for the next several days.

Time out for Mass. And peace to Fr. Maguire, but I must say the Monsignor's Mass at Roslindale was unbeatable. About Pentecost and God's individualized plan for us, collectively. And I couldn't help but think that though my career at BC is virtually ended, my mission is not: as a writer, I continue to "teach" (not indoctrinate the invisible student body—relationships—wherever and whatever). So, I feel very good this morning, despite having breathing problems. I so wanted to attend yesterday's evening Mass and to sing for Mary and I feel especially close to you because of Bonnie's letter and I know you two have a mission, and I am grateful to be on its healing (not cutting) edges.

Just as I enjoy, vicariously, the wonderful times you are having/*will* have in the Philippines…despite difficulties you might be having, breathing.

Tina is off to Orlando; Luisa will be back Tuesday night.

Above all, God is not through with us yet. Love, Len. May 31, 1998.

*

Linda sweetheart,

Last night, (the last day of May) I wasn't sure that I'd be around to write you. We were the target of violent storms and occasional tornadoes that started in the Dakotas (10 dead) and did a lot of damage in Michigan and Upper NY state, brought down big oaks in Worcester and well, they warned that the East Coast should be on the alert until 2am; but by 10pm I was so sleepy, I turned over the outdoor chairs and brought in your plants from that table, then went to bed. Not with my clothes on but with them nearby. They say that tornadoes sound like heavy freight trains, and I awakened several times last night, thinking that's what I heard, and downpours like the typhoons I remember from Malabon, but the lightning never was followed by thunder, and it seemed the worst track was along the north Massachusetts, lower New Hampshire border. We'll know later today where whatever damage was done occurred. It may be mostly fallen trees, with only rare deaths from trees falling on occupied cars.

We (the entire neighborhood) had no damage at all. I awoke at 5:30 this morning to a bright clear day. I even saw a male cardinal flying around.

So all my prayers last night (plenty of them) *were* answered. I went to Market Basket after breakfast and returned in time for Mass on TV. And also with enough money left to buy a spreader and some weed-and-feed from Home Depot later. Then I cut the grass in front and had lunch. (I'm almost through with all the good food left in the fridge, now I'll inventory the freezer.)

I took enough time yesterday to read through *The Circular Firing Squad* and am happy to find that it is worth offering for publication: it is rough in terms of violent action (though undescribed), and the characters are not as memorable as I would wish, but *some* of the metaphors are fresh and striking. And 1983 was a moment in history (though I could never compete with *your* profound insights and remarkable language) so I'll copy it and send it to Anvil. If she rejects it I'll ask her to send it to Giraffe. If neither...

Speaking of books, the mailman just delivered a check and royalty statement from Ateneo for *Common Continent* and *10,000 Seeds!* Still selling reasonably well. Though I don't know what she means by Version 1/2/3/4: it has nothing to do with paper (book or newsprint). Anyway, she sent pesos, about the equivalent of $46, And though I know it's a risk, I'm going to mail it to you *there* so you can use it to celebrate, (You're apparently getting only10% royalty).

I'm proud of, and I like to speculate on who your readers are and what they think, and…Love, Len. June 1, 98.

*

Dear Linda,

It's almost 6 pm, I've finished a ham and your meal, I know what tomorrow's weather will be (autumn cool and very windy) so I'll first sit here in the porch, digest and write you the news of the day.

No Marist showed up this morning; so Randy Hogan suggested we do the readings and gospel, the Lord's Prayer and receive pre-consecrated hosts. That we did. (I imagine something of this sort goes on in the world where priests are not always handy.) I think it worked well.

I have been somewhat housebound, these past few days (except for the Post Office and today's Mass).

I have avoided outside work: no hedge trimming. I really hope to do some of that before visiting Tina, though I may not do it as thoroughly as last year. My body is resisting me, not the germs, or books.

The blue flowers are gone, the white (daisies?) are splendid; and the mountain laurels are beginning to look pale, and the rhododendrons are really through. I think the hostas will soon start. I like the leisure but not the laziness, which I think can become unhealthy. I read a lot now, either books I'll teach in a month, or books by the same authors so I can speak of them in depth.

Some news I'll tell you by phone (especially when I hear how Larry continues to be): but McAleer called and has written his referee piece; Luisa returned –but being independent didn't want me to pick her up; Tina called once from their Orlando hotel–weather and exhibits are both better than they expected; Dora took to church the letter you got from some Marianist group for the Daily Mass Group, and several people asked about you, in church today.

Luisa is wondering how Baby's health is.

I sent about 200 words about *DreamEden* to the News Notes bulletin of *MELUS* (Multi Ethnic Literature US) one never knows who will notice it and what they'll do, but…

It's so nice sometimes: I have to remind myself just to sit; occasionally, on the porch & enjoy nature. Only one cardinal once day but plenty of jays and finches. Despite heavy rains, the apple leaves seem to be drying fast. Thanks for letting us keep this house/location.

I hope you are getting over your jet lag and that friends find a way to get to you, since traffic for you is so disgustingly slow. Give my regards to the Ramiros, thank Ranvin for turning over the phone to you so fast, and of course my heartfelt wishes for Brother Francisco when you meet. But above all, my love to you. Len. June 4, 1998.

*

Dear Linda,

This letter will be a pastiche, from time to time telling you whatever I can, although "breaking news" as they say on TV—I'd have called you about. But only the good news then.

It rained hard last night, so once again, I'm delaying hedge work. Besides I feel tried from having helped Luisa pick up Mama at Logan last night (almost 10 pm arrival) and I always wake up at dawn now 5:30-6am. so I simply got a few things at Market Basket, and I'm doing this now before lunch: tomatoes and chicken bleu which you left.

The priest pointed out the Greek roots of euthanasia means "God is in us" (I should have remembered that from the 17th century concern with people being too fanatically "enthusiastic" religiously. Holly Rollers., etc., like todays' charismatics. Anyway, I told myself I'm still low on energy because of my chest cold; but I do feel God is in us--and you, too, in me--like a guardian angel. That's more important than the cycles of nature outside and about controlling them. (The rhododendrons are through, and the lilacs; the peonies at least did bloom this time—no reason to transplant them. Gradually the mountain laurels will give up also.) About time for the hostas to start; and several poppies opened; and pots of gold, the bleeding hearts are hanging on; the mille fleures are about ready. All these compensate for the return of insects to the leaves of trees in back.

And I saw a slow heron fly by this morning during breakfast.

I left word for Tina, last night, to call me because the news has been of bad fires (forests) around Orlando, and I worried that they'd be delayed. But they had come in on Saturday; not Sunday, because she's teaching today. She called and said neither felt very good (no details) and she'd contact me tonight. Probably a form of cold.

Mama seemed full of pep and good memories. They had put her in an empty Class A seat and she had wheelchairs, etc. So I'm offering to take her to Chinatown this week.

Hey, guess what! Either I have more to say than I thought, or this airletters don't hold much. So there's no point in not finishing this letter. The so-called anthology that months ago accepted three of my "nature" poems, actually used only two. So I've reread the third, like it very much, and will try it now as a loner. And the ex-student Mike Brien who wanted me to write a preface for his collection meanwhile sent me a new story. (He's the ex-composer of spirituals. So what the other priest said last week—about the importance of patience applies. And I remember long ago when we returned from Malabon to find our non-paying renter gone and our picture frames burned, we bought our first big Persian rug.

Way to go! Depression is too depressing. God keeps testing us. *He* loves *us*. I love *you*. Len. June 9, 1998.

*

Dear Linda,

Yes, it's still officially Independence Day here, and the Philippine flag is still in front. But it is 1:30 pm, not 8:30 when you called this morning. (apparently 9:30 pm your time, according to the operator. I'm sitting in the porch, an eye out for raindrop, the first sign of which will make me furl the flag. We are promised rain, sometimes heavy today, (Friday) Saturday through Wednesday at least. I hope it has cleared by late that day since 6 am I fly to California. Well, nature is not that adaptable, so *we* must be. In your case, at least, drink plenty of liquids.

We hung up just in time for me to watch Mass. Then I decided to go to BC since I've spent days reading what I *wanted/ needed* to check my mail there and also my plants. One was drying up so I was able to keep it going until I return. The other one a jade plant has needed repotting for a long time; so I brought it home and after a quick lunch of canned mackerel (that will be my supper, too), I got a small bag of potting soil from Star.

I felt good to do that little rescue job, and I think your call restored me as well (though I had planned to call today 8:30 pm Boston time. There were two good pieces of mail the *Columbia Journal of American Studies* will use two articles of mine sometime this year yet: "A Curandero Triptych: Albuquerque (Anaya), Ceremony (Silko), and *Dreaming in Cuban* all of which grew out of my diversity course at BC. That's in addition to my two (old) poems being published in California by the Dept of Education.

Then Russell Leung of *Amerasia* (UCLA) has asked not to use my article on you (& 3 other Filipinas) for their magazine, but instead to put it into Volume 2 (due for September 1) in a commemorative sequence on Philippine-US Relations. I wish the essay would have been on *your* work only (as it was in an encyclopedia entry that I did a few months ago) but I know some editors fear some *other* critic's complaining of "nepotism" or "incest" if a husband spoke only of his wife's work. This is all so unfair: I have tried to train myself and others in objectivity, but as only you too well know Filipinos like to question my honesty by ignoring the special value in *your* writing. *Sayang*! Except for Frankie, NVM and Franz.

Incidentally, Leung asked if I knew that (a new version of NVM's "Winds of April" is out (the 1940 prize-winner). I don't know who the publisher is but you can possibly bring home a copy.

Meanwhile I have to put *Amerasia's* article on diskette by July 30. I'll check to see if it's already been "saved," as you always warn me to do. If not, maybe Luisa can instruct me here how to do it.

It's good to hear that, despite heat and congestion, you are not wholly housebound. I hope your P1000 check arrives safely. Until I have good news again, Love, Len. June 12, 1998.

*

Dear Linda,

It's 7:30 am, and even the river is quiet. I've lost track of how many days (4-5) we've had of heavy rain—I bailed, I mopped a fraction of an inch in our basement, scooped the garage which would dry if the sun ever comes out again. I think I told you that inside 128 there was real flooding (cars in underpasses; basements) so I decided it wasn't safe to go to Father Woods' anniversary Mass in West Roxbury. Seeing couples pushing cars in underpasses in Route 9 reminded me of Tom, and I told myself not to be heroic. The big rivers--Neponset and Charles--were beyond their banks; the Sudbury was not too bad, although water from these major rivers were being diverted. But though it still rains daily, no more downpours; and I've decided Thursday, the 18th, just to drive directly to Logan on the Turnpike. That way, coming home late at night, I can just find the car and take off. By the time you receive this I would have seen Tina and made my turnaround. I'll write again when I'm home.

I'll show Tina your first letter. It's so good to know that you can exercise, a little in the morning; and occasionally not just talk with friends but see them & go to Barasoain, etc. You lead just as active (ever busy) life here, I suppose adjusting to the slower tempo (& heat and traffic) these must be frustrating at time, although Freida surely enjoys your company. Here, although I seem caught up in "trivia" (mailings, food preparation—there's plenty left, I'm on lechon, pochero--this week, hedge trimming (still unfinished), time goes quite fast. As we turn to July, of course, I will be slightly overwhelmed for a while. I hope the weather is June-July like, back to normal.

Luisa and Mama took me to Ruby Tuesday, this Sunday, and I'll be at Dora's tonight—with Kay and Ed. After Mass this morning, I'll pick up my "Four Filipinas" ms and the diskette which Kinko's put the ms onto and mail them both to *Amerasia* and UCLA both. I wrote your (anonymous) advertising manager at U Washington, suggesting they make whatever deal is required to have *DreamEden* listed on *Filipinas* "collectible page": we'll see if anything happens.

Today, I'll remember also to leave a "Stop Mail" at the Post Office, for the weekend. I'm half packed (90% clothes), and I'll do the mid-week watering of your indoor plants and think if there's anything else I should/can do about the house before I leave very early, before sun-up—on Thursday. (Today is Tuesday).

I see that someone wants Imelda acquitted; and Marcos will be buried among real heroes. How short memories are! But not mine, of you: sometimes I literally feel your presence still in this house. Love, Len. 6/16/98.

*

Dear Linda,

I really hadn't planned to write you today, since as usual--trying to be prudent—I will roam the house today to make sure I haven't forgotten to pack anything important for tomorrow. But I have been struck by how good and often very relevant the homilies have been on the TV Masses. Even McFarland had things to say today, without facial muscular movements. He remarked that the Mass, though satellite, goes all over the nation; and many write to "ask if such a Mass is doing them any good."

And he explained that it is the next best thing to the Eucharist. It is an act of faith and participation. And I couldn't help thinking that that is what I feel when I say that even in your absence you are present. I don't mean simply that I look up in the direction that you typically have been, or I wish I had followed your instruction and saved on diskette my 21-page essay on "Four Filipina Writers" which *Amerasia* will use. (To resolve the problem without bothering Luisa who won't know or a while if she has a job with Company or not, I had Kinki scan the article for $9.95 and put it on disk.)

Done. Mailed. Or I wish I had learned more on how to use your camera. (Tina's rose has 6 flowers so far!) or exactly where that plant should be. Or I dream of touching your legs, etc, in bed. But even beyond that, I feel we are less remote than space says. Then McFarland read the gospel about Elijah leaving his son behind & going straight to heaven. What a nice Fathers' Day parable.

That reminds me that I read your letter to Tina over the phone last night.

Dora gave a scrumptious Fathers' Day meal--Kay, Ed, me-- more of despedida for me.

The rain has basically stopped, though the flowers (bent and battered) could use sunshine. I will wake tomorrow at 3, leave at 4, to arrive at Logan by Turnpike, by 5 for the 6am flight. I expect no special trouble, though there may be some early fog.

Some things I can't do anything about. Just go to bed early, hope I can sleep; & pray.

Josie also called last night. They've been back from Turkey; several days. The priest–leader was excellent (except that he recommended massages in Turkey without realizing that—young men, not women were the masseuse). She was asking when you return and of course was inviting me, until I told her how tied up I'll be until the first week of July.

Hey, this letter is beginning to take shape, so maybe I'll mail it today anyway. Glad you're exercising in the morning. Can go to Barasoain, Thousand Islands and Pansol. Away from major pollution. And Clark Field.

I have eaten papaya here, too, though I know it can't compare with Doding's tree in back. And I will have lechon that you left & pochero. etc. when I return from California. I'm sure that I won't be able to run out of foods that you prepared.

I wish I knew the names of the flowers you planted, so many surviving the storm: many blues, and whites, and the coral bells are trying to stand up again. When I return will be time enough to fertilize, top the evergreen tree-hedge. Yesterday was clear enough so that I took a chance: literally rolled out our bedroom window onto the roof, to clear the gutter and to re-attach a vertical gutter which the weather and horrific torrents some days ago separated.

I've seen ducks again. But not your swan. The birds must have taken a beating. The squirrels, too.

Well, I'll call when I get back from Tina—next Tuesday? Remember to rest. Remember that I love you and know that you love me. Len. June 17, 1998.

*

Dear Linda,

Tina as you well know never holds anything back; and she planned a great weekend, even though she often has a cough about which she was to see a doctor yesterday after I left. (I tried to call her on my return—near midnight here—but she was out. I'll try again tonight.) It worked out for the first several days. Tina and I were a pair, and that seemed like old times.

Now, here's the schedule-that-was. Tina took me to the Discovery Museum (basic archeology) next to the RR Museum in old Sacramento, then we had a great meal a block away at the Rio City Café on the waterfront (chicken fusilli). That night we all three ate at the Little Prague in Davis, my favorite spot now, really Czech food amid central European décor; the owner/manager very genuine. I had smoked pork chops with sauerkraut and potato pancakes and Czech beer.

Day 2: 6/19

Tina and I went to the Sacramento Zoo: very big and varied, though lots of kids (well-behaved though). We ate at a tiny place, which alas, I hardly remember, Le Bou, but it, too was pleasant. I had clam chowder and French bread sandwich with eggplant, pesto. tomato, lettuce. Tina said one of the good things about going "vegetarian" is that it does away with constipation. Very thoughtful. Now a small friendly restaurant. Lentils, yellow peas, collard greens, eggplants; no silverware but all of these foods fairly easy, (if messy) to pick up by hand using what they're served on a plate-sized very thin pancake material, easily broken off and twisted around the food. Quite spicy.

Afterwards to the latest Disney movie about a Chinese girl who replaces her old father when the emperor calls for defense against the Huns who have breached the walls of China. Of course, she has to dress like a boy, but is heroic and exemplary and impresses the general's son who has replaced his dead father. Beautifully drawn so that one would wish it were longer, though Tina points out that, for kids' sake, Disney things are usually kept to 1 ½ hours.

One of the previous nights, Tina had shown a sample video, at home, of the places they visited in Orlando, and she explained in detail each of the exhibits they visited. She loves to talk, has a memory for detail—like yours—and therefore makes a great teacher—and therefore I hope she can get rid of her cough fast: my throat was always one of my concerns.)

Day 3. 6/20.

Sunday. Farmer's Market in Davis. Then a visit to the State Capitol Museum, largely to see the Assembly and the Senate legislative areas, and on to Fort Sutter Museum, where people play appropriate roles the way they do at the Plymouth Plantation here. Minor reenactments. Some personnel played roles well. Then into another part of Sacramento, to eat Ethiopian; remember the place. Le Bou, a clean modern place, proud be a bakery, and it serves only small items. Then Tina and I went to the Crocker Art Museum, a gorgeous mansion with the most beautiful woodwork, that I have ever seen in a house, so that the ballroom for example was better than the art they collected—which included a whole room of someone's fishing scenes. But the sculpture was okay, and some Korean pottery. Then Tina showed me new portions of UC Davis, including llamas and cows, an equestrian section under development. (Hey, I just looked outside and saw a bright male cardinal!) Dinner, with David, we had at Symposium:

not a pretentious place but with a menu better than the Greek restaurant near here: retsina, vegetarian moussaka, pistachio cake.

Day 4: 6/21.

Fathers' Day 8 am Mass at Saint James. A lovely place as you remember; and everybody sang! Then we picked off a few more picnic items and off to Muir Woods, down near San Francisco. Hard to find a parking space at first but well worth the walk that followed. We had to eat in the car: apricots, big turkey and ham sandwiches on Farmers' Market bread (poppy, sesame and caraway) with an underlay of dried tomato spread.

But what a gorgeous walk through the woods (we did the midwalk Bridge 3, if you recall) We were all so glad that you recommended Muir. Not only the height of the trees, but the way they made burls out of which new growth proceeded which buttressed the original tree, so that trees had several collective trunks. And yes they did resemble Gothic pillars in a cathedral! Very tiring, but...Stellar jays, butterflies, redwoods, laurels...I got you one of several booklets of the place to tickle your own recollections.

Back to Davis and dinner at the Saigon Café: a sweet and sour shrimp soup which Tina and I shared, lemongrass chicken, catfish in a clay pot, rice, chicken curry and coconut juice. A place as simple as what I recall the Cambodian restaurant (no longer there) but the food was good. To top off the night we went to Little Prague for dessert, especial teas and Black Forest cake. And so bed after final; packing.

Day 5: 6/22

In the morning I went to ARC with Tina for her "lab" which again she handled so efficiently; students were to do things with about a dozen skeletal pieces. I liked watching her instruct and guide; then they broke up to make their examinations and she circulated among them, I read part of the text they use. Her lab was followed by her lecture course (some of the same students whom we had met at the Zoo, doing an assignment there), so we had to say our final goodbyes;

and David who had been at Sierra meanwhile, came in good time and whisked me away to the airport—and insisted on staying with me because there was an unusually large crowd there (other fathers I presume). Safely off.

Three of the four planes which I took that weekend were 2x2 across and the meals were only breakfast and lunch, so First Class was not imposing, but it did allow plenty of leg room and a choice of no conversation; so I do thank you for your frequent flyers.

From St. Paul to Boston we had a big DC 10 (maybe picking up bigger load in Boston for overseas), and there was only a scattering of us in First Class. So I went to a window (to avoid storms we flew at 20,000, not 30 thousand feet), and the food was Chinese pork and noodle dish with wine. I missed Tina as a meal companion, but at least the food seemed special. The alternative was chicken teriyaki: and I had had enough chicken by then. Our landing was perfect, and the car was handy and I was home by midnight.

It was so good to hear your voice on Father' Day, since we had been thinking of you in Muir Woods already: and Tina was in a nice reminiscent mood earlier in the weekend though she keeps apologizing she was only two years old when she first went to Hong Kong But what she remembers, she remembers well and I know she was a happy child and is happy now. I will remember that most of all; I know that you are responsible for shaping, sharpening her life's perceptions, and for that reason I felt close to you also by being so much with her this weekend. If I say I love you (and I do) and you ask why; well, here's one overwhelming reason. I'm proud of her intellect (one older student said I should be proud of her) but above all, her attitude towards life and all living things; for that, too; like Dumas, she's a good Christian and a fine Christian example to us all (especially me) and I think you are most responsible for that, too, And for that you are lovable, worthy of love.

And now I had better have some coffee and get this in the mail. 3:30 pm. before I fall asleep. Love, more than ever, Len 6/23/98.

*

Dearest Linda,

Here I sit, 7:15 am, no humidity, 60° on the porch (must remember to write bigger), with two letters from you nearby and a typically loving birthday card from Tina. Gretchen must be busy, readying for California but her birthday gift—a Thai wooden frame for a picture is in the next room.

All is peaceful here. The last days of Roma and Natalie were deceptively peaceful: that is, frankly boring. We had done Boston earlier, the college campuses, Plimoth Plantation, Concord, Colonial brunch, Longfellow Inn—all those during their first days, and I guess they were beginning to feel overfed and in need of leisure. By the weekend they were prostrate. I still wanted to show them Maine, we did go to the Aegean but that was a major concession on their part; and did go once to Hopkinton State Park—so Nat could get a tan!

All the more reason I treasured you call and Tina's—and look forward to holding you again (take care of your back). Apparently Roma's sinuses have kept bothering her; so I'm glad they came and am grateful; and life goes on.

Fr. John Coss appeared yesterday, and we cut down that dogwood, leaving a multi-stump some 3 ft high which he said can serve to hold a bird bath and some kind of ikon. He took away nearly a dozen small red cut leaf maple trees, and we have a tentative date when I will take him for lunch.

My body aches now (I dragged off only about 85% of the cuttings). I had every intent of carrying off the rest today; or cutting the grass in back but my body says those can wait. And I have a class tonight and need the energy for that.

With occasional showers, summer so far has been like a good springtime. Must take shots of your flowers. (Neither Roma nor Natalie wanted to pose). Your mail has piled up, as usual, but nothing so significant that I should send it ahead.

Cris Castro says there will be a rondalla exhibition in Lexington (Museum of National Heritage) two days after you return, but I didn't commit us.

I washed and replaced the beddings, and will prepare our bed one more time for your return (in my mind I touch you now: just for practice).

I seem to have a settled 13-14 students. The ones who have committed themselves seem very good. Have fun. Love to all. But a special love to you. Len. 7/98.

*

Dear Linda,

We are in the first (and I hope last) heat wave: over 90 for three days. But at least some rain is promised, and a return to the 80s.

I hope that Doding when he arrived remembered that I called yesterday (one day late!) to wish you a happy anniversary. Our 42nd. Sorry I was too bushed on the 14th to make a call then, but...

There's much to be done out of doors, and my energy flags. Not a good excuse, however. Tina didn't forget and called when I got back from class (a stable 13 people). We had a good talk. Gretchen had called earlier principally to say they have their tickets ready for Boston, for the Labor Day Conference, which they will attend for several days, then if one of us can pick them up from their hotel the following Wednesday (I have a class until 10 am), they'll join us at home for a few days. She seemed happy but extremely busy, as you can imagine, and when our conversation grew thin, she had to go. I'm so happy, myself, for them that I simply appreciated her call.

What I really thought I should do in this letter is to give you some idea of what to expect when you return. Above all, expect lots of loving body contact—along with whatever opportunities you need to refresh and recover. We still have rice and many of the smaller frozen containers of food which you made. I have gotten 4 days' worth of meals from the two spaghetti dishes.

The lechon and chicken stew are finally gone. But there are plenty of veggie meals which I probably need, and oranges and apples. Twice this weekend, I will be eating out with Fr. Coss and the Garcias. Doding said you have managed to see the Brothers, so I can relay that news to Coss. Did I tell you that Leon Miller's sister died?

Two days after you arrive, the IP mandolin players will present a rondalla at American Heritage in Lexington. And Birthright will be in touch with you. Everyone else has been fairly considerate. Protect your back and don't bring anything heavy, even if you're carrying only one suitcase.

Aside from my destroying the ricer, the house is in good shape; and I hope I can keep improving on the outdoors before the end of the month. Many many flowers are blooming though I don't know them well enough to give them names (I did take a few pictures); the cones are great as are the brown centered yellow flowers, the hostas of course, some pansies, the mille-fleures, the beebalm (I think those fuzzies around the apple trees, etc), lots of daylilies of various colors. The yuccas haven't started yet. Things around the peach tree probably need pruning, but not by me. You'll see. What I'm trying to say is your garden is alive and self-sustaining, so you won't have to be out there in this terrible heat, puttering about.

I'm also trying to say that I really do love you and am missing you terribly now/looking forward to climbing all over you. I don't want to think of any details or I will start to come unstuck. Luckily there will always be enough work to keep me monastic until you come.

I sent your novel to Bonnie; and a letter of inquiry to Rodriguez. Now I want to be a clinging husband again. Until then, and even then, Len. July, 1998. Both my calves hurt—like a double Charliehorse: the result of being too long on a ladder, clipping our bushes (on one side only).

23

2002

Linda dearest,

The Post Office claims they no longer make airletters, so…Anyway, this is *our* day: Dec 23rd years ago you accepted my proposal.

So the sun comes out, and the temperature no longer is night-time's 20. We had about an inch of wet rainlike snow, last night, now melting fast (1 pm).

It was good to hear your voice and that you had arrived safely. I will call Tina right away; and Gretchen some hours later. Since then Tina called on her own. So, the lonesomeness gets some relief. Gretchen asked *what* (not just how) I'm doing: and I told her I was "working up" Bulosan, sometimes for hours (rereading all of his letters e.g.) for the Monday lecture on Bulosan and Ben Santos. The problem will come with trying to say only what is most significant about each— *in one hour!* Without presuming that anyone has ever read either one. They just may have read something about Steinbeck and Saroyan, however, and that would help. And most seem of an age that they were kids during the Depression. Anyway, besides revealing some of the difficulties of the poor, especially abroad where they might have had unfulfillable expectations, what I want to emphasize is *resilience:* what beauty sometimes emerges from the dispossessed—as when Spanish restrictions on clothes produced the loveliest barongs.

I had hoped to send you word about your email; but though I have seen some (useless) email directed towards me, so far I have not managed to find *yours*. When I explained that to Tina, she immediately reached your mail, but said that Javier has not yet acknowledged your information.

Putting together two meals a day (breakfast is a breeze), I have come to appreciate more fully the problem you have of doing the same—except that thanks to you, I have the ready-mades you froze (plus 12 pieces of KFC) I've decided I'll reward myself on Mondays by making them on principal days that I eat out, after work.

Speaking of work: I raked all the leaves, to hold a cover around your flower beds yesterday, to help protect against the snow. And I replaced a cover that wind had blown off (not away, luckily). I also repacked my schoolbag to hold a copy apiece for my class—copies of *Stranded Whale* which we will be discussing as the course winds down in December.

The days seem fairly organized (less than a dozen of us at Mass these days: yesterday I missed in order to get a haircut.) And I sleep warm and well. I feel your presence (and even Tina's and Gretchen's since their phone calls) in the house, and so far I have allowed myself no time to feel lonely—time flies. (The porch light stopped working again, but…)

I forgot to ask you just when you go to Marikina; but you surely will be there by the time this letter arrives. I'll mail it now before the sun sets and the weather turns night-time wintry. The news is stable: the sniper remains uncaught and is making threats unless he is given $10 million! The French have offered a clue: a sharpshooter from their military supposedly disappeared after leaving for America…but no one has mentioned that again, so just maybe it *will* turn out to be true.

I love you intently and am so glad (as are both your daughters) that you are getting *some* of the attention you richly deserve. My best to the Ramiros—and to Edna; and (if they show up) to Jimmy Abad, Sister Teresa, Father Galdon...

I hope someone takes pictures of your "moment."

I want to keep very busy, so the time seems to move and you'll be back before...it really does comfort me, whenever I touch the chain around my neck. You are there, you are here. I do love you.

Love, Len. 10/23/02.

24

LEONARD CASPER PASSES AWAY

Len passed away in his sleep, on his 95th birthday yesterday. He wanted to be cremated and didn't want an obituary but I wrote down something to remember him by. We'll have a private service for him. Please keep him in your prayers. Love, Linda

*

Leonard Ralph Casper passed away in his sleep on his 95th birthday, July 6, 2018. He was born in Fond du Lac, Wisconsin to Louis Casper and Caroline Eder. He had three brothers and four sisters. Louis; Rose; Ruth; Leo; Larry; Rita; and Roma.

He married Linda Ty-Casper at San Juan Rizal, Philippines on July 14, 1956. They have two daughters, Gretchen G. Casper, professor of Political Science at Pennsylvania State University, and Kristina Elise Casper-Denman, professor of Anthropology at American River College, Sacramento.

Len was inducted into the US Military during World War II; and saw active service starting May 26, 1943; serving in Foreign Service 4 months, 6 days; in Continental Service, 2 years, 4 months, 11 days.

His specialty was Cannoneer, # 864. He was qualified as a Marksman Carbine June 13, 1944; was Grade Pfc. Army serial # 36 821 365. Organization: Battery A 389 the FA Battalion; 99th Infantry Division, 38th Field Artillery Regiment.

His battle campaigns included the Rhineland, Central Europe, Belgium, Czechoslovakia, Ruhr Valley. His decorations and citations were the World War II Victory Ribbon, American Theater Ribbon, EAME Theater Ribbon, Good Conduct Ribbon, 2 Bronze Stars. He received his Honorable Discharge, 2/12/46 at Camp Chafee, Arkansas.

Leonard with three brothers—Louis, Leo and Larry—and a sister, Rita, served in the US Army during World War II. Larry received the Purple Heart.

Len attended grade school at St, Joseph Church, Fond du Lac High School; and received his BA, MA and PhD from the University of Wisconsin where he was a graduate assistant.

He taught at Cornell University, University of the Philippines, Ateneo de Manila University, Philippine Normal College, was lecturer at several colleges in the Philippines, in Taiwan and in Thailand on grants from the American Philosophical Society, the Ford Foundation, ACLS-SSRC, Asia Society, and Fulbright.

He was a Creative writing Fellow at Stanford, 1951; directed the Creative Writing Program at the University of Rhode Island, summer of 1958; Writing Fellow at Bread Loaf, 1961; a Fellow of the Rockefeller Foundation at Bellagio, 1994. He served on the editorial board of several literary magazines such as Literature East and West. He was a speaker at the Bi-Centennial of the Philippine Republic, in 1996.

In 1956 he began teaching Contemporary American Literature and Creative Writing at Boston College; and in 1962 received the "Heights" Man of the Year Award in "recognition of his loyalty and service to the University and to its Young men." After retirement in 1999, Len continued teaching at Boston College as Emeritus

Professor; then teaching at the SOAR Federal Program—Seniors teaching Seniors—in Wellesley, MA.

Several of Len's creative writing students became published writers, poets, and editors, including George Higgins, whose first novel was *The Friends of Eddie Coyle*; Gemino Abad who dedicated his latest anthology, *Philippine short Fiction in English from 1990-2008*, to Leonard and three other of his professors; Michael J. Brien, editor, Amoskeag.

He wrote critical essays in his field which included American and Philippine literature. In 1966, his book on Robert Penn Warren, *The Dark and Bloody Ground*, the first on the author, was published by the University of Washington Press; his last book on *Robert Penn Warren, The Blood Marriage of Earth and Sky*, was published in 1997 by Louisiana State University Press.

Among his books are: *Six Filipino Poets* (1955), *Wayward Horizon* (1961), *The Wounded Diamond* (1964), *New Writing from the Philippines* (1966), *Firewalker* (1987), *In Burning Bush* (1991), *The Opposing Thumb* (1995), *Sunsurfers Seen from Afar* (1996), *The Circular Firing Squad* (1999), *Green Circuits of the Sun* (2002). With Thomas A. Gullason, he co-authored a textbook *The World of Short Fiction*: International Collection, Harper and Row, (1952).

While training for service and during active service in the US Army, his short stories were published in *Southwest Review* of the Southern Methodist University, Texas; whose editors encouraged him to continue submitting his stories from the front. In 1971 the Southern Methodist University Press published these short stories in a book, *A Lion Unannounced*, a National Council of the Arts Selection.

Len was a daily communicant at St. Jeremiah, Framingham until the church closed after 48 years. He was a communicant at St. George in Saxonville, and at the Sons of Mary Health of the Sick Missionaries, Framingham.

Responses

Dr. Thomas Byrne called the same day, remembering Len. Fr James Woods, Dean of Continuing Education at Boston College and Bishop Walter Edyvean, one of Len's first students at BC, called that they had offered Masses for Len. There were many Mass cards and prayers.

Cecilia Brainard. My heart feels very heavy with this news…I did not know the details of his wonderful life. I just know he has a great mind and was a force in Philippine literature. I have always felt privileged and grateful that this Great Mind took the time to read and comment on my work. May I share this sad news of his passing in social media? … There are many responses in Facebook. I can't keep up. People are commenting not just on my Facebook but in the sites that I have shared my post. I hope you find comfort in that Len was/is so beloved and highly respected…

Jaime An Lim. I will always be grateful to Len Casper. He was my dissertation adviser at Indiana University, and he wrote the introduction to my book of criticism, Literature and Politics: The Colonial Experience in Nine Philippine Novels. Will miss him.

Linda Nietes-Little. To my Tocaya, Linda. Sorry to hear about Len's passing and we share in your grief. But he is in a better place now, free from all the turmoils of the world and the aches and pains of old age. He is now sitting at the foot of the Master, together with all the other writers who have gone ahead of him. Len is in our prayers and may he rest in Peace. Please take care of yourself!

Albert B. Casuga. Rest in peace, Dr. Len. Your Bamboo and Greenwood Tree was a primer to me. Like Jim Abad, I continued to write the expected books. Rest well, your job here is done. Sad news.

Leny Strobel. Love to you, Linda Ty Casper!

Jean Vengua. Wow, end of an era...

Dr. Georgina C. Perry. We walked from the college of education to LA (Liberal Arts) to see if Len was in his office. We all had a crush on him.

Mila D. Aguilar. Sorry to hear that...Len lived a long and full life.

Cristina Pantoja Hidalgo. Filipino writers--particularly writers in English--are in his debt because he was one of the first critics to focus on Philippine literature in English.

Noelle de Jesus. We read his literary criticisms in college in a class taught by Fr. Galdon and I read Linda Ty's work on my own. In 1985, my father was a Fulbright and we lived in Ann Arbor. I worked as Prof Paz Naylor's teaching assistant for her Tagalog/Linguistics courses at the University of Michigan, and his daughter Gretchen, was in the advanced class. My sincere condolences to the family. His was a life well lived. May he rest in peace.

Simeon Dumdum Jr. Leonard Casper reviewed and said good words about my and Christine Godinez Ortega's books of poems in Philippine Studies. May he rest in peace.

Carol Nunez. Prayers for the eternal repose of Len & condolences to Linda, Gretchen and Tina...this news about the dies natalis – "birth in heaven" of Len Casper... prayer for Len at once.

MacArthur Corsino. An exceptional American with a heart for the PH has fallen.

Sonia Ziegler. So very sorry for your loss. He lived quite a full and amazing life.

Herminia Coben. May Professor Casper rest in peace. He lived a long and highly productive life. Linda, my prayers and condolences. Menez Coben.

Eve La Salle Caram. What a wonderful picture for him to be remembered by. Blessings.

Amelia Bojo. What a life! May he rest in peace.

Thelma Arambulo. A gift, I think, to cross over to the other side on the anniversary of the day you crossed over to this side.

Juan Y. Arcellana. From the old arcellana family of maginhawa street up village, our prayers and condolences.

Mahar Mangahas. Condolences to Linda and family.

Dick Malay. Sitting in his class in UP earl 60s was a visceral pleasure, though he sent me out once for chatting with a seatmate as he was lecturing. That ethical breach and penalty from an American Jewish professor added verve and color to my college days.

Steven P.C. Fernandez. Highest honors to a Great Man.

Connie J. Maraan. A good life will have its reward. I'm imagining all the writers who are coming to greet him.

Aida CF Santos. Condolences to his family and loved ones

Asuncion A. Lopez. Thank you, Leonard Casper, for giving time and passion to educating our writers.

Denver Torres. His critical essays helped Philippine Literature in so many ways ... May he rest in peace.

Beverly Wico Siy. oo nga po, mam sunod sunod haaay (Are you related to Professor David Wico? After my AA, UP Diliman, I went to the history department to register. Professor Wico said, Go to the Law College. If they reject you, come back. I did get my law degree but ended up writing historical novels.)

Gemma Nemenzo. Sincerest condolence from Irwin and me. We felt so privileged to have met both of you during our 2015 road trip. Your beautiful backyard and river is still the stuff of our dream

Don Bino (Bino Realuyo). So sad. May he travel well.

Aloy Polintan. I have a copy of *Green Circuits*. I'm halfway finishing it. This would be my only tribute to an astounding literary critic who gave attention to Philippine lit.

Erlinda Alburo. wow, 95! Baby, I used his critical works in my dissertation. To complete my appreciation of Len, I'd like to read his creative pieces.

Joel David. Haven't heard his name in years. No wonder since he moved back to the US. So sad to hear about his passing.

Ailil B. Alvarez. May Sir Leonard rest in peace. Will offer a prayer for his soul.

Luz de Leon. Nakikiramay sa iyong pagdadalamhati. He is now at peace, be at peace, too; that he is now in heaven that we all wish for.

Ralph Rodriguez. I have no words to tell of my sadness at Len's passing—my deepest condolence. You have that legacy to continue with the good that he did.

Michael Brien. There is probably not a day that passes that I don't think of him and thank him for his mentoring. I wish you and your daughters, peace.

Anne O'Reilly. I never had him as a professor, but his reputation was stellar. My sympathy to you and your family on the loss of a wonderful person.

Glicerio Abad. Our heartfelt thoughts. Len is now in a safe and happy place. Let us be happy for him. Much love.

Nim Gonzalez. Our prayers from the Gonzalez family, much love, too.

Lakshmi G. Yokohama. I received a text from Ibarra about the sad news of Len's passing. My parents adored him. Our sincere condolence.

Sara Miranda. May the knowledge that he is experiencing eternal life provide some measure of comfort in these days of grief.

Odel Perez. Nakikiramay kami. I have this image of Len in my mind with smiling eyes and a warm glow about him. I picture him wearing a short sleeve barong.

Jimmy and Mercy Abad. Our good Lord welcome him to his kingdom. I shall always remember his encouragement in the craft of writing and his lucid analysis of Philippine literature. I will always remember how Len admitted me to his class in Ateneo, and of course, in UP I enrolled in his class. He truly loved our literature in English, and definitely he inspired me to do anthologies in poetry and fiction. More, much more than THANKS to you, Len!

Edna Z. Manlapaz. There is a small altar by my bedside…From time to time, I light a candle to hold close to my heart those for whom I pray. Just now, after learning of Len's peaceful passing, I have lit a votive candle for him and for you.

Tony Joaquin. I offer my prayers for Len's immortal soul resting by the bosom of our beloved Jesus Christ.

Nilda S. Rimonte. Your news though expected, came as a shock all the same…he taught me about Philippine literature. I liked Len.

Susan Severino Lara. O my, another great one leaves us.

Gloria Cajipe, Ev Laserna. By any measure, a life well-lived and deservedly blessed. We will remember him and all of you in our prayers.

Luisa Garcia. It's just like Len not wanting any fuss over him.

Karen Sayward. What an incredible life he had, and so inspiring to read about Len's illustrious accomplishments, including his tenure at BC.

Helen K. Heineman. Thoughts and prayers are with you. Len is surely in a better place.

Emily Lyle. I'm so sorry. Thank you for the outline of Len's very interesting life

Joel Pablo Salud, Editor in Chief, *The Philippine Graphic*: First news for this lazy weekend: Dr. Leonard Casper, fiction writer and literary critic, passed away in his sleep on his 95th birthday, 06 July.

Last time I heard Dr. Casper's name, I was yet a writer at the *Manila Standard*. That's a lifetime ago. I recall bringing with me a tattered Leonard Casper book, the title I could not recall, wherever I went. It was a thin volume, a collection of his critical essays, one of the books which had ushered me into the literary life.

Never had the pleasure of meeting him in person, but his words had served as a roadmap during my first fumbling attempts to write short fiction. Can't say I followed everything to the letter, being headstrong and all. Nonetheless, he was one of the great influences who shaped my writing during the early years.

It saddens me to receive news of his passing. But then again, Len, as he was fondly called by family and friends, lived a full life. While this may mark the end of an era for many writers, a new one also has been born. To continue the task of writing: I believe Len wouldn't have it any other way.

Rest in peace, sir. It was an honor to have made your acquaintance through your books.

Thanks for sharing the news, Cecilia Brainard. Please send her our warm condolences. We share in her grief.

Linda Ty-Casper's note: *There were many names whose messages I was not able to read: Marra Lanot, Sylvia Mayuga, Reynaldo Caturza, Ian Rosales Casocot, Krip Yuson, Maria Karina Africa Bolasco, Edwin Lozano, Ambeth R. Ocampo, Christine Godi, Christopher Fallarme, Krip Yuson, Felice Prudente Sta. Maria; and many names I could not see...*

And: **Paulino Lim Jr.**, "I just reread Len's *In Burning Ambush*...so much love in what he wrote, light in what he said."

Gretchen Casper: Leonard Casper embodied intellectual curiosity, modesty, and affection. For my father, intellectual curiosity included wordplay. We can see from his letters how he reveled in words and languages. Even after being diagnosed with macular degeneration and dementia, my father would solve the Sunday *New York Times Magazine's* Spelling Bee, where readers are asked to construct words using as many of the seven randomly selected letters as possible. In particular, he loved playing with the fullest meanings of phrases to create sentences that resonated well beyond their strings of letters. However, he believed that knowledge and scholarship were not solely gained through working in a university office, but also required experience and adventure in the world, to help him more fully understand what he was reading and writing, not to mention understand himself. It was this desire for education and experience, not a bucket list, that led him to his adventures: enlisting for World War II, visiting Manila, and traveling around the world.

Second, my father was a modest man. He was proud of his working-class roots. He shared stories of his parents' lives before he was born: his father and mother living above a tavern where his father worked, their moving to Fond du Lac where his father's last job was as a railroad porter, his mother working within scarcity to feed and clothe eight children during the Depression, and her creation of a home filled with laughter and games. My father taught his children to never brag and to never talk about money. Yes, he was ambitious, but in a quiet way. Regarding his literary criticism of Robert Penn Warren's work, what he wanted to convey was Warren's creative process; he feared that visiting Warren in Connecticut or New York might focus his attention on the man rather than the work. He continued his style of quiet probing when he wrote his literary criticism of Philippine literature. My father was comfortable in his own skin: he was content, he had self-knowledge. He did not aspire to wear the title of department chair or dean. His professional goal was to be the best literary critic and writer that he could be, quietly.

Finally, my father valued affection. There was an exuberance about him. He was always telling jokes. It didn't matter to him if the jokes were funny; what mattered was the sense of playfulness. He was close to his brothers and sisters, visiting them often in Wisconsin, Hawaii, and Tennessee. His sister Rita helped my father purchase the engagement ring that he presented to my mother. He was so deeply in love with my mother – "Lindissima" – that he agreed to wait several years until she had graduated from UP before setting the wedding date in Manila. From the very beginning, he encouraged Mom's writing, offering feedback on her short stories and novellas and, most importantly, constant intellectual support. His sense of family extended to include Filipino writers whom he met in the United States and in the Philippines. He was grateful for their camaraderie, for their friendship. He reciprocated by championing their work and hosting them when they visited the US. My father embraced his siblings, his family, and his friends with his generosity and playfulness.

*

Kristina Casper-Denman: Born in 1923 in Fond du Lac, Wisconsin, Leonard Casper loved nature from the start. He spent time at the lakes in his home state and the seashore and rivers of his adopted state of Massachusetts. He loved all sorts of music, often singing along with the radio even if he made up the words as he went, and he joined in Christmas caroling with the Boston-based Iskwelahang Pilipino. Partially, he joined caroling because he loved socializing and Filipino food. Len loved dinosaurs and thought he would pursue a career in paleontology or perhaps journalism but ended up teaching and writing after his military service in Czechoslovakia in WWII. He did not talk much about his time in Europe, but visited important battle sites as a tourist, especially in honor of his brother who landed at Normandy. Len loved to travel, to make new friends, and to spend quiet time in museums and cathedrals. He wrote and taught from the heart, injecting diversity and inclusion in his lessons at Boston College over four decades.

ACKNOWLEDGEMENT

Deepest gratitude to Cecilia Brainard for making Len's Memoir "happen".

BIOGRAPHY

Linda Ty-Casper's short stories and novels have been published in the Philippines and abroad. "The character of their wisdom and strength give the stories their distinct nationality": Mauro Avena. They "must first be read as information…then as knowledge, which is power, which empowerment leads to wisdom…": Franz Arcellana. The novels, both historical and contemporary, are set in periods critical to the country, beginning with the Spanish to the American period, up to the martial law years.

She was a member of the UP Writers, Radcliffe Fellow, Wellesley P.E.N. Women, the Boston Authors which was founded in 1909 by Julia ward Howe. Among her honors are the Southeast Asia WRITE Award, Parangal from ALIWW, PAMANA Arts Legacy Award. She received fellowships from Harvard, Radcliffe. Her degrees are from the University of the Philippines and Harvard. A resident of the United States, she has remained a citizen of the Philippines.

LINDA TY-CASPER

www.ingramcontent.com/pod-product-compliance
Lightning Source LLC
Chambersburg PA
CBHW030134170426
43199CB00008B/63